SCOTLAND

1001 THINGS TO SEE

D0988370

CONTENTS

ii How to use this book

iii Abbreviations

iv Information for disabled visitors

v Maps

1 **Scotland: 1001 Things to See**

184 Advertisements

197 Index

206 Of further interest

ACKNOWLEDGEMENTS

The Scottish Tourist Board would like to thank everyone who has helped in the provision of information for this publication, especially: the National Trust for Scotland, the Ancient Monuments Division of the Scottish Development Department, and staff of many of Scotland's Area Tourist Boards.

The information quoted in this book is as supplied to the Scottish Tourist Board and to the best of the Board's knowledge was correct at the time of going to press. The Scottish Tourist Board can accept no responsibility for any errors or omissions.

November 1985

INTRODUCTION

A wide selection of the many thousands of things to see and places to visit in Scotland are described in this book— 1001 of the most important and most interesting.

Many visitors will want to discover the Scotland of old, and see the castles, abbeys and other historic buildings which are reminders of Scotland's colourful and romantic past.

There are reminders too of the life and work of the Scottish people, in the folk and clan museums, the visitors centres and the industrial and military relics which have been carefully preserved to bring the past to life.

Modern Scotland is also well presented in this book:— Scotland at Work in its distilleries, workshops and mills; and Scotland at Leisure in its theatres, art galleries, museums, wildlife reserves and parks and gardens, especially in Spring. Here we list only the main gardens open regularly; other gardens are open for a few days each year under Scotland's Garden Scheme, and you can find out more by contacting the Scheme at 31 Castle Terrace, Edinburgh EH1 2EL, tel: 031-229 1870.

HOW TO USE THIS BOOK

Entries in this book are listed alphabetically by name, eg Burns Mausoleum, and not by the nearest town unless that is part of the name. However, because there are so many, entries for the cities of Aberdeen, Dundee, Edinburgh and Glasgow are, for simplicity, listed under the name of the city.

There is a series of maps covering the whole of Scotland at the beginning of the book, with the entries marked for easy reference. The numbers on the map are the same as the numbers of the entries in the text. Also, each entry in the text has a reference to help you locate it on the correct map.

In the entries, the section in italics gives details where applicable of location, opening hours, admission charges, group rates, ownership, and telephone number for a last minute check in that order. **You are always advised to check these details of properties, particularly before making a long journey.** *Child* generally means under 14; *closing time* refers to the latest time that visitors are admitted, and this may be up to 45 minutes before the establishment closes. The second section of the entries tells you what you can see, with some history and general details where appropriate.

ABBREVIATIONS

The abbreviations used in the entries are listed below, together with the head offices of the organisations concerned.

AM   Ancient Monuments in the care of the Secretary of State for Scotland and maintained on his behalf by the Scottish Development Department, Ancient Monuments Division, 3-11 Melville Street, Edinburgh EH3 7PE. Tel: 031-226 2570.

FC   Forestry Commission (Scotland), 231 Corstorphine Road, Edinburgh EH12 7AT. Tel: 031-334 0303.

NCC   The Nature Conservancy Council, 12 Hope Terrace, Edinburgh EH9 2AS. Tel: 031-447 4784.

NTS   The National Trust for Scotland, 5 Charlotte Square, Edinburgh EH2 4DU. Tel: 031-226 5922.

RSPB   The Royal Society for the Protection of Birds, 17 Regent Terrace, Edinburgh EH7 5BN. Tel: 031-556 5624.

SWT   The Scottish Wildlife Trust, 25 Johnston Terrace, Edinburgh EH1 2NH. Tel: 031-226 4602.

OPENING STANDARD

This refers to the hours during which Ancient Monuments are open to the public:

April to September: Mon.-Sat. 0930-1900, Sun. 1400-1900.

October to March: Mon.-Sat. 0930-1600, Sun. 1400-1600.

DISTANCES

The distances indicated in the location of entries are approximate and are normally the shortest by road, except in a few remote places where they are ''as the crow flies''.

INDEX

There is an index in this book (pages 197-205), breaking down the entries into different interests: Gardens, Folk and Clan Museums, Castles, etc.

SCOTTISH TOURIST BOARD COMPANION PUBLICATIONS

Scotland: Touring Map

This gazetteer is produced as a companion to the Scottish Tourist Board's Touring Map of Scotland, which shows the places listed here and also the places in Scotland where you can enjoy beaches and outdoor sports like golf, sailing and pony trekking.

Scotland: Walks and Trails

Another useful Scottish Tourist Board publication which lists over 200 easy walks throughout Scotland which are suitable for families without specialist equipment. Many are signposted and have leaflets or guide books for sale.

Scotland: Hillwalking

Detailed descriptions of over 60 or more difficult walks and scrambles on hills in different parts in Scotland. Written by an expert and completely revised this year.

INFORMATION FOR DISABLED VISITORS

This is the first time that detailed information for disabled visitors has been included in *Scotland: 1001 Things to See.* We hope that it will enable you to get out and about. Please use your own discretion and telephone the site in advance if you require further details. A telephone number is printed in the entry where appropriate. We would be delighted to hear from you if you have made use of this information. Your experiences will enable us to help others.

The information given in this publication is as supplied to the Scottish Tourist Board and to the best of the Board's knowledge was correct at the time of going to press. The Scottish Tourist Board can accept no responsibility for any errors or omissions.

The sites have not been personally inspected by Scottish Tourist Board staff.

DEAF PEOPLE   We assume that all sites in this book will be sympathetic to visitors with hearing problems. Any special facility will be mentioned in the text.

BLIND PEOPLE   We assume that all sites in this book will welcome guide dogs. If they do not, this will be mentioned in the text. Any special facility will also be mentioned in the text.

   ♿   **EASY WHEEL CHAIR ACCESS**   Most or all of the site easily accessible. No more than one step but entrance may be made by a side door. No rough terrain but not all the footpaths may be suitable.

   ♿   **ACCESS WITH ASSISTANCE**   Two or more
A   steps but not as many as a flight. It has been evaluated as "possible with strong help". This help may sometimes be available on site. Please ring—it may be easy.

   ♿   **PARTIAL ACCESS**   (P/A With Assistance) Easy
P   access to part of the site but the rest may not be possible because of stairs etc. Please ring for advice on how much you will be able to see.

   ♿   **VERY DIFFICULT/NO ACCESS**   Knowing the determination of some of our visitors, we hesitate to say impossible but from the information supplied to us we can say daunting, strenuous, dangerous, eg spiral stairs, stiles, rocky paths. . . . Your comments on these sites will be particularly interesting.

T   **TOILET DOOR 26″ (700mm) OR MORE**   Some of these toilets are specially adapted. Some are known to be large and easily accessible. Please ring the site if this is essential.

Where there is no information shown in the text, we have not received a completed questionnaire. Can you help us by sending in your comments?

MAPS

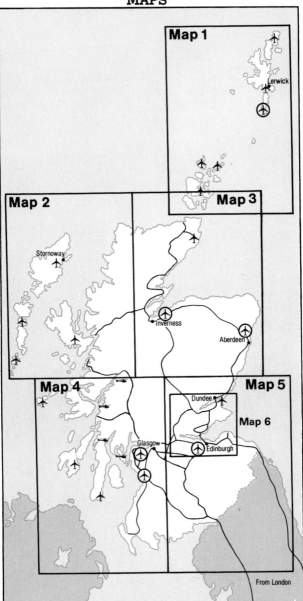

Railway routes

⊕ Major airports

✦ Airports with scheduled flights

⊶ Heliports

These maps are for "1001" locations only. Holiday attractions and touring routes can be found on the "Scotland Touring Map" published by the Scottish Tourist Board.

Produced for the Scottish Tourist Board by Baynefield Carto-Graphics Ltd. 1986

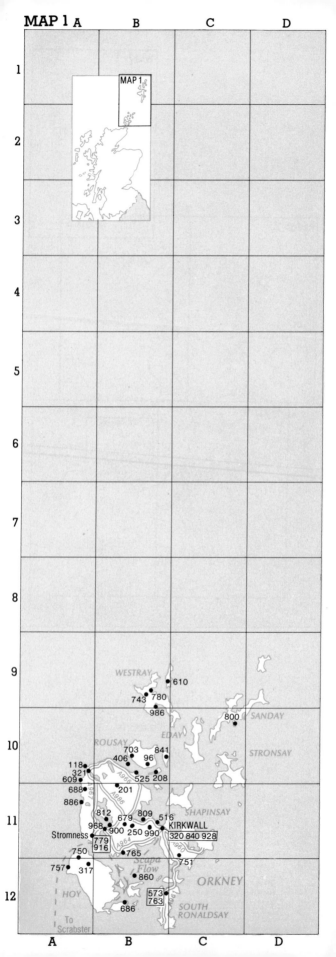

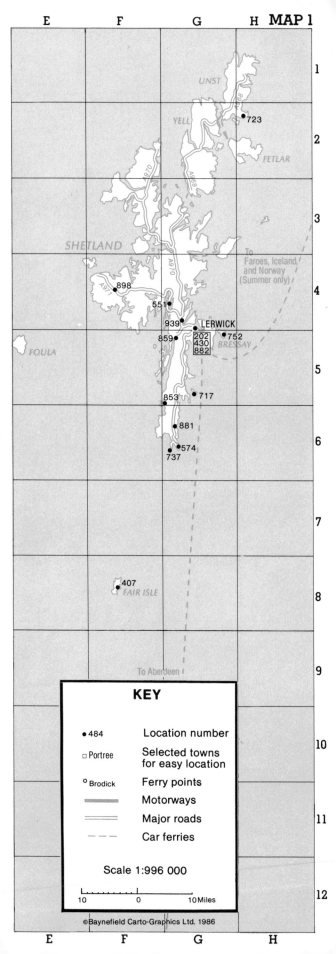

MAP 1

E   F   G   H

UNST

YELL

FETLAR

•723

A970   A968

SHETLAND

A970

To
Faroes, Iceland,
and Norway
(Summer only)

A971   •898

551•

939•   LERWICK
859•   202   •752
        430   BRESSAY
        882

FOULA

853•   •717

881•

•574
737•

407
FAIR ISLE

To Aberdeen

KEY

•484	Location number
□ Portree	Selected towns for easy location
○ Brodick	Ferry points
▬▬▬	Motorways
═══	Major roads
─ ─ ─	Car ferries

Scale 1:996 000

10   0   10 Miles

©Baynefield Carto-Graphics Ltd. 1986

E   F   G   H

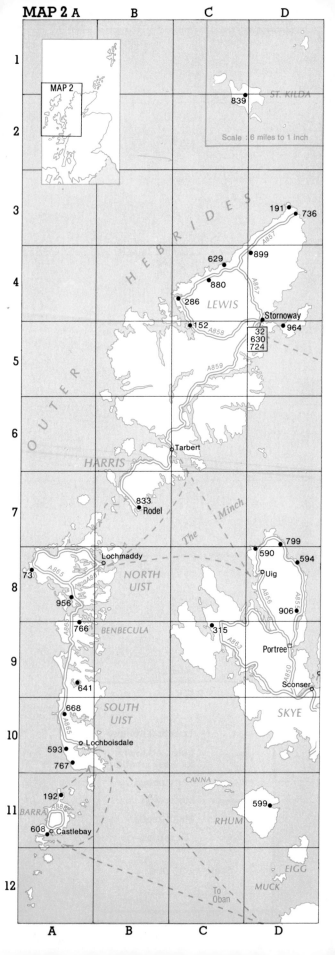

MAP 2

A   **B**   **C**   **D**

MAP 2

ST. KILDA

839

Scale : 6 miles to 1 inch

H E B R I D E S

191
736

A857

629
899

880
A852

286

LEWIS

152   A858

Stornoway

32
630   964
724

A859

O U T E R

Tarbert

HARRIS

833
Rodel

The Minch

799
590   594

Lochmaddy   Uig

73   NORTH
A865   UIST   A856   A855
A865
956   906

766   BENBECULA

315

A865   A863

Portree

641   A850

Sconser

668   SOUTH
UIST   SKYE
A865

593   Lochboisdale
767

CANNA

192
A888   599

BARRA   RHUM

608   Castlebay

EIGG

MUCK

To
Oban

A   **B**   **C**   **D**

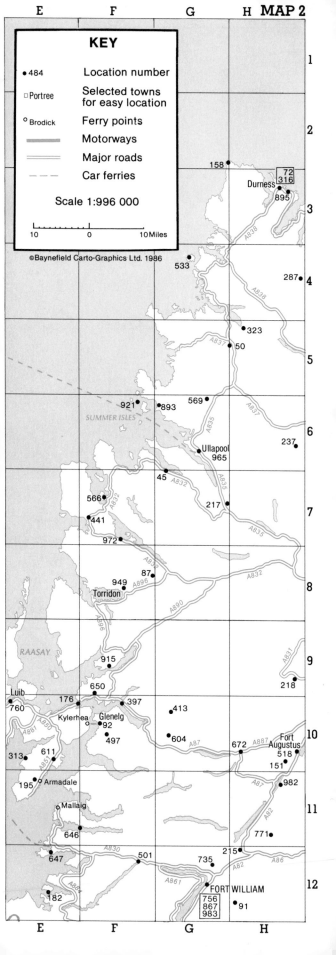

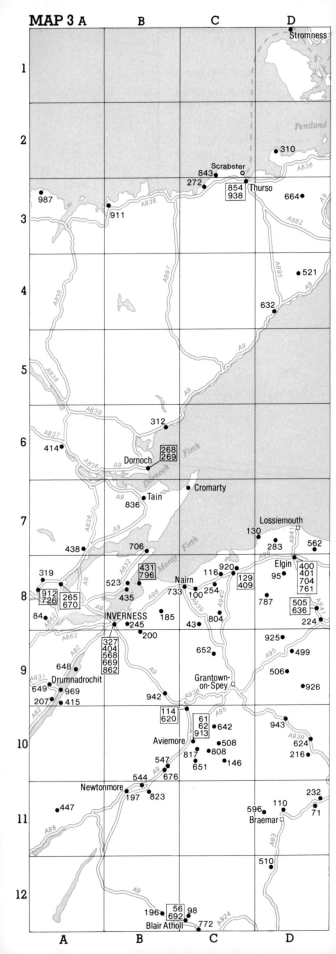

MAP 3

A   **B**   **C**   **D**

Stromness

Pentland

310

Scrabster
843
272   854 938   Thurso
987
911   *A836*   664

A897   *A895*   521   *A9*

632

A836   *A838*   *A9*

A839

A837   312

414   *A836*   268 269   *Firth*

Dornoch   *Dornoch*   Cromarty

Tain   *A9*
836   Lossiemouth
130   *A941*
438   706   *Moray Firth*   283   562

319   431 796   *A832*   116   920   Elgin   400 401 704 761
523   Nairn   129 409   95
912 726   265 670   435   733   254   787   505 636
84   *A96*   100   *A939*   224
INVERNESS   185   43   804
245   925
327 404 568 669 862   200   652   499   *A95*
648   *A9*   506
A831   Drumnadrochit   Grantown-on-Spey   926
649   969   *A938*
207   415   942   114 620   61 62 913   642   943   *A939*
Aviemore   508   624
547   817 808   216
544   676   651   146
Newtonmore   232
197   823   596   110   71
447   *A86*   Braemar
A93
510
A9
196   56 692   98
Blair Atholl   772   *A924*

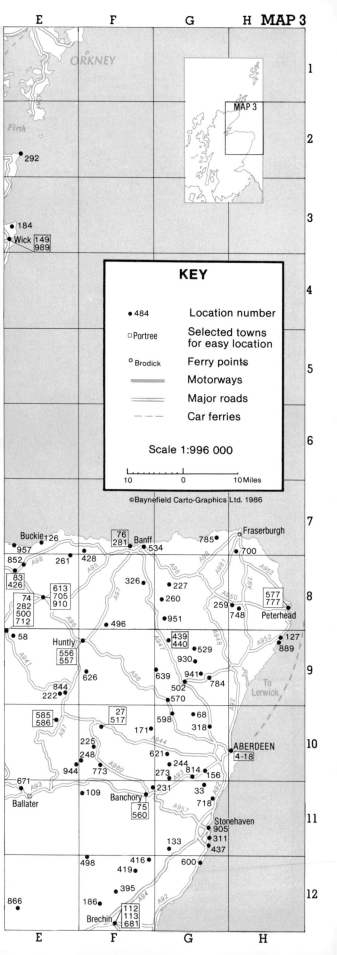

MAP 3

E   F   G   H

ORKNEY

Firth

1

2

● 292

3

● 184
● Wick 149
      989

4

KEY

● 484   Location number
□ Portree   Selected towns
             for easy location
○ Brodick   Ferry points
             Motorways
             Major roads
─ ─ ─   Car ferries

Scale 1:996 000

10   0   10 Miles

©Baynefield Carto-Graphics Ltd. 1986

7

Buckie 126   Fraserburgh
● 957   76   ● 785   ● 700
● 852   261   428   281 Banff
                              ● 534
83   577
426   777
74   613   326   227   259   ● 748 Peterhead
282   705   260
500   910   951
712

8

● 58   439
Huntly   440
556   ● 529   ● 127
557   626   930   ● 889
             844   639 941
             222   502 784   To
                     570   Lerwick

9

585   27
586   517
225   171   ● 68
248   598 318
944   773
       621   244
       273   814   156
671 109   33
Ballater Banchory 718
          75
          560

Stonehaven
● 905
● 311
● 437

11

498   416   600
       419
       395
866   186
       Brechin 112
               113
               681

12

E   F   G   H

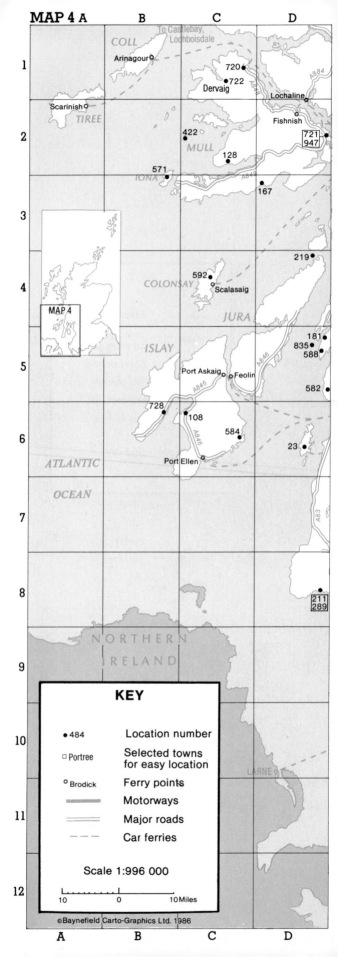

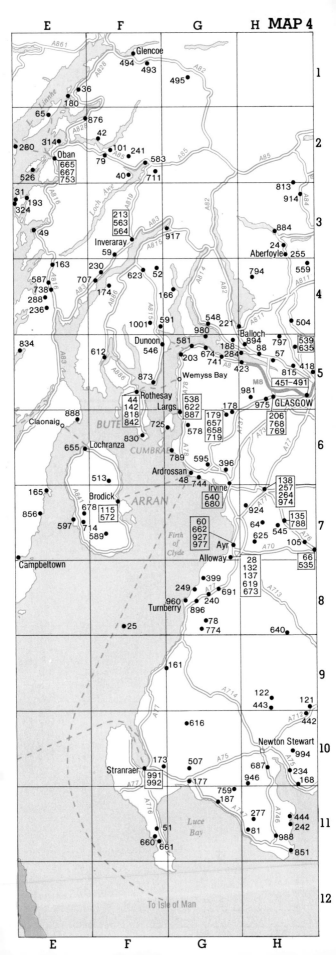

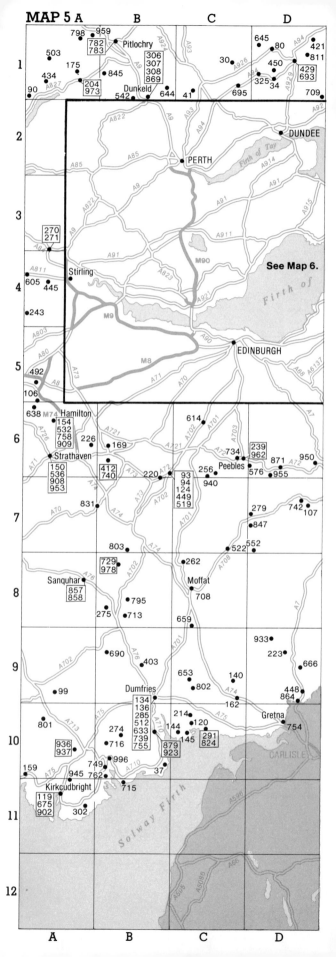

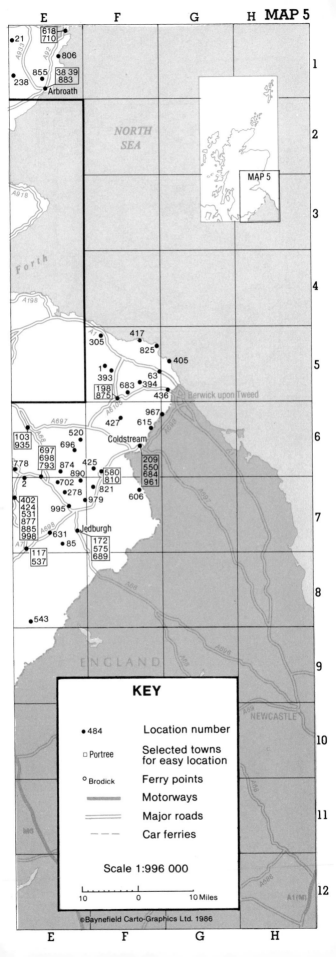

MAP 5

E F G H

NORTH
SEA

MAP 5

1
2
3
4
5
6
7
8
9
10
11
12

618
710
21
806
855
238
38 39
883
Arbroath

Forth

417
305
825
405
1
393
63
683
394
198
875
436
Berwick upon Tweed

967
427
615

103
935
520
696
Coldstream

697
698
793
874
425
209
550
684
961
778
2
890
580
810
702
821
278
979
606

402
424
531
877
885
998
995
631
85
Jedburgh
117
537
172
575
689

543

NEWCASTLE

ENGLAND

KEY

• 484   Location number

□ Portree   Selected towns
               for easy location

○ Brodick   Ferry points

               Motorways

               Major roads

- - -   Car ferries

Scale 1:996 000

10   0   10 Miles

©Baynefield Carto-Graphics Ltd. 1986

E F G H

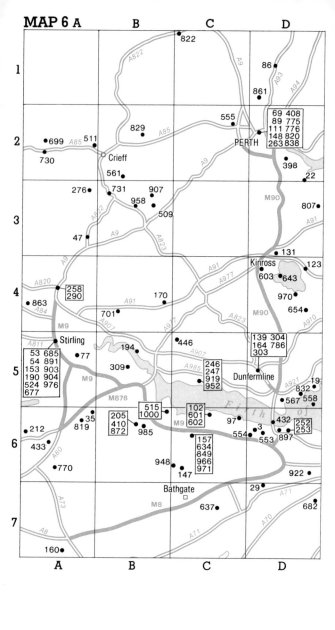

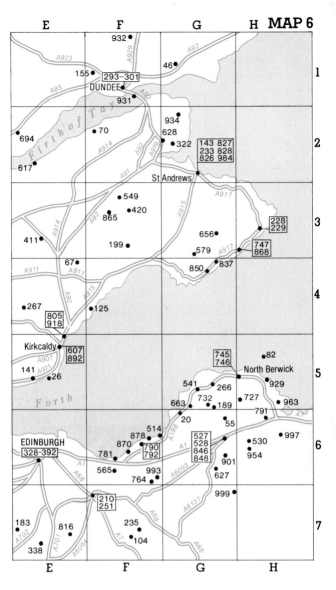

MAP 6

E F G H

932
46
155
293–301
DUNDEE
931
A923 A929 A92

Firth of Tay
694
70
617
934
628
322
143 827
233 828
826 984
St Andrews

549
420
865
411
199
656
579
850
228
229
747
868
837

67
125
267
805
918
Kirkcaldy
607
892
141
26
Forth

745
746
82
North Berwick
929
541
266
663
732
189
727
963
791
20
55
514
878
527
528
846
848
530
997
790
792
954
870
781
565
993
901
764
627
999
EDINBURGH
328–392
210
251
183
816
235
104
338

E F G H

1
2
3
4
5
6
7

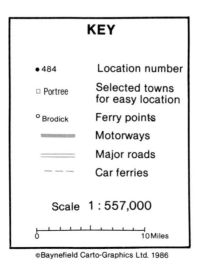

SCOTLAND

1001 THINGS TO SEE

1   ABBEY ST BATHANS TROUT FARM   5F5

7m N of Duns, take unclassified road 3m from Duns on B6355. May-Sep, daily 1100-1700, Oct-Apr, Sun 1100-1700. Free. (Trout Feeding) Adult: 40p, child: 20p. Group rates on application. Tel: Abbey St Bathans (036 14) 242 and 237.

Interpretive centre, with murals depicting the life in the valley from prehistoric times to the present. Fresh trout for sale, tea room, craft shop, working potter, toilets, car park, picnic area, woodland and river walks.

---

2   ABBOTSFORD HOUSE   5E6

A7, 2½m SSE of Galashiels. Late Mar-end Oct. Mon-Sat 1000-1700, Sun 1400-1700. Adult: £1.20, child: 60p. Group rates subject to revision. (Mrs P Maxwell-Scott, OBE). Tel: Galashiels (0896) 2043.

Sir Walter Scott's romantic mansion built 1817-1822. Much as in his day, it contains the many remarkable historical relics he collected, armouries, the library with some 9,000 volumes and his study. He died here in 1832. Free car park, with private entrance for disabled drivers. Teashop and gift shop.

---

3   ABERCORN CHURCH   6D6

Off unclassified road 2m N of A904, by Hopetoun, South Queensferry. All year, daily. Free. Tel: 031-331 1869.

Ancient church dedicated to St Serf, founded in 5th century. Present building, on site of 7th century monastery, dates from 12th century (see Norman Arch in S wall), reconstructed in 1579 and 1893. Display of 8th century Anglian crosses and hogback monuments; Duddingston aisle 1603; Binns aisle 1618. Also Hopetoun gallery and retiring rooms.

---

4   ABERDEEN ART GALLERY AND MUSEUMS   3H10

&
P
T

Schoolhill. All year. Mon-Sat 1000-1700 (Thu 1000-2000), Sun 1400-1700. Free. Parking available. (City of Aberdeen District Council). Tel: Aberdeen (0224) 646333. Artline: 24-hour recorded information service, tel: Aberdeen (0224) 632153.

Permanent collection of 18th, 19th and 20th century art with the emphasis on contemporary works. A full programme of special exhibitions. Music, dance, poetry, events, film, coffee shop, gallery shop, reference library, print room. Disabled access: A lift is available in the Gallery for disabled visitors which takes them to the first floor galleries and also gives access to the McBey print room and reference library. Guide dogs permitted.

---

5   ABERDEEN, BRIDGE OF DEE   3H10

Built in 1500 by Bishop Gavin Dunbar in James V's reign. Its seven arches span 400 feet and it formerly carried the main road south. The medieval solidity of the structure is enlivened by heraldic carvings.

---

6   ABERDEEN, JAMES DUN'S HOUSE   3H10

&
A
P

Schoolhill. All year. Mon-Sat 1000-1700. Free. Tel: Aberdeen (0224) 646333.

This former residence of James Dun, master and rector of Aberdeen Grammar School, is now a museum featuring special temporary exhibitions of particular interest to families. Museum shop.

7 ABERDEEN, DUTHIE PARK WINTER GARDENS   3H10

& *Polmuir Road/Riverside Drive. All year, daily, 1000-dusk. Free.*
T

Winter gardens with exotic plants and flowers, birds, fish and turtles. Cactus house. Banks of crocuses and daffodils and a 'hill of roses'.

Aberdeen Fishmarket

8 ABERDEEN, FISHMARKET   3H10

Off Market Street.

Aberdeen is one of the major fishing ports of Britain, landing hundreds of tons of fish daily. Every morning (Mon-Fri) the fishing fleets unload their catches, which are auctioned off amid tense bustle. Best visited 0730-0930.

9 ABERDEEN, GORDON HIGHLANDERS REGIMENTAL MUSEUM   3H10

Regimental Headquarters, Viewfield Road. All year. Sun & Wed 1400-1700; at other times by prior arrangement. Free.
Tel: Aberdeen (0224) 318174.

Fine displays relating the regiment's varied campaigns. There are collections of uniforms, colours and banners, silver and medals (with a special Victoria Cross exhibition), and a library with historical material and photographic albums.

10 ABERDEEN, HIS MAJESTY'S THEATRE   3H10

& *Rosemount Viaduct in city centre. Tel: Aberdeen (0224) 638080.*
P
T

Aberdeen's main theatre, opened in 1906 to the designs of Frank Matcham, seats 1,500. It offers a varied programme of entertainment, including ballet, opera, musicals, plays and concerts. Lounge bars.

11 ABERDEEN, MARISCHAL COLLEGE   3H10

Broad Street. Museum only: Mon-Fri 1000-1700, Sun 1400-1700. (University of Aberdeen). Tel: Aberdeen (0224) 40241, ext 243.

An imposing granite structure of the 19th century. In the quadrangle, entered by a fine archway, are older buildings of 1836-44, with the graceful Mitchell Tower. The anthropological museum houses local, classical, Egyptian and Chinese antiquities, and a general ethnographic collection.

12 ABERDEEN, MARITIME MUSEUM 3H10

Provost Ross's House, Shiprow. All year, Mon-Sat 1000-1700. Free.
Tel: Aberdeen (0224) 585788.

Situated in one of Aberdeen's oldest buildings (1593), the museum uses models, paintings and audio-visual displays to tell the story of local shipbuilding, the fishing industry, and North Sea oil and gas developments. Museum shop.

13 ABERDEEN, MERCAT CROSS 3H10

Castle Street.

Built in 1686, and paid for out of Guild wine funds, the Cross is decorated with medallion heads of the Stuart monarchs.

14 ABERDEEN, PROVOST SKENE'S HOUSE 3H10

Broad Street. All year. Mon-Sat 1000-1700. Free.
Tel: Aberdeen (0224) 641086.

Erected in the 16th century, this house bears the name of its most notable owner, Sir George Skene, Provost of Aberdeen 1676-1685. Remarkable painted ceilings and interesting relics. Period rooms suitably furnished and displays of local history. Provost Skene's kitchen (for tea, coffee and light meals).

15 ABERDEEN (OLD), BRIG O' BALGOWNIE 3H10

Also known as the 'Auld Brig o' Don', this massive arch, 62 feet wide, spans a deep pool of the river and is backed by fine woods. It was completed c. 1320 and repaired in 1607. In 1605 Sir Alexander Hay endowed the bridge with a small property, which has so increased in value that it built the New Bridge of Don (1830), a little lower down, at a cost of £26,000, bore most of the cost of the Victoria Bridge, and contributed to many other public works. Now closed to motor vehicles.

16 ABERDEEN (OLD), CRUICKSHANK BOTANIC GARDENS 3H10

Chanonry. All year, Mon-Fri 0900-1630, also May-Sep, Sat and Sun 1400-1700. Free. (University of Aberdeen).
Tel: Aberdeen (0224) 40241, ext 5247.

Extensive collection of shrubs, herbaceous and Alpine plants, heather and succulents. Rock and water gardens.

17 ABERDEEN (OLD), KING'S COLLEGE 3H10

High Street. All year, weekdays 0800-1700, Sat 0800-1200. Free.
(University of Aberdeen).

Founded 1494. The chapel, famous for its rich woodwork, is 16th century and the notable 'crown' tower is 17th century.

18 ABERDEEN (OLD), ST MACHAR'S CATHEDRAL 3H10

Chanonry. All year, 0900-1700. Free. Tel: Aberdeen (0224) 45988
9am to 5pm weekdays.

This granite cathedral was founded in 1131 on an earlier site, through the main part of the building dates from the mid-15th century. The west front with its twin towers is notable, and the painted wooden heraldic nave ceiling is dated 1520. The nave is in use as a parish church.

Aberdour Castle

19   ABERDOUR CASTLE   6D5

At Aberdour, A92, 10m E of Dunfermline. Opening standard, except closed Thurs morning and Fri. Adult: 50p, OAP, child: 25p; 10% discount for parties of 11 or more persons. (AM) Tel: 031-226 2570.

Overlooking the harbour at Aberdour, the oldest part is the tower, which dates back to the 14th century. To this other buildings were added in succeeding centuries. A fine circular doocot stands nearby, and here also is St Fillans Parish Church, part Norman, part 16th century.

20   ABERLADY CHURCH   6G6

& *In Aberlady, A198, 7m SW of North Berwick. All reasonable times. Free.*

Largely rebuilt 100 years ago, the church has a fortified 15th-century tower. In the chancel is the Aberlady Stone, part of a Celtic Cross, 8th century, and there are notable stained-glass windows.

21   ABERLEMNO SCULPTURED STONES   5E1

At Aberlemno, B9134, 5m NE of Forfar. All times. Free. (AM) Tel: 031-226 2570.

In the churchyard is a splendid upright cross-slab with Pictish symbols; three other stones stand beside the road.

22   ABERNETHY ROUND TOWER   6D2

At Abernethy, A913, 9m SE of Perth. Free: apply Keykeeper. (AM) Tel: 031-226 2570.

A round tower, 74 feet high, dating from the 11th century. Tradition has it that Malcolm Canmore did homage to William the Conqueror here. Beside it is a Pictish symbol stone. (See also No 113).

23   ACHAMORE HOUSE GARDENS   4D6

& *Isle of Gigha, off the Mull of Kintyre. All year, daily, 1000-dusk. Adult:*
P *£1, child: 50p (Gardens only—house not open to the public). Car and*
T *passenger ferry from Tayinloan. (D W N Landale).*
Tel: Gigha (058 35) 254.

Rhododendrons, camellias and many semi-tropical shrubs and plants may be seen at these gardens developed over the past 30 years. Elsewhere on this fertile island, see the ruined church at Kilchattan, which dates back to the 13th century. Boathouse bar, visitor reception centre and Gigha Hotel ½ mile away.

Achnaba Church: see No 42.

24 ACHRAY FOREST DRIVE 4H3

&
A
P
T

Off A821, 4m N of Aberfoyle. Easter-end Sep, daily 1000-1800. £1 per car. Tel: Aberfoyle (087 72) 383.

Scenic drive on Forestry Commission roads with fine views of the Trossachs. Walks, picnic places, play area and toilets.

Adam Smith Centre: see No 892.

---

25 AILSA CRAIG 4F8

Island in Firth of Clyde, 10m W of Girvan. Contact Mr McCrindle for party rates, tel. Girvan (0465) 3219. Visitors must obtain permission from the Marquis of Ailsa, Blanefield House, Kirkoswald, tel: Kirkoswald (065 56) 646.

A granite island rock, 1,114 feet high with a circumference of 2 miles. The rock itself was used to make some of the finest curling stones and the island has a gannetry and colonies of guillemots and other seabirds.

---

26 ALEXANDER III MONUMENT 6E5

By A92 S of Kinghorn at Pettycur Promontory. All times. Free. Tel: Burntisland (0592) 872667.

On the King's Crag, a monument marks the place where Alexander III was killed in a fall from his horse in 1286.

---

27 ALFORD VALLEY RAILWAY 3F10

&
A
T

Murray Park, Alford. Weekends only Apr/May/Sep; daily 1100-1700 Jun/Jul/Aug. Tel: Alford (0336) 2326.

Narrow gauge railway running from Alford Station and Museum to Haughton Country Park (approx 1 mile) and Haughton Country Park to Murray Park (1 mile). Terminus near Alford Transport Museum.

Alloway Kirk

28 ALLOWAY KIRK 4G7

&
A

In Alloway, 2½m S of Ayr. All reasonable times. Free. Tel: Alloway (0292) 41252 (mornings).

Ancient church, a ruin in Burns' day, where his father William Burns is buried. Through its window, Tam saw the dancing witches and warlocks in the poem *Tam o' Shanter*. Adjacent to Burns Centre, Burns Monument Hotel and ½ mile from Burns Cottage/Tearoom.

29 ALMONDELL COUNTRY PARK 6D7

On B7015 (A71) at East Calder or off A89 at Broxburn. 12m SSW of
Edinburgh. Free except for barbecues (small booking charge).
Tel: Mid Calder (0506) 882 254.

In the valley of the River Almond, a network of paths
and bridges, constructed by young people from all over
the world through Enterprise Youth. Visitor Centre
with aquaria showing life in various water habitats.
Nature trails link with old drovers' roads over the
Pentland Hills.

30 ALYTH FOLK MUSEUM 5C1

Off A94, 3m N of Meigle. May-Sep, Tue-Sat 1300-1700. Free.
Tel: Perth (0738) 32488 (Perth Museum).

A collection of rural agricultural and domestic
artefacts.

31 AN CALA GARDEN 4E3

On B844 on Isle of Seil, 16m SW of Oban via Clachan Bridge,
Apr-mid Sep, Mon and Thu 1400-1800. Adult: 40p, child (accompanied):
10p. (Blakeney family). Tel: Balvicar (085 23) 237.

Cherries, azaleas, roses, water and rock gardens.
Panoramic view of inner Hebridean islands. There is a
hotel by the garden (Easdale Inn) and also a tearoom
in the village.

An Lanntair Gallery

32 AN LANNTAIR GALLERY 2D4

Town Hall, South Beach Street, Stornoway. All year, Mon-Sat
1000-1800. Free. Tel: Stornoway (0851) 3307.

The gallery operates a lively contemporary and
traditional exhibitions programme, which changes
monthly. The visual arts programme is supplemented
by musical, literary and performing events with a
strong emphasis on traditional Gaelic culture.

33 ANDERSON'S STORYBOOK GLEN 3G11

At Maryculter, off Lower Deeside Road, 5m WSW of Aberdeen.
1 Apr-31 Oct, 1000-1900. Adult: £1.50, child: 75p. Group rates: 10%
discount if party is over 20 and under 80; above 80, 20%.
Tel: Aberdeen (0224) 732941.

The Glen is the result of 11 years work by the
Anderson family, who are famed for their roses. In 20
scenic acres, there are many attractions. For children
there are the Old Woman's Shoe and the Three Bears'
House amongst others, and elsewhere the Glen is
landscaped with waterfalls, there are seating areas and
a restaurant seating 250 which serves snacks and
3-course meals.

34 ANGUS FOLK MUSEUM 5D1

 ♿
P
T

Off A94 at Glamis, 6m SW of Forfar. 28-31 Mar, 1 May-30 Sep, daily 1200-1700, last admission 1630. Adult: 90p; child: 40p; no reduction for parties. (NTS) Tel: 031-226 5922.

Kirkwynd Cottages, a row of 19th-century cottages with stone-slabbed roofs, containing relics of domestic and agricultural life in the county in the 19th century and earlier.

35 ANTONINE WALL 6A6

From Bo'ness to Old Kilpatrick, best seen off A803 E of Bonnybridge, 12m S of Stirling. All reasonable times. Free. (AM) Tel: 031-226 2570.

This Roman fortification stretched from Bo'ness on the Forth to Old Kilpatrick on the Clyde. Built about AD 142-143, it consisted of a turf rampart behind a ditch, with forts about every two miles. It was probably abandoned about AD 163. Remains are probably best preserved in the Falkirk/Bonnybridge area, notably Rough Castle (see No 819), and at Bearsden (see No 815).

36 APPIN WILDLIFE MUSEUM 4E1

 ♿

On A828 at Appin House, 20m N of Oban. All year, daily 1000-1800. Donation. Tel: Appin (063 173) 308.

The Forest Ranger (John Scorgie) has over the years collected specimens of the local wildlife, to let visitors know what to look for in the area.

37 ARBIGLAND 5B10

 ♿
P
T

By Kirkbean, off A710, 12m S of Dumfries. May-end Sep: Tue, Thu, Sun 1400-1800. In 1986 house open daily afternoons, Sat 24 May-Sun 1 June and Sat 23 Aug-Sun 31 Aug. Adult £1, child: 50p, groups by arrangement. (Captain J B Blackett). Tel: Kirkbean (038788) 213.

These extensive woodlands, formal and water gardens are arranged round a sandy bay which is ideal for children. John Paul Jones' birthplace is nearby, and his father was the gardener at Arbigland. Tearoom.

Arbroath Abbey

38 ARBROATH ABBEY 5E1

In Arbroath. Opening standard. Adult: 50p, OAP, child: 25p. 10% discount for parties of 11 or more persons. (AM) Tel: 031-226 2570.

Founded in 1178 by William the Lion and dedicated to St Thomas of Canterbury, it was from here that the famous Declaration of Arbroath asserting Robert the Bruce as King was issued in 1320. Important remains of the church survive; these include one of the most complete examples of an abbot's residence.

39 ARBROATH ART GALLERY   5E1

*Arbroath Library, Hill Terrace. All year, Mon-Sat 0930-1700. Free.
(Angus District Council).*

Changing exhibitions offer work of Angus artists and
subjects of local interest.

---

40 ARDANAISEIG GARDENS   4F2

*E of B845, 22m E of Oban. 31 March-31 Oct, daily 1000-dusk.
Adult: £1, child: free. Tel: Kilchrenan (08663) 333.*

Rhododendrons, azaleas, rare shrubs and trees.
Magnificent views across Loch Awe and of Ben
Cruachan. The hotel restaurant is open for morning
tea, luncheon and afternoon tea.

---

41 ARDBLAIR CASTLE   5C1

*On A923 1m W of Blairgowrie. Open Thurs afternoons only by
arrangement with Tourist Information Centre, tel: Blairgowrie
(0250) 2960. Parties at other times, tel: Blairgowrie (0250) 3155.
Adult: £1.25, child: 60p, group rates: £1. (Mr L Blair Oliphant).*

Mainly 16th-century castle on 12th-century
foundations, home of the Blair Oliphant family.
Jacobite relics and links with Charles Edward Stuart.
Room containing relics of Lady Nairne (née
Oliphant), author of *Charlie is My Darling* and other
songs.

---

42 ARDCHATTAN PRIORY   4F2

*On the N side of Lower Loch Etive, 7m NE of Oban. Open all times.
Free. (AM) Tel: 031-226 2570.*

One of the Valliscaulian houses founded in Scotland in
1230, and the meeting place in 1308 of one of Bruce's
Parliaments, among the last at which business was
conducted in Gaelic. Burned by Cromwell's soldiers in
1654, the remains include some carved stones. The
gardens of Ardchattan House, adjoining the Priory, are
open Apr-Sep; admission charge. Achnaba Church,
near Connel, has notable central communion pews.

---

43 ARDCLACH BELL TOWER   3C8

*Off A939, 8½m SE of Nairn. Opening standard. Free: apply keykeeper.
(AM) Tel: 031-226 2570.*

A two-storey tower of 1655 whose bell summoned
worshippers to the church and warned the
neighbourhood in case of alarm.

---

44 ARDENCRAIG GARDENS   4F5

*At Ardencraig, by Rothesay, Isle of Bute. 1 May-30 Sep, Mon-Fri
0900-1630, Sat and Sun 1300-1630. Free. (Argyll and Bute District
Council). Tel: Rothesay (0700) 4644.*

Bought by the Royal Burgh of Rothesay in 1968, this
garden now produces plants for floral displays
throughout Bute. Contains propagation, educational
and show unit, aviaries containing many foreign bird
species, and tearoom. Ornamental ponds with
interesting varieties of fish.

45 ARDESSIE FISHERIES 2G7

 ♿
P
T

*On A832, by Little Loch Broom, between Gairloch and Ullapool.
Easter-15 October, Mon-Sat 1000-1900. Adult: 50p, child: 25p, group
rates by arrangement only. Tel: Dundonnell (085 483) 252 (any time).*

A fish farm with many facilities under cover. Rainbow
trout reared for the table, and local restocking service
with rainbow trout, brown trout and salmon. Visitors
can see the fish at all stages of growth and feed the
larger fish. Fresh trout always available. Locally caught
wild salmon on sale in season (June-August); smoked
salmon and smoked trout also available.

Carlungie Earth-House

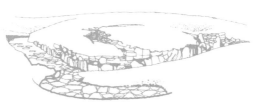

46 ARDESTIE AND CARLUNGIE EARTH-HOUSES 6G1

*N of A92. Ardestie: about 6m E of Dundee, at junction with B962.
Carlungie: 1m N on unclassified road to Carlungie. All times. Free. (AM)
Tel: 031-226 2570.*

Two examples of large earth-houses attached to surface
dwellings. At Ardestie the gallery is curved and 80 feet
in length: the Carlungie earth-house is 150 feet long,
and is most complex; used in first centuries AD.

47 ARDOCH ROMAN CAMP 6A3

*A822 at Braco, 10m S of Crieff. All reasonable times. Free.
(Ardoch Estate). Tel: Dunblane (0786) 824000.*

One of the largest Roman stations in Britain, dating
back to the 2nd century. There is a roman fort and
several camps in the surrounding area.

48 ARDROSSAN CASTLE 4G6

*Ardrossan, on a hill overlooking Ardrossan Bay. All year, all reasonable
times. Free.*

Mid 12th-century castle on a hill with fine views of
Arran and Ailsa Craig. Castle was destroyed by
Cromwell and only part of the north tower and two
arched cellars remain. Car park.

49 ARDUAINE GARDENS 4E3

*Arduaine, A816, 20m SSW of Oban. Apr-Oct, Sat-Wed 1000-1800.
Adult: £1, child (under 14): free. (Messrs E & H Wright).*

Beautiful coastal garden, noted especially for
rhododendrons and azalea species, also magnolias and
other rare and interesting trees and shrubs, water and
rock gardens. This is a plantsman's garden rather than
a tourist attraction.

50 ARDVRECK CASTLE 2H5

A837, 11m E of Lochinver, on Loch Assynt. All reasonable times. Free.

Built c. 1490 by the MacLeods, who in the mid-13th
century obtained Assynt by marriage; the three-
storeyed ruins stand on the shores of Loch Assynt.
After his defeat at Culrain, near Bonar Bridge, in
1650, the Marquess of Montrose fled to Assynt but
was soon captured and confined here before being sent
to Edinburgh and executed.

Ardwell House Gardens

51 ARDWELL HOUSE GARDENS 4F11

Ardwell, 11m SSE of Stranraer. Mar-Oct, daily 1000-1800. Admission by donation. (Mr and Mrs John Brewis). Tel: Ardwell (077 686) 227.

Daffodils, rhododendrons, crazy paving, foliage and flowering shrubs. Also pond walks with sea view.

52 ARGYLL FOREST PARK 4F4

W and NW from Loch Long almost to Loch Fyne: A815, B839, B828 and A83. (FC)

Three forests — Ardgartan, Glenbranter and Benmore — cover 60,000 acres of superb scenery. There are scores of forest walks as walkers may use virtually all the forest roads. Many leading through forests to high tops are arduous, but there are others, like the paths from the Younger Botanic Garden (see No 1001), by Loch Eck, which lead to Puck's Glen. The Arboretum at Kilmun should also be seen (No 591).

53 ARGYLL'S LODGING 6A5

Castle Wynd, Stirling. Seen from the outside.

This fine example of an old town residence was built c. 1632 by Sir William Alexander of Menstrie, later Earl of Stirling, who eleven years earlier helped to found Nova Scotia (New Scotland). It is now a youth hostel. (See also No 50).

54 ARGYLL AND SUTHERLAND HIGHLANDERS' MUSEUM 6A5

In Stirling Castle. Easter to end Sep, Mon-Sat 1000-1730, Sun 1100-1700. Oct, Mon-Fri 1000-1700. Free. Tel: Stirling (0786) 75165.

Fine regimental museum, with a notable medal collection.

Armadale Castle: see No 195.

55 ATHELSTANEFORD CHURCH 6G6

Off B1343, 4m N of Haddington. All reasonable times. Free; donations. Tel: Athelstaneford (062088) 243 or (062088) 378.

The plaque by the church tells the story of the origins of St Andrew's Cross (the Saltire), which was first adopted as the Scottish flag at this place. A floodlit flag flies permanently on the site.

56 ATHOLL COUNTRY COLLECTION 3C12

Blair Atholl. Open every afternoon 1330-1730 during the summer season, also weekday mornings from 0930 during Jul and Aug, or by arrangement. Adult: 50p, schoolchildren: 25p, group rates on application to John Cameron. Tel: Blair Atholl (079681) 232.

Folk Museum with blacksmith's 'smiddy' and crofter's stable and byre. Emphasis on the importance of flax growing and spinning to the economy of the district. Road, rail and postal services, the school, the kirk, the vet and gamekeeper are all featured. Picnic area and adjacent to Blair Castle Craft Centre.

57 AUCHENTOSHAN DISTILLERY 4H5

A82, 10m NW of Glasgow. All year. Mon-Fri 0900-1200, 1400-1600. Tel: Duntocher (0389) 79476.

Guided tours showing the brewing, distilling and warehousing of whisky, with a dram at the end. Reception centre and gardens.

58 AUCHINDOUN CASTLE 3E9

In Glen Fiddich, 3m SE of Dufftown, ½m off A941. All times: viewed from the outside only. Free. (AM) Tel: 031-226 2570.

A massive ruin on the summit of an isolated hill, enclosed by prehistoric earthworks. The corner stones were removed to Balvenie (see No 74). In Queen Mary's wars the castle was the stronghold of the redoubtable 'Edom o' Gordon' who burned Corgaff (see No 216). Jacobite leaders held a council of war there after Dundee's death at Killiecrankie.

Auchindrain Museum

59 AUCHINDRAIN MUSEUM 1F3

On A83, 5½m SW of Inveraray. Easter-Sep 30 (other times by arrangement). Apr, May, Sep: 1100-1600 (not Sat); Jun, Jul, Aug: 1000-1700. Adult: £1.50, child, OAP: £1. Group visits: contact curator. Tel: Furnace (049 95) 235.

Original communal-tenancy Highland farm, now a fascinating folk museum. Dwellings and barns of 18th and 19th centuries, furnished in period, traditional crops and livestock. Display centre, shop, picnic area, car park and toilets.

60 AULD KIRK 4G7

Off High Street, Ayr. All reasonable times. Free. Tel: Ayr (0292) 262938.

A fine church, dating from 1654, with notable lofts inside. Robert Burns was baptised and sometimes attended church there.

Aultroy Cottage: see No 87.

---

61 AVIEMORE BIRD GARDEN 3C10

&

Within the grounds of Aviemore Centre. All year, daily 1000-1800 (subject to weather conditions in winter). Groups by arrangement. Adult: £1, child: 50p; group rates on application. (Mr Iain Brodie). Tel: Aviemore (0479) 811259.

A collection of birds, many of which are rare or endangered. Pheasants, waterfowl, owls and rare breeds of domestic poultry. Every effort is made to assist disabled visitors.

---

62 AVIEMORE CENTRE 3C10

Off A9, 32m S of Inverness. All year, daily 1000 onwards. Admission free (charge for facilities). Group rates on request from Marketing Office, London, tel: 01-637 4002. Tel. Aviemore (0479) 810624.

Leisure, sport and conference centre with wide range of recreational and entertainment facilities, including: cinema/theatre, swimming pool, ice rink, saunas, artificial ski slope, go-karts, discos, restaurants, and many more.

Avondale Castle: see No 908.

---

63 AYTON CASTLE 5F5

&
A

At Ayton, by Eyemouth, on A1, 8m N of Berwick. Sun 1400-1700, or by appointment. Adult and OAP: £1, child under 14: free. Tel: Ayton (03902) 212.

Scottish Baronial style castle built in 1846 in red sandstone. Now fully lived in as a family home.

---

64 BACHELORS' CLUB 4H7

&
A
P

Tarbolton, B744, 7½m NE of Ayr off A758. 28 Mar-31 Oct, daily 1000-1800; other times by arrangement. Adult: 60p, child: 30p. (Custodian: Mr Sam Hay, 7 Croft Street, Tarbolton.) Tel: Tarbolton (0292) 541 940.

A 17th-century house where in 1780 Robert Burns and his friends founded a literary and debating society, the Bachelors' Club. In 1779, Burns attended dancing lessons here, and in 1781 he was initiated as a Freemason. Period furnishings, with reminders of Burns' life at Lochlea Farm. Small coffee shop.

---

65 BACHUIL 4E2

&
A

On Isle of Lismore, Argyll. (Ferry from Oban or Port Appin). Daily, by arrangement. Free. (Alastair Livingstone of Bachuil). Tel: Lismore (063 176) 256.

The Bachuil Mor or Pastoral Staff of Saint Moluag is kept in the house, the Baron of Bachuil being its Hereditary Keeper.

---

66 BAIRD INSTITUTE MUSEUM 4H7

&
A
T

Centre of Cumnock, off the Square. All year, Tue and Fri 1330-1600, Sat 1100-1300. Free. Groups free, by arrangement. Tel: Cumnock (0290) 22024.

The Baird Institute dates back to 1891 when it was built from money bequeathed by a local draper named John Baird. In late Victorian Gothic-style the building is of locally quarried red sandstone. Temporary exhibitions include local Victorian pottery from Cumnock, wooden souvenirs, Ayrshire embroidery and general displays of local history.

67 BALBIRNIE CRAFT CENTRE 6E4

In Balbirnie Estate, Markinch, on eastern outskirts of Glenrothes New Town. All year, Tue-Sat 1000-1800, Sun 1330-1730. Free.

Seven craft workshops of potter, leatherworker, jeweller and silversmith, modern furniture maker, stained glass artist, fashion designer and reproduction furniture maker. Glenrothes itself has fine examples of modern sculpture.

68 BALBITHAN HOUSE AND GARDEN 3G10

Unclassified road (Hatton of Fintry to Inverurie). 2½m NE of Kintore. Open by arrangement only. May-Jul. Adult: 80p, child: 20p. (Mrs McMurtrie). Tel: Kintore (0467) 32282.

A fine 17th-century house with an interesting 'old-world' garden including old roses, yew hedges, and herbs. The house contains a small museum with a collection of Scottish kitchen antiques. There is usually an exhibition of paintings in the galleried music-room with prints and cards from original paintings for sale.

69 BALHOUSIE CASTLE (BLACK WATCH MUSEUM) 6D2

Facing North Inch Park, Perth. Entrance from Hay Street. Mon-Fri 1000-1630 (Winter 1000-1530), Sun (Easter-Sep) 1400-1630. Free. Advance notice required for groups. Tel: Perth (0738) 21281, ext 30.

The castle houses the regimental headquarters and museum of the Black Watch (Royal Highland Regiment) and displays in chronological order the history of the famous Regiment from 1740 to the present time. Garden, museum shop.

70 BALMERINO ABBEY 6F2

On S shore of River Tay on unclassified road 5m W of Newport. View from outside only. Free. Tel: Gauldry (082 624) 733.

Cistercian abbey founded in 1229 by Queen Ermingade, second wife of William Lyon. Ruined during period of Reformation. Gardens.

Balmoral Castle

71 BALMORAL CASTLE 3D11

On A93, 8m W of Ballater. Grounds and exhibition of paintings and works of art in the Ballroom of the castle. May-Jun-Jul daily except Sun 1000-1700 (may be closed when members of the Royal Family are in residence). Adult: £1.10, child: free. Donations from entry fee to charities. Tel: Crathie (03384) 334.

The family holiday home of the Royal Family for over a century. The earliest reference to it, as Bouchmorale, was in 1484. Queen Victoria visited the earlier castle in 1848; Prince Albert bought the estate in 1852; the castle was rebuilt by William Smith of Aberdeen with modifications by Prince Albert and was first occupied in 1855. Souvenir shops, refreshment room, country walks and pony-trekking.

72   BALNAKEIL CRAFT VILLAGE   2H3

1m W of Durness. 1 Apr-30 Sep, 1000-1800. Free.
Tel: Durness (097 181) 342.

Twelve independently-owned businesses operated by craft workers, specialising in pottery, woodwork, tapestry, jewellery, bookbinding, candlemaking and many other crafts. The village was originally a Ministry of Defence early warning station, restored for crafts in 1964. Coffee shop, exhibition.

73   BALRANALD NATURE RESERVE   2A8

3m NW of Bayhead, North Uist, turn off main road. Reception cottage at Goular near Hougharry. Apr-Sep, daily. Free. (RSPB)
Tel: 031-556 5624.

Hebridean marsh, machair and shore. Important for plants and nesting birds.

Balvenie Castle

74   BALVENIE CASTLE   3E9

At Dufftown, A941, 16m SSE of Elgin. Apr-Sep, standard opening; closed Oct-Mar. Adult: 50p, OAP/child: 25p. Group rates: 10% discount for parties of 11 or more persons. (AM) Tel: 031-226 2570.

Picturesque ruins of 14th-century moated stronghold originally owned by the Comyns. Visited by Edward I in 1304 and by Mary Queen of Scots in 1562. Occupied by Cumberland in 1746. The corner stones came from Auchindoun (see No 58).

75   BANCHORY MUSEUM   3F11

High Street. Jun-Sep, Mon, Tue, Wed, Fri, Sun 1400-1700. Free. (North East of Scotland Museums Service). Tel: Peterhead (0779) 77778.

A small display of local history in a room in the old Council Chambers.

76   BANFF MUSEUM   3F7

On A947 at Banff. Jun-Sep, 1400-1715 (not Thu). Free. (North East of Scotland Museums Service). Tel: Peterhead (0779) 77778.

There is a fine display of birds in Britain in their settings and an interesting local history exhibition, including local silverware.

Bannockburn

77 BANNOCKBURN 6A5

   Off M80, 2m S of Stirling. (Tourist Information Centre). Mar-Oct, daily
T *1000-1800. Entry to site: 10p. Audio-visual presentation. Adult: 60p,*
   child: 30p. (NTS) Tel: Bannockburn (0786) 812664.

The audio-visual presentation tells the story of the
events leading up to the significant victory in Scottish
history (1314). In June 1964 the Queen inaugurated
the Rotunda and unveiled the equestrian statue of
Robert the Bruce. Information available on cassette.

---

78 BARGANY GARDENS 4G8

   4m from Girvan, 18m S of Ayr on B734. Mar-Oct, 0900-1900 or sunset,
   whichever is the earlier. Freewill contribution box (suggested
   contributions—Adult: 75p, child: 10p).
   (N E F Dalrymple Hamilton). Tel: Old Dailly (046 587) 249/221.

Woodland garden centred on a lily pond surrounded
by azaleas and rhododendrons. Fine trees, rock garden
and extensive walled garden. Small picnic area near the
car park.

---

79 BARGUILLEAN GARDEN 4F2

   3m W of Taynuilt on Glenlonan Road. Apr-Oct, daily, daylight hours.
   Adult: 40p, child: free; group rates by arrangement.
   (Mr and Mrs Neil Macdonald). Tel: Taynuilt (08662) 333.

Lochside gardens, featuring daffodils, rhododendrons,
azaleas, flowering shrubs and heathers. Particularly
attractive May-July. Barguillean Nurseries welcome
visitors but regret no retail sales. Gardens and
wholesale nursery.

---

80 BARRIE'S BIRTHPLACE 5D1

   9 Brechin Road, Kirriemuir. 28-31 Mar, 1 May-30 Sep, Mon-Sat
P *1100-1750, Sun 1400-1830, last admission 15 mins before closing.*
   Adult: 60p, OAP/child: 30p (Mrs Elizabeth M Drainer,
   tel: Kirriemuir (0575) 72646 or 72538 (Home)). (NTS)
   Tel: Kirriemuir (0575) 72646.

Here in this white-washed cottage Sir J M Barrie was
born in 1860. Manuscripts, personal possessions and
mementoes of actors and producers associated with his
plays are shown.

81   BARSALLOCH FORT   4H11

Off A749, 7½m WNW of Whithorn. All reasonable times.
Free. (AM) Tel: 031-226 2570.

Remains of an iron-age fort on the edge of a raised
beach bluff. 60-70 feet above the shore, enclosed by a
ditch 12 feet deep and 33 feet wide.

Bass Rock

82   BASS ROCK   6H5

Off North Berwick. Boat trips from North Berwick go round the
Bass Rock. Tel: North Berwick (0620) 2197 (Tourist Information Centre).

A massive 350-feet-high rock whose many thousands
of raucous seabirds include the third largest gannetry
in the world.

83   BAXTERS VISITORS CENTRE   3E8

½m W of Fochabers on main Aberdeen-Inverness road (A96). Apr-Oct
(Guided tours), Mon-Fri 1000-1130 and 1400-1530. Centre open
1000-1600 except holidays. Free. Tel: Fochabers (0343) 820 393.

Slide show with commentary, Old Baxter Shop,
replica of the original George Baxter and Sons
establishment where Baxters of Speyside were formed.
George Baxter cellar, shop and tearoom. Highland
cattle nearby.

84   BEAULY PRIORY   3A8

At Beauly, A9, 12m W of Inverness. Opening standard, but closed Mon
and Tues in winter. Adult: 50p, OAP/child: 25p. Group rates:
10% discount on parties of 11 or more persons. (AM) Tel: 031-226 2570.

Ruins of a Valliscaulian Priory founded in about 1230.
Notable windows and window-arcading.

85   BEDRULE CHURCH   5E7

&   *Bedrule, nr Denholm, off A698, Bedrule/Chesters Road.*
Tel: Hawick (0450) 506.

Bedrule Church, with its remarkable stained glass and
armorial bearings and picturesque location high above
the river, is the focus of the area from which 'fighting
Turnbulls' came, numbers amongst them William
Turnbull, born 1400, Bishop of Glasgow and founder
of Glasgow University (1451). Although nothing
remains of Bedrule Castle, the mound of Fast Castle
still dominates this reach of the Rule.

86   BEECH HEDGE   6D1

A93, just S of Meikleour, 12m NNE of Perth.

Listed as the highest of its kind in the world the Beech
Hedge was planted in 1746 and is now 600 yards long
and 85 feet high. Information board.

87 BEINN EIGHE NATIONAL NATURE RESERVE

2F8

W of A896/A832 junction at Kinlochewe. (NCC)

The first National Nature Reserve in Britain, of great geological and natural history interest. Car park and nature trails on A832 NW of Kinlochewe. Aultroy Cottage Visitor Centre on A832, 1m nearer Kinlochewe. Car park, toilets.

88 BELL OBELISK

4H5

Off A82 W of Bowling. All times. Free.

The obelisk at Douglas Point erected to commemorate Henry Bell, who launched the *Comet*, the first Clyde passenger steamer. Bowling is where the Forth and Clyde Canal enters the Clyde, and where the first practical steamboat, Symington's *Charlotte Dundas* was tried out in 1802 and in 1812.

89 BELL'S SPORTS CENTRE

6D2

Off Hay Street, Perth. All year, daily, 0900-2300. Charges based on activities, full details from Centre. Tel: Perth (0738) 22301/2.

The Sports Centre provides facilities for the majority of indoor sports, and details of activities and charges can be obtained from the Centre. It stands in the North Inch, a large park beside the River Tay, where in 1396 the notable clan combat between Clan Chattan and Clan Kay took place. Cafeteria.

90 BEN LAWERS

5A1

Off A827, 14m WSW of Aberfeldy. Visitor Centre open Easter-May and 1-30 Sep, 1100-1600; 1 Jun-31 Aug, 1000-1700; daily. Adult: 60p, child: 30p. (NTS) Tel: Killin (056 72) 397.

Perthshire's highest mountain (3,984 feet) noted for its variety of alpine flowers. There is a Visitor Centre, Nature Trail and a variety of guided walks in summer.

91 BEN NEVIS

2H12

Near Fort William.

Britain's highest mountain (4,406 ft/1,344 m) and most popular mountain for both rock-climber and hillwalker. It is best seen from the north approach to Fort William, or from the Gairlochy Road, across the Caledonian Canal. (See also No 867).

92 BERNERA BARRACKS

2F10

At Glenelg, on unclassified road W of A87 at Shiel Bridge. All times. Free.

The remains of Bernera Barracks, erected c 1722 and used continuously until after 1790.

93 BIGGAR GASWORKS MUSEUM

5B6

Gasworks Road, near the War Memorial, Biggar. Sundays in summer months, 1100-1700 (dates advertised locally). Free. Tel: 031-225 7534.

Biggar Gasworks was built in 1839 and closed in 1973 on the arrival of natural gas. It is now the only surviving coal gasworks in Scotland. The buildings, plant and associated displays give a concise picture of the coal-gas industry. Working machinery and gas lights, guided tours, display of gas appliances, video show. Limited car parking.

94   BIGGAR KIRK   **5B6**

&   *Kirkstyle, Biggar. Daily till dusk. Sunday services 1100, also 0930 Jun-Aug. Free.(Church of Scotland).*

Collegiate Church built in 1545 (on site of earlier building) by Malcolm, Lord Fleming of Biggar, uncle of Mary, Queen of Scots. Alternative wheelchair entrance at rear.

The Binns: see No 554.

---

95   BIRNIE CHURCH   **3D8**

Unclassified road off A941, 3m SE of Elgin. All year, daily. Free.

Small Romanesque church built in the early 12th century on the site of the church (c 550) of St Brendan the Navigator. Believed to be the oldest parish church in continuous use for worship in Scotland, and standing on a pre-Christian site (standing stones in churchyard).

Bishop's Palace: see No 320.

---

96   BLACKHAMMER CAIRN   **1B10**

N of B9064, on the south coast of the island of Rousay (Orkney). All times. Free. (AM) Tel: 031-226 2570.

A long cairn containing a megalithic burial chamber divided into seven compartments or stalls; probably third millennium BC.

Black Watch Memorial: see No 973.

Black Watch Museum: see No 69.

Blackness Castle

97   BLACKNESS CASTLE   **6C6**

B903, 4m NE of Linlithgow. Opening standard, except Oct-Mar closed Mon afternoon and Tue. Adult: 50p, OAP/child: 25p. Group rates: 10% discount for parties of 11 or more persons. (AM) Tel: 031-226 2570.

This 15th-century stronghold, once one of the most important fortresses in Scotland, was one of the four castles which by the Articles of Union were to be left fortified. Since then it has been a state prison in Covenanting time, a powder magazine in the 1870s, and more recently, for a period, a youth hostel.

Blair Castle

98   BLAIR CASTLE   3C12

 ♿
P
T

Near A9, 6m NNW of Pitlochry. Easter-mid Oct, Mon-Sat 1000-1700,
Sun 1400-1700. Adult: £2, OAP: £1.50, child: £1.20, family ticket:
£6.50. Group rates: 20p off full admission prices, ie Adult: £1.80,
OAP: £1.30, child: £1. (Duke of Atholl).
Tel: Blair Atholl (079 681) 207.

A white turreted baronial castle, seat of the Duke of
Atholl, chief of Clan Murray. The oldest part is
Cumming's Tower, 1269. Mary, Queen of Scots,
Prince Charles Edward Stuart and Queen Victoria
stayed here. When the castle was in Hanoverian hands
in 1746, General Lord Murray laid siege to it on the
Prince's behalf, making it the last castle in Britain to
be besieged. The Duke is the only British subject
allowed to maintain a private army, the Atholl
Highlanders. There are fine collections of furniture,
portraits, lace, china, arms, armour, Jacobite relics and
masonic regalia. Licensed restaurant, gift shop, deer
park, pony-trekking, nature trails, picnic areas and
caravan park. Free car and coach parks.

99   BLOWPLAIN OPEN FARM   5A9

Balmaclellan, Castle Douglas. Easter-end Oct, 1400 every day except Tue.
Adult: £1, child: 50p. Group rates on request. (Mrs Mary Blyth).
Tel: New Galloway (06442) 206.

Guided tour showing day-to-day life on a small hill-
farm, and in particular the different types of animals
and their uses.

100   BOATH DOOCOT   3C8

Off A96 at Auldearn, 2m E of Nairn. Donation box (NTS)
Tel: 031-226 5922.

A 17th-century doocot (dovecote) on the site of an
ancient castle where Montrose flew the standard of
Charles I when he defeated the Covenanters in 1645.
The plan of the battle is on display.

101   BONAWE IRON FURNACE   4F2

At Bonawe, 12m E of Oban, off A85. Opening standard, Apr-Sep only.
Adult: 50p, OAP: 25p, child: 25p. Group rates: 10% discount for parties
of 11 or more persons. Tel: 031-226 2570.

The restored remains of a charcoal furnace for iron-
smelting , established in 1753, which worked until
1876. The furnace and ancillary buildings are in a
more complete state of preservation than any other
comparable site.

102 BO'NESS & KINNEIL RAILWAY   **6C6**

♿ A

Off Union Street, Bo'ness. All year, Sat and Sun. As line awaits opening of extension, fares structure is uncertain at present. Tel: Bo'ness (0506) 822298.

Working steam railway system, with historic locomotives and rolling stock. Steam trains run summer weekends regularly from 1200-1700, open to visitors all year at weekends. Refreshments and sales stand. Buffer Stop Cafe (snacks), picnic area, visitor trail and visitor centre. Free car parking.

103 BORDER COUNTRY LIFE MUSEUM   **5E6**

♿ P

At Thirlestane Castle, Lauder, off A68. 11 May-30 Jun, all Sep, Wed and Sun only, daily Jul and Aug except Fri. (Grounds) 1200-1800, (Museum and Castle) 1400-1700. (Castle and Museum) Adult: £2, (Museum only) £1. Tel: Lauder (05782) 560 or 254.

The Border Country Life Museum Trust was established in 1981 to set up a museum to depict country life in the Scottish Borders from prehistoric times to the present day. Displays reflect the traditions, folklore and land use of the Borders. Demonstrations of vintage tractors and traditional farming methods are organised periodically by the Border Vintage Agricultural Association. (see also No 935). Tearoom, gardens and gift shop.

104 BORTHWICK CHURCH   **6F7**

Off A7, 13m SE of Edinburgh.

Nearby is Borthwick Castle (seen from outside only), built about 1430, with twin towers and two wings, one of the strongest and biggest of Scotland's tower houses. Mary, Queen of Scots visited the castle after her marriage to Bothwell. Borthwick Church, largely Victorian with two medieval aisles and sandstone effigies.

Boswell Museum and Mausoleum

105 BOSWELL MUSEUM AND MAUSOLEUM   **4H7**

♿ P

In Auchinleck. A76, 17m E of Ayr. Seen from outside at all times. For entry and guided tour, contact Mr G P Hoyle, 131 Main Street, Auchinleck; prior notice appreciated. Free: donations welcome. (Auchinleck Boswell Society). Tel: Cumnock (0290) 20757.

The ancient Parish Church, formerly a Celtic well, was enlarged by Walter fitz Alan in 1145-65, and again by David Boswell in 1641-43. It is now a museum of the Boswell family, and also contains a memorial to William Murdoch (1745-1839), a pioneer of lighting and heating by gas. The Boswell Mausoleum, attached, built by Alexander Boswell (Lord Auchinleck) in 1754, is the burial place of five known generations, including James Boswell, Dr Johnson's famous biographer. (Tour 1½ hrs.) Small car park. 2 miles away at Lugar a walking tour on Murdoch, including his birthplace at Belo Mill, opened in 1984.

Bothwell Castle

106 BOTHWELL CASTLE   **5A5**

At Uddingston on A74, 7m SE of Glasgow. Opening standard, except Oct-Mar closed. Thu afternoon and Fri. Adult: 50p, OAP, child: 25p. Group rates: 10% discount for parties of 11 or more persons. (AM) Tel: 031-226 2570.

Once the largest and finest stone castle in Scotland, dating from the 13th century and reconstructed by the Douglases in the 15th century. In a picturesque setting above the Clyde Valley.

107 BOWHILL   **5D7**

&
T

Off A708, 3m W of Selkirk. Grounds and Playground open 1 May-31 Aug. House open 4 Jul-15 Aug. Daily (not Fri) 1200-1700, Sun 1400-1800. Last day 1 Sep. Adult: £2, child: 75p. Grounds: Adult: 75p. Group rates on application. Tel: Selkirk (0750) 20732.

For many generations Bowhill has been the Border home of the Scotts of Buccleuch. Inside the house, begun in 1812, there is an outstanding collection of pictures, including works of Van Dyck, Reynolds, Gainsborough, Canaletto, Guardi, Claude Lorraine, Raeburn, etc. Also porcelain and furniture, much of which was made in the famous workshop of Andre Boulle in Paris. In the grounds are an adventure woodland play area, a riding centre, garden, nature trails, tearoom and gift shop.

Bowmore Round Church

108 BOWMORE ROUND CHURCH   **4C6**

&
A
P

Bowmore, Isle of Islay. Daily. 0900-dusk. Free.

Also known as Kilarrow Parish Church, was built by the Campbells of Shawfield as part of Daniel Campbell's planned village in 1769. Believed to be a copy of an Italian design, it possibly owes its shape to the belief that no evil spirits could hide in any corners. The builder was Thomas Spalding.

109 BRAELOINE INTERPRETIVE CENTRE 3F11

Glentanar, near Aboyne. Apr-Sep 1000-1700, other times by arrangement. Donations. (Hon Mrs Bruce). Tel: Aboyne (0339) 2072.

There are signposted walks and trails and an exhibition about the wildlife, farming, forestry and land use of this fascinating estate. Picnic area. Guided walks can be arranged by contacting countryside ranger.

Braemar Castle

110 BRAEMAR CASTLE 3D11

& *A93, at Braemar. May-early Oct, daily 1000-1800. Adult: £1.10, child 13 and under: 55p. Group rates: parties of 30 and over 85p per head. (Farquharson of Invercauld). Tel: Braemar (033 83) 219.*

This turreted stronghold, built in 1628 by the Earl of Mar, was burnt by Farquharson of Inverey in 1689. It was rebuilt about 1748 and garrisoned by Hanoverian troops. There is a round central tower, a spiral stair, barrel-vaulted ceilings and an underground pit prison. Fully furnished family residence. Interesting historical relics. Free car and bus park.

111 BRANKLYN GARDEN 6D2

& *Dundee Road (A85). Perth. 1 Mar-31 Oct, daily 0930-sunset. Adult: 80p, child: 40p. No dogs. (NTS) Tel: Perth (0738) 25535.*

Described as the finest two acres of private garden in the country, this outstanding collection of plants, particularly rhododendrons, alpines, herbaceous and peat garden plants, attracts gardeners and botanists from all over the world.

112 BRECHIN MUSEUM 3F12

& *In Library, St Ninian's Square. All year, Mon-Tue-Wed-Fri 0930-1800, Thu 0930-1900, Sat 0930-1700. Free. (Angus District Museums). Tel: Montrose (0674) 73232.*

Housed in Public Library. New displays to include archaeology, medieval burgh and Cathedral, civic and industrial history, folk life and paintings by local artist David Waterson.

113 BRECHIN ROUND TOWER 3F12

At Brechin. Viewed from the churchyard. All reasonable times. (AM) Tel: 031-226 2570.

One of the two remaining round towers of the Irish type in Scotland, dating back to the 11th or 12th century. Now attached to the cathedral (c 1150, partially demolished 1807, restored 1900-02; interesting tombstones). (See also Abernethy, No 22).

114 BRIDGE OF CARR
3C10

  Carrbridge. All times.

High and narrow single-arch bridge. Built by John Niccelsone, mason, in summer 1717, for Sir James Grant. Tearoom in village.

115 BRODICK CASTLE, GARDEN AND COUNTRY PARK
4F7

1½m N of Brodick pier, Isle of Arran. Castle: 28 Mar-30 Apr (including Easter weekend) Mon, Wed and Sat 1300-1700. 1 May-30 Sept, daily 1300-1700. Goatfell, park and gardens: all year, daily 1000-1700. Tearoom: Mon-Sat 1000-1700, Sun 1200-1700. Last admission 20 minutes before closing. (Castle, gardens and country park) Adult: £1.40, child: 70p; group rates. (Gardens and country park only) Adult: 80p, child: 40p. (NTS) Tel: Brodick (0770) 2202.

This ancient seat of the Dukes of Hamilton dates in part from the 13th century, with extensions of 1652 and 1844. The contents include silver, porcelain and fine paintings, sporting pictures and trophies. There are two gardens: the woodland garden (1923) is now one of the finest rhododendron gardens in Britain; the formal garden dates from 1710. In 1980 the gardens became a country park, supported by the Countryside Commission for Scotland, with a ranger service. Nature trail specially designed for wheelchair users. Tearoom, shop, nature trails and adventure playground.

116 BRODIE CASTLE
3C8

Off A96, 4½m W of Forres. Easter and 1 May-31 Oct. Mon-Sat 1100-1800. Last admission 1715. Sun 1400-1800. Adult: £1.40, child: 70p; group rates. Entry to grounds only by donation. (NTS) Tel: Brodie (030 94) 371.

The castle was largely rebuilt after the earlier structure was burned in 1645; it is based on the 16th century 'Z' plan, with additions made in the 17th and 19th centuries. The house contains fine French furniture, English, Continental and Chinese porcelain, and a major collection of paintings. A woodland walk has been laid out in the gardens by the edge of a 4-acre pond. Picnic area, adventure playground, car park, shop and small tearoom.

117 BROOK COTTAGE WORKSHOPS
5E7

Stobs, 5m S of Hawick on B6399. Apr-Oct 1000-2000, closed Sat; Nov-Mar 1000-1800, closed Sat. Free. Tel: Hawick (0450) 73113.

Hand-crafted furniture and gift items made from local timbers. Workshop and showroom open to all visitors who have the opportunity to see the whole process of furniture making from seasoning the timber to hand finishing.

118 BROUGH OF BIRSAY
1A10

At Birsay, N end of mainland, 11m N of Stromness, Orkney. Tides permitting. Opening standard, except Oct-Mar closed Mon and Tue morning. Adult: 50p, OAP/child: 25p. Group rates: 10% discount for parties of 11 or more persons. (AM) Tel: 031-226 2570.

The remains of a Romanesque church and a Norse settlement on an island accessible only at low tide. A replica of a Pictish sculptured stone discovered in the ruins is in the grounds, (original in the Royal Museum of Scotland, Queen Street, Edinburgh, No 360).

119 BROUGHTON HOUSE 5A11

    High Street, Kirkcudbright. Apr-Oct, Mon-Sat 1100-1300, 1400-1700.
A   *Nov-Mar, Tues, Thurs 1400-1700. Adult: 50p; child: 30p.*
    Tel: Kirkcudbright (0557) 30437.

This early 18th-century mansion belonged to the late 19th-century artist E A Hornel. There is a display of his pictures, antique furniture, a library and an attractive ornamental garden.

120 BROW WELL 5C10

    On B725, 1m W of Ruthwell. All times. Free.
    Tel: Dumfries (0387) 53862.

Ancient mineral well visited by Robert Burns in July 1786, when at Brow sea bathing under his doctor's orders.

Bruce's Stone

121 BRUCE'S STONE 4H9

    6m W of New Galloway by A712. All reasonable times. Free. (NTS)
    Tel: 041-552 8391.

This granite boulder on Moss Raploch records a victory by Robert the Bruce over the English in March 1307, during the fight for Scotland's independence.

122 BRUCE'S STONE 4H9

    E side of Loch Trool, unclassified road off A714, 13m N of Newton
A   *Stewart. All reasonable times. Free. Tel: Newton Stewart (0671) 2431.*

A massive granite memorial to Robert the Bruce's first victory over the English leading to his subsequent success at Bannockburn. Fine views of Loch Trool and the hills of Galloway.

123 MICHAEL BRUCE'S COTTAGE 6D4

    Kinnesswood, off A911, 4m E of Milnathort. Apr-Sep, daily 1000-1800.
    (Keys at The Garage, Kinnesswood.) Admission by donation.
    (Michael Bruce Memorial Trust) Tel: 031-667 1011/4311.

A cottage museum in the birthplace of the Gentle Poet of Loch Leven (1746-1767), who wrote and improved some of the Scottish Paraphrases.

124 JOHN BUCHAN CENTRE 5B6

    S end of Broughton, 5m E of Biggar. Easter-mid Oct, daily 1400-1700.
A   *Adult: 50p, OAP: 50p, child, 20p; group rates. (Biggar Museum Trust).*
    Tel: Biggar (0899) 21050.

The Centre, formerly Broughton United Free Church, tells the story of the life and work of John Buchan, 1st Lord Tweedsmuir, set against his family background. Broughton village was his mother's birthplace, and a much-loved holiday home.

125 BUCKHAVEN MUSEUM 6F4

Above Buckhaven Library, College Street, Buckhaven. All year, Mon 1400-1900, Tue 1000-1200, 1400-1700, Thu 1000-1200, 1400-1900, Fri 1400-1700, Sat 1000-1230. Free. (Kirkcaldy District Museums). Tel: Buckhaven (0592) 260732.

Buckhaven was once described as 'a full-flavoured fisher town' and its past importance in the East Coast fisheries is reflected in displays on the fisherfolk themselves, their lifestyle and their fishing techniques.

126 BUCKIE MARITIME MUSEUM 3E7

Cluny Place. All year, Mon-Fri 1000-2000, Sat 1000-1200. Free. Tel: Forres (0309) 73701.

Displays on fishing methods, coopering, lifeboats, navigation and local history. The Peter Anson Gallery houses watercolours of the development of fishing in Scotland. Shop.

Bullers of Buchan

127 BULLERS OF BUCHAN 3H9

Off A975, 7m S of Peterhead.

A vast chasm in the cliffs, 200 feet deep, *which no man can see with indifference* said Dr Johnson in 1773. A haunt of innumerable seabirds.

128 BURG 4C2

5m W on track from B8035 on N shore of Loch Scridain, Isle of Mull. Only accessible at low tide. Free. (NTS) Information from Miss McGillivray at Burg Farm.

The area contains MacCulloch's fossil tree, possibly 50 million years old, which can be reached at low water. Cars inadvisable beyond Tiroran. 5-mile walk, very rough in places.

129 BURGHEAD MUSEUM 3C8

Burghead. All year. Tue 1330-1700, Thu 1700-2030, Sat 1000-1200. Free. (Moray District Council). Tel: Forres (0309) 73701.

Museum of local history, including archaeology (Pictish fort), geology, the Lairds of Duffus, the harbour and fishing.

130 BURGHEAD WELL 3D7

At Burghead, 8m NW of Elgin. Opening standard. Free. (AM) Tel: 031-226 2570.

This remarkable rock-cut structure within the wall of an Iron Age fort is possibly an Early Christian Baptistry.

Burleigh Castle

131 **BURLEIGH CASTLE** 6D3

Off A911, 2m NE of Kinross. Opening standard. Free: key-keeper at farm opposite. (AM) Tel: 031-226 2570.

A fine tower house dating from about 1500. The seat of the Balfours of Burleigh, several times visited by James VI.

132 **BURNS COTTAGE AND MUSEUM** 4G7

& *B7024, at Alloway, 2m S of Ayr. All year. Jun-Aug 0900-1900, Apr, May, Sep, Oct 1000-1700 (Sun 1400-1700); Nov-Mar 1000-1600 (not Sun). Adult: £1, child: 50p; (includes Burns Monument). (Trustees of Burns Monument). Tel: Ayr (0292) 41215.*

In this thatched cottage built by his father, Robert Burns was born, 25 January 1759, and this was his home until 1766. Adjoining the cottage is a leading museum of Burnsiana. This is the start of the Burns Heritage Trail which can be followed to trace the places linked with Scotland's greatest poet. Tearoom, gift shop, museum and gardens. Information available on cassette. (See also Nos 138 and 619).

133 **BURNS FAMILY TOMBSTONES
AND CAIRN** 3G11

Off A94, 8m SW of Stonehaven at Glenbervie Church. All times. Free.

The Burnes (Burns) family tombstones in the churchyard were restored in 1968 and a Burns memorial cairn is nearby.

134 **BURNS HOUSE, DUMFRIES** 5B9

Burns Street. All year. Mon-Sat 1000-1300, 1400-1700, Sun 1400-1700. Closed Sun and Mon Oct-Mar. Adult: 30p, child: 15p. Tel: Dumfries (0387) 53374.

In November 1791 Robert Burns moved to Dumfries as an Exciseman and rented a three-room flat (not open to public) in the Wee Vennel (now Bank Street). In May 1793 he moved to a better house in Mill Vennel (now Burns Street) and here he died on 21 July 1796, though his wife Jean Armour stayed in the house until her death in 1834. The house has been completely refurbished and many relics of the poet are on show.

135 BURNS HOUSE MUSEUM, MAUCHLINE   4H7

   *Castle Street, Mauchline, 11m ENE of Ayr. Easter-31 Oct, Mon-Sat
P 1100-1230, 1330-1730, Sun 1400-1700 (or by arrangement). Adult: 50p,
child: 20p. Tel: Mauchline (0290) 50045.*

On the upper floor is the room which Robert Burns
took for Jean Armour in 1788. It has been kept intact
and is furnished in the style of that period. The
remainder of the museum contains Burnsiana and a
collection of folk objects. There is a large collection of
Mauchline boxware and an exhibition devoted to
curling and curling stones which are made in the
village. Nearby is Mauchline Kirkyard (scene of *The
Holy Fair*) in which are buried four of Burns'
daughters and a number of his friends and
contemporaries. Other places of interest nearby are
15th-century Mauchline Castle and Poosie Nansie's
Tavern. (See No 788).

136 BURNS MAUSOLEUM   5B9

   *St Michael's Churchyard, Dumfries. All reasonable times. Free.
A Tel: Dumfries (0387) 53862.*

Burns was buried in St Michael's Churchyard near to
the house in Mill Vennel where he died in 1796 (see
No 134). In 1819 his remains were moved into the
present elaborate mausoleum.

Burns Monument, Alloway

137 BURNS MONUMENT, ALLOWAY   4G7

   *B7024 at Alloway, 2m S of Ayr. Apr-mid Oct, daily 0900-1900.
A Adult: £1, OAP/child: 50p (including Burns Cottage). (Trustees of Burns
P Monument). Tel: Ayr (0292) 41321.*

Grecian monument (1823) to the poet with relics
dating back to the 1820's. Nearby is the attractive
River Doon, spanned by the famous Brig o' Doon, a
single arch (possibly 13th century), central to Burns'
poem *Tam o' Shanter*. Museum, gift shop, gardens. (see
also No 927).

138 BURNS MONUMENT AND MUSEUM, KILMARNOCK   4H7

   *Kay Park. Closed till further notice. Admission by arrangement.
Tel: Kilmarnock (0563) 26401.*

The Monument is a statue by W G Stevenson,
offering fine views over the surrounding countryside.
The Kay Park Museum houses displays on the life and
works of Burns, and has an extensive Burns library.

139 MURISON BURNS COLLECTION 6D5

Dunfermline Central Library, Abbot Street. All year. Mon, Tue, Thu, Fri 1000-1300, 1400-1900, Wed 1000-1300, Sat 1000-1300, 1400-1700. Free. Tel: Dunfermline (0383) 723661 (Contact Mr C Neale, Senior Reference Librarian).

A collection of books, pamphlets, portraits, prints and commemorative pottery relating to the life and work of Robert Burns. Housed in a room in the first Carnegie Library, built in 1883.

140 BURNSWARK 5C9

A

By unclassified road, 1½m N of B725, Ecclefechan-Middlebie road. All reasonable times. Free. Tel: (057 65) 203.

A Roman artillery range and a native hill fort with extensive earthworks, thought to have been a series of Roman practice siege works, best seen from the hilltop. The excavated ditches and ramparts of Birrens fort are nearby.

141 BURNTISLAND MUSEUM 6E5

Above library, High Street. Open library hours. Free. Tel: Burntisland (0592) 260732.

A permanent display of the local history of Burntisland, including shipbuilding. The nearby church, with octagonal shape, is also interesting.

142 BUTE MUSEUM 4F5

A
P

Stuart Street, Rothesay. Apr-Sep, Mon-Sat 1030-1230, 1430-1630 (June-Sep, Sun 1430-1630); Oct-Mar. Tue-Sat 1430-1630. Adult: 50p, OAP: 30p, child: 20p, children from Strathclyde Schools: Free. (Buteshire Natural History Society). Tel: Rothesay (0700) 3380.

Exhibits relating to the Island of Bute, including geology, prehistory, Clyde steamers, recent bygones, birds and mammals.

The Byre Theatre

143 THE BYRE THEATRE 6G2

T

Abbey Street, St Andrews. Group rates: discounts for 20 or more persons; discounts for OAPs/students; 2 for price of 1 on 1st nights. Tel: St Andrews (0334) 76288.

Repertory theatre, housed in a modern, purpose-built theatre with resident repertory company during the summer months. Bar. Lunchtime offers tea and snacks in summer, evening meals for 20 or more.

144 CAERLAVEROCK CASTLE 5C10

Off B725, 9m S of Dumfries. Opening standard. Adult: 50p, OAP/child: 25p. Group rates: 10% discount for parties of 11 or more persons. (AM) Tel: 031-226 2570.

This seat of the Maxwell family dates back to 1270. In 1330, Edward I laid siege to it and in 1638 it capitulated to the Covenanters after a siege lasting 13 weeks. The castle is triangular with round towers. The heavy machicolation is 15th century and over the gateway between two splendid towers can be seen the Maxwell crest and motto. The interior was reconstructed in the 17th century as a Renaissance mansion, with fine carving.

145 CAERLAVEROCK NATIONAL NATURE RESERVE 5C10

B725, S of Dumfries, by Caerlaverock Castle. All year. Free. (NCC) Tel: Alexandria (0389) 58511.

13,594 acres of salt marsh and intertidal mud and sand flats between the River Nith and the Lochar Water. A noted winter haunt of wildfowl, including barnacle geese. Access unrestricted, except in sanctuary area (600 acres), but intending visitors should contact the warden for advice on safety. Care must be taken relating to tides and quicksands.

Cairn Baan: see No 589.

146 CAIRNGORM CHAIRLIFT 3C10

A951 from A9 at Aviemore, then by Loch Morlich to car park at 2,000 feet. All year, daily 0900-1630, depending on weather. Prices vary according to journey. Group rates: 10% discount for 10-19 persons, 15% for 20-39 and 20% for 40 and over. Two free tickets for bus driver or courier. (Cairngorm Chairlift Company Limited). Tel: Cairngorm (047 986) 261.

At the car park is a large Day Lodge containing restaurant, bar, shop and snack bar. At the top of the chairlift is the Ptarmigan snack bar, the highest observation building in Great Britain at 3,600 feet with magnificent views to west and north-east. Also alpine garden.

147 CAIRNPAPPLE HILL 6C6

Off B792, 3m N of Bathgate. Apr-Sep, standard opening, but closed Mon (am) and Fri Oct-Mar. Adult: 50p, OAP/child: 25p. Group rates: 10% discount for parties of 11 or more persons. (AM) Tel: 031-226 2570

Sanctuary and burial cairns. Originally a Neolithic sanctuary remodelled in the Early Bronze Age (c 1800 BC) as a monumental open-air temple in the form of a stone circle with enclosing ditch. Later (c 1500 BC) it was despoiled and built over by a Bronze Age Cairn, considerably enlarged several centuries later. Now excavated and laid out.

148 CAITHNESS GLASS (PERTH) 6D2

Inveralmond, Perth. On A9 north of the town. All year. Free. Factory Shop: Mon-Sat 0900-1700, Sun 1300-1700, Sun 1100-1700 (Jul and Aug). Factory viewing: Mon-Fri 0900-1630. (Caithness Glass Plc.) Tel: Perth (0738) 37373.

Visitors are welcome at the factory to see the fascinating process of glass-making. Factory shop, paperweight museum and gallery, and licensed restaurant. Ample car/coach parking.

149   CAITHNESS GLASS (WICK)   3E3

*Harrowhill, Wick. All year. Free. Factory Shop: Mon-Fri 0900-1700,
Sat 0900-1300 (all year), Sat 0900-1600 (summer only). Factory viewing:
Mon-Fri 0900-1630 (all year). (Caithness Glass Plc).
Tel: Wick (0955) 2286.*

See hand-made glass blowing from the raw materials
stage through all the processes to the finished article.
Cafe and factory shop. Ample car/coach parking.

150   CALDERGLEN COUNTRY PARK   5A6

&

A
P
T

*Strathaven Road, East Kilbride. Park: all times, Children's Zoo:
daily, 1000-dusk, Visitor Centre (summer): Mon-Fri 1100-1700, Sat and
Sun 1100-2000; (winter): Sat and Sun 1100-1700. Free. (East Kilbride
District Council). Tel: East Kilbride (03552) 36644.*

Park consists of over 300 acres of wooded gorge and
parkland 5km in length. Extensive path system, nature
trails, picnic sites, woodland and river with large
waterfalls. Visitor Centre gives history of the landscape
in the area. Ornamental garden, children's zoo and
adventure playground. Ranger service.

151   CALEDONIAN CANAL   2H10

Tel: 041-332 6936 or Inverness (0463) 233140.

Designed by Thomas Telford and completed in 1822,
the Caledonian Canal links the lochs of the Great Glen
(Loch Lochy, Loch Oich and Loch Ness). It provides a
coast to coast shortcut between Corpach near Fort
William and Clachnaharry at Inverness. The Canal has
been described as the most beautiful in Europe—the
spectacular Highland scenery of lochs, mountains and
glens is unusual for a canal. There are a number of
pleasure cruises available on the canal and small boats
are available. (See also No 735).

152   CALLANISH STANDING STONES   2C5

*Callanish, off A858, 12m W of Stornoway, Lewis. All times. Free. (AM)
Tel: 031-226 2570.*

A unique cruciform setting of megaliths second in
importance only to Stonehenge. It was probably
carried out in a series of additions between 3000 and
1500 BC. An avenue of 19 monoliths leads north from
a circle of 13 stones, with rows of more stones fanning
out to south, east and west. Inside the circle is a small
chambered tomb.

153   CAMBUSKENNETH ABBEY   6A5

*1m E of Stirling. Standard opening. Closed winter. Adult: 50p,
OAP/child: 25p. Group rates: 10% discount for parties of 11 or more
persons. (AM) Tel: 031-226 2570.*

Ruins of an abbey founded in 1147 as a house of
Augustinian Canons. Scene of Bruce's Parliament,
1326.

**154   THE CAMERONIANS (SCOTTISH RIFLES)
         REGIMENTAL MUSEUM**   5A6

&
T

*Mote Hill, off Muir Street, Hamilton. All year. Mon-Sat 1000-1200,
1300-1700 (Wed morning only). Free. Tel: Hamilton (0698) 428 688.*

Display of uniforms, medals, banners, and documents,
relating to the regiment and also to Covenanting
times.

155 CAMPERDOWN WILDLIFE CENTRE 6F1

Off A923, near junction with A972, 3m NW of Dundee.
Oct-Apr 1000-1600, May and Sep 1000-1700, Jun, Jul, Aug 1000-1800.
Adult: 40p, OAP/child: 40p. Group rates: 20p per person in party of 12 or
more. (City of Dundee District Council). Tel: Dundee (0382) 623555.

Indigenous wildlife collection including deer
paddocks, wildcats, pinemartens, European brown
bear, lynx, wolves, arctic foxes, pheasants, golden eagle
and buzzards. Wildfowl ponds, bantams and large
selection of domestic stock. Guided tours for
educational parties. Snack bar and souvenir shop,
restaurant 250 yards away, large play complex adjacent
(free). Free parking. (See also No 295).

156 CAMPHILL VILLAGE TRUST 3G10

  ᠼ
  P *Newton Dee Community, Bieldside. Mon-Fri 0900-1200, 1400-1700, Sat*
0900-1200. Groups by arrangement. Free. Tel: Aberdeen (0224) 868701.

Sheltered craft workshops with mentally handicapped
adults making soft toys, and wood, metal, woven and
batik goods. Wholemeal bakery, confectionery,
laundry, health and wholefood store. Craft shop and
coffee bar. Organic/biodynamic garden and two farms.

157 CANAL MUSEUM 6C6

  ᠼ *The Basin, Union Canal, Linlithgow. Apr-Sep, Sat and Sun 1400-1700.*
Free.

Records, photographs, audio-visual display and relics of
the history and wildlife of the Union Canal, in former
canal stables, built c 1822 when the canal was opened.
The museum is run in conjunction with the canal
passenger boat *Victoria*. (See Nos 966 and 971).

158 CAPE WRATH 2G2

12m NW of Durness.

The most northerly point of Scotland's north-west
seaboard. A passenger ferry (summer only) connects
with a minibus service to the cape.

Cardoness Castle

159 CARDONESS CASTLE 5A10

On A75, 1m SW of Gatehouse-of-Fleet. Opening standard. Adult: 50p,
OAP/child: 25p. Group rates: 10% discount for 11 or more persons. (AM)
Tel: 031-226 2570.

This 15th-century tower house was long the home of
the McCullochs of Galloway. It is four storeys high,
with a vaulted basement. Features include the original
stairway, stone benches and elaborate fireplaces.

160　CARFIN GROTTO　　6A7

   A
   T

Carfin Village, 2m N of Motherwell. Daily. Outdoor devotions only on Sun (May-Oct) at 1500. Free. Tel: Motherwell (0698) 63308.

Grotto of Our Lady of Lourdes and a place of pilgrimage. Hall open for teas during the summer (Sunday only).

161　CARLETON CASTLE　　4F9

A77, 6m S of Girvan. All reasonable time. Free.

One in a link of Kennedy watchtowers along the coast. Now a ruin, it was famed in ballad as the seat of a baron who got rid of seven wives by pushing them over the cliff, but was himself disposed by May Cullean, his eighth wife.

162　CARLYLE'S BIRTHPLACE　　5C9

   A
   P

A74 at Ecclefechan, 5½m SE of Lockerbie. Easter-31 Oct, Mon-Sat 1000-1800. Adult: 30p. (NTS) (Mrs Nancy Walter). Tel: Ecclefechan (05763) 666.

Thomas Carlyle (1795-1881) was born in this little house built by his father and uncle, both master masons, and itself of considerable architectural interest.

163　CARNASSERIE CASTLE　　4E4

Off A816, 9m N of Lochgilphead. All reasonable times. Free. (AM) Tel: 031-226 2570.

The house of John Carswell, first Protestant Bishop of the Isles, who translated Knox's *Liturgy* into Gaelic, and published it in 1567, the first book printed in that language. The castle was captured and partly blown up during Argyll's rebellion in 1685.

164　ANDREW CARNEGIE BIRTHPLACE MUSEUM　　6D5

   P
   T

Moodie Street, Dunfermline. Apr-Oct, Mon-Sat 1100-1700 (Wed: till 2000), Sun 1400-1700; Nov-Mar, daily 1400-1600. Free. Tel: Dunfermline (0383) 724 302.

Weaver's cottage, birthplace of Andrew Carnegie in 1835, and linked Memorial Hall. New displays for the 150th Anniversary tell the story of the poor Scots boy who emigrated to America and made himself one of the world's richest men—and gave away 350 million dollars.

165　CARRADALE HOUSE GARDENS　　4E7

Off B842, 12½m NNE of Campbeltown. Apr-Sep, daily 1000-1600. Adult: 20p, child: free. (Naomi Mitchison). Tel: Carradale (05833) 234.

Walled garden dating from about 1870; flowering shrubs, rhododendrons, azaleas. Wild garden with paths and iris pond, best visited April-June. The remains of a vitrified fort stand on an island (access by foot except at high tide) south of the harbour at Carradale village.

166　CARRICK CASTLE　　4G4

On W bank of Loch Goil, 5m S of Lochgoilhead. All reasonable times. Free.

Built in the 14th century and first recorded in 1511, the walls of this great rectangular keep are entire though roofless. The Argylls kept their writs and charters here, and used it as a prison. Fortified in 1651 in expectation of a siege by Commonwealth forces, it was burned by the Earl of Atholl's troops in 1685.

167 CARSAIG ARCHES

4D3

On shore 3m W of Carsaig, South Mull. All times. Free.
Tel: Tobermory (0688) 2182.

A 3-mile walk from Carsaig leads to these remarkable
tunnels formed by the sea in the basaltic rock.
Reached only at low tide. On the way is the Nun's
Cave, with curious carvings; it is said that nuns driven
out of Iona at the time of the Reformation sheltered
here. Tearoom facilities available at Pennyghael.

168 CARSLUITH CASTLE

4H10

A75, 7m W of Gatehouse-of-Fleet. Opening standard. Free. (AM)
Tel: 031-226 2570.

A roofless 16th-century tower house on the L-plan,
built in the 1560s for the Browns.

169 CARTLAND BRIDGE

5B6

On A73 W of Lanark. All times. Free.

An impressive bridge built by Telford in 1822 over a
gorge, carrying the Mouse Water. It is one of the
highest road bridges in Scotland.

Castle Balliol: see No 640.

Castle Campbell

170 CASTLE CAMPBELL

6B4

In Dollar Glen, 1m N of Dollar. Opening standard, except Oct-Mar
closed Thu afternoon and Fri. Adult: 50p, OAP/child: 25p. Group rates:
10% discount for 11 or more persons. (AM) Tel: 031-226 2570.

On a steep mound with extensive views to the plains
of the Forth, this castle was built towards the end of
the 15th century by the first Earl of Argyll, and it was
at one time known as Castle Gloom. It was burned by
Cromwell's troops in the 1650s. The courtyard, great
hall, and the great barrel roof of the third floor are
well worth seeing. The 60 acres of woodland of Dollar
Glen (NTS) make an attractive walk to the castle. The
glen has a variety of steep paths and bridges through
spectacular woodland scenery.

171 CASTLE FRASER

3F10

3m S of Kemnay off B993. Castle: 1 May-30 Sep, daily 1400-1800 (last
tour 1715). Gardens and Grounds: all year, daily 0930-sunset. House:
Adult: £1.40, child: 70p; group rates (Grounds) by donation. (NTS)
Tel: 031-226 5922.

Castle Fraser, begun about 1575, belongs to the same
great period of native architectural achievements as
Crathes and Craigievar Castles, and is the largest and
grandest of the Castles of Mar. Two notable families of
master masons, Bel and Leiper, were involved in its
construction, completed in 1636. Garden, picnic area
and tearoom.

Castle Girnigoe: see No 184.

Castle Gloom: see No 170.

---

172 CASTLE JAIL   5E7

&
P
T

Castlegate, Jedburgh. Weekdays 1000-1200, 1300-1700, Sun 1300-1700.
Adult: 40p, OAP, child, student and the unemployed: 20p. Group rates:
5% discount for parties of 20 or more persons.
(Roxburgh District Council). Tel: Jedburgh (0835) 63254.

On the site of Jedburgh Castle, a 'modern' reform jail
was built in 1825. Rooms have been interestingly
reconstructed to re-create the 'reformed' system of the
early 19th century. The jail is set in a grassy area,
suitable for picnics and also forms part of the Jedburgh
Town Trail.

---

173 CASTLE KENNEDY GARDENS   4F10

&
A
P

N of A75, 3m E of Stranraer. Apr-Sep, daily 1000-1700. Adult: £1,
OAP: 80p, child (under 16): 50p.
Tel: Stranraer (0776) 2024 or (05814) 225.

The Earl and Countess of Stair live at the adjoining
Castle. These are nationally famous gardens
particularly well known for their rhododendrons,
azaleas, magnolias and embothriums. The notable
pinetum was the first in Scotland. Tearoom and plant
centre.

---

174 CASTLE LACHLAN   4F4

Off B8000, 8m SW of Strachur.

Castle Lachlan was first mentioned in a charter of 1314
and the ruins stand on a promontory overlooking
Loch Fyne. Its internal double tenement structure has
only one parallel in Scotland and is probably the result
of 16th-century modifications. It is the ancient home
of MacLachlan of MacLachlan.

Castle Menzies

---

175 CASTLE MENZIES   5A1

&
P

On B846, Weem, 1m W of Aberfeldy. In process of restoration by
Menzies Clan Society. Apr-Sep, Mon-Sat 1030-1700, Sun 1400-1700.
Adult: £1, OAP: 50p, child: 30p; group rates on application.
(Menzies Clan Society). Tel: Aberfeldy (0887) 20932.

Fine example of 16th-century Z-plan transitional
fortified tower house with elaborately carved dormers
added in 1577. Castle also houses Clan Menzies
Museum.

---

176 CASTLE MOIL   2E10

&

Near Kyleakin pier, Skye. All reasonable times. Free.

Earlier known as Dunakin, these rather scant ruins
were once a lookout post and a fortress against raids
by Norsemen. For centuries this keep was a
stronghold of the MacKinnons of Strath. Now known
as Castle Moil ('the roofless castle').

177 CASTLE OF PARK   4G10

Off A75, by Glenluce, 9m ESE of Stranraer. Not yet open to the public; may be viewed from the outside. (AM) Tel: 031-226 2570.

A tall, imposing castellated mansion, still entire, built by Thomas Hay of Park in 1590.

178 CASTLE SEMPLE COLLEGIATE CHURCH   4G6

At Castle Semple, 1½m NE of Lochwinnoch. Not open to the public; may be viewed from the outside. (AM) Tel: 031-226 2570.

The church is a rectangular structure. A square tower projects from the west gable. The apse is three-sided, each side having three windows of debased Gothic form.

179 CASTLE SEMPLE COUNTRY PARK   4G6

   A P T

Off Largs Road, Lochwinnoch, 9m SW of Paisley. 0900-dusk; closed for Christmas and New Year holidays. Free, but charges (various) for use of loch. (Strathclyde Regional Council). Tel: Lochwinnoch (0505) 842882.

Country park based on Castle Semple Loch; about 200 acres. Bring your own boat or hire (no motor boats or keel boats). Bank angling. Next to RSPB visitor centre. Picnic areas and information centre.

Castle Sinclair: see No 184.

180 CASTLE STALKER   4E1

On a tiny island offshore from A828, 25m NNE from Oban. Mar-Sep, open by appointment. Adult: £2.50, child: £1 (including boat trip). Group rate: £2 per person. (Lt Col D R Stewart Allward). Tel: Upper Warlingham (088 32) 2768.

This picturesque ancient home, c. 1500, of the Stewarts of Appin, and associated with James V, has recently been restored.

181 CASTLE SWEEN   4D5

On E shore of Loch Sween, 15m SW of Lochgilphead. All reasonable times. Free. (AM) Tel: 031-226 2570.

This is probably the oldest stone castle on the Scottish mainland, built in the mid-12th century. It was destroyed by Sir Alexander Macdonald in 1647.

Castle Tioram

182 CASTLE TIORAM   2E12

On an islet in Loch Moidart, reached by unclassified road N of A861, 6m NNW of Salen. All times. Free.

The ancient seat of the Macdonalds, of Clan Ranald, built in the early 14th century, well situated on a small island and accessible at low tide. It was burned by the orders of the then chief when he joined the 1715 Rising, fearing it might be taken by his enemies the Campbells. The castle offers fine views of Loch Moidart.

183 CASTLELAW FORT 6E7

Off A702, 7m S of Edinburgh. Opening standard. Free. (AM)
Tel: 031-226 2570.

A small Iron Age hill fort consisting of two concentric
banks and ditches. In the older rock-cut ditch an
earth-house is preserved. Occupied into Roman times
(2nd century AD).

184 CASTLES GIRNIGOE AND SINCLAIR 3E3

*3m N of Wick. Take airport road towards Noss Head Lighthouse. All
times. Free.*

Two adjacent castles on a cliff-edge above Sinclair's
Bay, one time strongholds of the Sinclairs, Earls of
Caithness. Girnigoe is the older, dating from the end
of the 15th century; Sinclair was built 1606-07. Both
were deserted c 1679 and 20 years later were reported
in ruins.

Cawdor Castle

185 CAWDOR CASTLE 3B8

    At Cawdor on B9090, 5m SW of Nairn. May-Sep, 1000-1700.
P *Adult: £1.80, child: 90p. Group rates (1985), adult party (20+): £1.60,*
T *child party (20+): 70p. (Rt Hon The Earl of Cawdor).*
    Tel: Cawdor (06677) 615.

The old central tower of 1372, fortified in 1454 (a
family home for over 600 years), is surrounded by
16th-century buildings, remodelled during the
following century. Notable gardens surround the
castle. Shakespeare's Macbeth was Thane of Cawdor,
and the castle is one of the traditional settings for the
murder of Duncan. Licensed restaurant, snack bar and
picnic area in grounds; beautiful gardens and extensive
nature trails; 9-hole pitch and putt golf course and
putting green.

186 THE CATERTHUNS 3F12

5m NW of Brechin. All times. Free. (AM) Tel: 031-226 2570.

These remains of Iron Age hill forts stand on hills on
either side of the road from Balrownie to Pitmudie,
beyond little Brechin. The Brown Caterthun has four
concentric ramparts and ditches; the White Caterthun
is a well-preserved hill fort with massive stone
rampart, defensive ditch and outer earthworks.

187 CHAPEL FINIAN 4G11

Off A747, 12½m WSW of Wigtown. All reasonable times. Free. (AM)
Tel: 031-226 2570.

A small chapel or oratory probably dating from the
10th or 11th century, in an enclosure about 50 feet
wide.

188 CHURCH OF ST MAHEW 4G5

  ♿
A

½m N of Cardross on Darleith Road, west of the golf course, and 4m NW of Dumbarton. All reasonable times. Free (donation box). Tel: Cardross (0389) 841 784.

The first church was dedicated by St Mahew (c 535), a prophet and disciple of St Patrick, but the present building, restored in 1955, is the work of Duncan Napier and dates from 1467. Formerly known as Kirkton Chapel, now Roman Catholic parish church for Cardross.

189 THE CHESTERS FORT 6G5

1m S of Drem, unclassified road to Haddington, East Lothian. All times. Free. (AM) Tel: 031-226 2570.

The Chesters is one of the best examples in Scotland of an Iron Age fort with multiple ramparts.

190 THE CHURCH OF THE HOLY RUDE 6A5

  ♿
A

St John Street, Stirling. May-Sep, daily 1000-1700. Free.

The only church in Scotland still in use which has witnessed a coronation, when in 1567, the infant James VI, age 13 months, was crowned. John Knox preached the sermon. The church dates from 1414, and Mary, Queen of Scots worshipped there. No guide dogs.

191 CHURCH OF ST MOLUAG 2D3

N end of the Isle of Lewis. Open all reasonable times. (Scottish Episcopal Church). Tel: (0859) 3609.

Known in the Gaelic as Teampull mhor (big temple) this chapel was probably built in the 12th century. Now restored; occasional services held.

192 CILLE BARRA 2A11

At Eoligarry, at N end of Isle of Barra. All times. Free.

The ruined church of St Barr, who gave his name to the island, and the restored chapel of St Mary formed part of the medieval monastery. Preserved there are four gravestones, thought to have come from Iona.

193 CLACHAN BRIDGE 4E3

  ♿

B844 off A816, 12m SW of Oban. All times. Free. Tel: Oban (0631) 63122.

This picturesque single-arched bridge, built in 1791, which links the mainland with the island of Seil, is often claimed to be the only bridge to 'span the Atlantic' (though there are others similar). The waters are actually those of the narrow Seil Sound, which joins the Firth of Lorne to Outer Loch Melfort, but they can with some justification claim to be an arm of the Atlantic.

194 CLACKMANNAN TOWER 6B5

On a hill W of Clackmannan (A907). No facilities for entry whilst restoration work is in progress; may be closely viewed from the outside. (AM) Tel: 031-226 2570.

Before the partial collapse of this tower with its 14th-century nucleus, it was one of the most complete of Scottish tower houses. In Clackmannan itself, see the old Tolbooth, the ancient 'Stone of Mannan' and the stepped Town Cross.

195 CLAN DONALD CENTRE 2E11

&. *At Armadale on A851, ½m N of Armadale Pier. Apr-Oct, Mon-Sat*
T *0900-1730, Sun (pm) mid-season. Adult: £1.20, child: 60p. Group rates:*
60p per person (10 or more in group). Tel: Ardvasar (047 14) 227.

The Museum of the Isles Exhibition is located in a
restored section of Armadale Castle and tells the story
of Clan Donald and the Lords of the Isles. Surrounded
by beautiful woodland gardens with a mature
arboretum, guided walks, nature trails and children's
play area. Audio-visual theatre, restaurant, gift shop,
toilets, car park. Countryside Ranger Service.

196 CLAN DONNACHAIDH MUSEUM 3B12

&. *Calvine, A9, 4m W of Blair Atholl. Apr-mid Oct, weekdays 1000-1730,*
A *Sun 1400-1730. At other times by arrangement. Free.*
Tel: Calvine (079 683) 264.

Clan Donnachaidh comprises Reid, Robertson,
MacConnachie, Duncan, MacInroy and others. Old
and new exhibits include items associated with the
Jacobite Risings of 1715 and 1745. Restaurant nearby.

197 CLAN MACPHERSON MUSEUM 3B11

&. *In Newtonmore on A9/A86, 15m S of Aviemore. May-Sep, Mon-Sat*
1000-1730, Sun 1430-1730. Free. Tel: Newtonmore (054 03) 332.

Relics and memorials of Clan Chiefs and other
Macpherson families. Exhibits include a letter to
Prince Charles Edward Stuart from his father, a
massive silver epergne depicting an incident in the life
of Cluny of the '45 after the Battle of Culloden, green
banner of the clan, Victorian royal warrants, crests,
James Macpherson's fiddle and other historical relics.

Clan Tartan Centre: see No 379.

198 JIM CLARK MEMORIAL TROPHY ROOM 5F5

&. *44 Newtown Street, Duns. Easter-end Sep, Mon-Sat 1000-1300,*
P *1400-1800, Sun 1400-1800. Adult: 50p, child: 25p. (Berwickshire District*
Council). Tel: Duns (0361) 82600, ext 36.

A memorial to the late Jim Clark, twice world motor
racing champion, with a large number of his trophies.

199 CLATTO COUNTRY PARK 6F3

&. *Dalmahoy Drive, off A972, 2m from Dundee city centre. All year,*
A *1000-dusk. Free. Tel: Dundee (0382) 89076.*
P

Reservoir area with 24 acres of water protected by a
shelter belt of conifer and mixed woodland.
Particularly popular for windsurfing (instruction
available). Rowing boats and windsurfing equipment
for hire.

200 CLAVA CAIRNS 3B9

Near Culloden, off B9006, 6½m ESE of Inverness. All reasonable times.
Free. (AM) Tel: 031-226 2570.

An extensive group of standing stones and cairns
dating from the Bronze Age.

201 CLICK MILL 1B11

Off B9057, 2m NE of Dounby, Orkney. All reasonable times. Free.
(AM) Tel: 031-226 2570.

The only working example of the traditional
horizontal water mill of Orkney.

202 CLICKHIMIN BROCH 1G4

About ¾m SW of Lerwick, Shetland. Opening standard. Free. (AM)
Tel: 031-226 2570.

This site was fortified at the beginning of the Iron
Age with a stone-built fort. Later a broch (which still
stands to a height of 17 feet) was constructed inside
the fort.

Cloch Lighthouse

203 CLOCH LIGHTHOUSE 4G5

A78, 3m SW of Gourock. Seen from the outside only.

This notable landmark stands at Cloch Point with fine
views across the Upper Firth of Clyde estuary. The
white-painted lighthouse was constructed in 1797.

204 CLUNY HOUSE 5A1

    Nr. Aberfeldy. 1 Mar-end Oct. Adult/OAP: £1, child: free. Group rates:
    10% off. (R S Masterton). Tel: Aberfeldy (0887) 20795.

Fine woodland garden of over 5 acres. Many species of
trees and shrubs. Spring bulbs and autumn colour
outstanding. The garden has been described as one of
the best woodland gardens in Scotland. Plant stall for
sale of rare plants.

205 COASTERS ARENA 6B6

Grangemouth Road, Falkirk. Arena (Skating): Thu 1830-2100, Fri
1900-2200, Sat 1330-1630, 1700-2000, 2030-2330, Sun 1900-2200.
Clubhouse: Thu-Sun 0900-1330. Thu: members only, Fri and Sun £1.50,
Sat (early) £1.00, (middle) £1.50, (late) £1.50; group rates by arrangement.
Skate hire: 50p. Tel: Falkirk (0329) 24101.

National basketball centre and largest indoor roller
skating rink in the country. Snack bar for fast food,
sports/skate shop and discotheque.

206 COATS OBSERVATORY 4H5

    Coats Observatory, Oakshaw Street, Paisley. Mon-Fri 1400-1700,
    Sat 1000-1300 and 1400-1700. Free. Groups by prior arrangement.
    (Renfrew District Council). Tel: 041-889 3151.

There has been a continuous tradition of astronomical
observation and meteorological recording since the
observatory was built in 1882. The recent updating of
seismic equipment and the installation of a satellite
weather picture receiver has made it one of the best
equipped observatories in the country.

207 COBB MEMORIAL 3A9

Between Invermoriston and Drumnadrochit by A82. All times. Free.

A cairn commemorates John Cobb, the racing
motorist, who lost his life near here in 1952 when
attempting to beat the water speed record, with his jet
speedboat, on Loch Ness.

208   COBBIE ROW'S CASTLE   1B10

On the island of Wyre, Orkney. Opening standard. Free. (AM)
Tel: 031-226 2570.

Probably the earliest stone castle authenticated in
Scotland. The *Orkneying Saga* tells how (c 1145)
Kolbein Hruga built a fine stone castle in Wyre. It
consists of a small rectangular tower, enclosed in a
circular ditch. In a graveyard near the castle is St
Mary's Chapel, a ruin of the late 12th century. It is a
small rectangular structure of nave and chancel. The
walls are built of local whinstone.

209   COLDSTREAM MUSEUM   5F6

Market Square. Whitsun-Sep, Mon, Fri & Sun 1400-1700, Sat
1000-1300. Adult: 35p, child: 15p. Tel: Coldstream (0890) 2630.

Small museum rebuilt in 1863 in the original headquarters of the Coldstream Guards (founded 1659).

210   COLLEGIATE CHURCH OF
ST NICHOLAS   6F7

Dalkeith. All reasonable times. Jun-Aug, Tue & Thu 1400-1600. Free.

Choir and apse of a 15th-century foundation endowed
by the Douglas family. There is the notable tomb of
Sir James Douglas, 1st Earl of Morton and his deaf
and dumb Countess, Joanna, daughter of James I.

211   COLUMBA'S FOOTSTEPS   4D8

W of Southend at Keil.

Traditionally it is believed that St Columba first set
foot on Scottish soil near Southend. The footsteps are
imprinted in a flat topped rock near the ruin of an old
chapel.

212   COLZIUM HOUSE AND PARK   6A6

Off A803 at Kilsyth, 10m NE of Glasgow. All year, daily, dawn to
dusk. House closed when booked for private functions. Free.
Tel: Kilsyth (0236) 823281.

19th-century residence, with museum containing
mainly local artefacts and a picture collection. Park
contains a large collection of trees and shrubs and the
ruins of Colzium Castle, destroyed by Cromwell.
Walled garden, museum, pets corner, tearoom and
arboretum.

213   COMBINED OPERATIONS MUSEUM   4F3

Cherry Park, near Inveraray Castle, Inveraray. 1st Sat in Apr-2nd Sun in
Oct. Apr, May, Jun, Sep, Oct, daily 1000-1300, 1400-1800, Sun
1300-1800, closed Fri. Jul-Aug, daily 1000-1800 incl Fri, Sun 1300-1800.
Last admissions: 1230 & 1730. Adult: 65p, OAP/child: 45p.
(The Trustees of the Tenth Duke of Argyll). Tel: Inveraray (0499) 2203.

The museum sets out to show by means of
photographs, models, posters and displays, the work of
the Combined Training Centre at Inveraray during
World War II.

214   COMLONGON CASTLE   5C10

Situated in Clarencefield, midway between Dumfries and Annan on
B724. Mar-Nov, daily 1030-1800. Adult: 60p, child: 30p. Group rates:
45p. Tel: Clarencefield (038787) 283.

Exceptionally well preserved mid-15th century Border
castle containing many original architectural features
including pledge chamber with pit, heraldic devices,
fireplaces and medieval ironwork. Picnic area, secluded
walks, aviary. Bed and breakfast is available at the castle.

Commando Memorial

215 COMMANDO MEMORIAL 2H12

Off A82, 11m NE of Fort William.

An impressive sculpture by Scott Sutherland, erected in 1952 to commemorate the Commandos of World War II who trained in this area. Fine views of Ben Nevis and Lochaber.

216 CORGARFF CASTLE 3D10

Off A939, 15m NW of Ballater. Opening standard, key-keeper in winter. Adult: 50p, OAP/child: 25p. Group rates: 10% discount for parties of 11 or more persons. (AM) Tel: 031-226 2570.

A 16th-century tower house, converted into a garrison post and enclosed within a star-shaped loopholed wall in 1748. The castle was burned in 1571 by Edom o' Gordon and the wife, family and household of Alexander Forbes, the owner, perished in the flames. (See also No 58).

217 CORRIESHALLOCH GORGE 2G7

A835 at Braemore, 12m SSE of Ullapool. All times. Free. (NTS)

This spectacular gorge, 1m long and 120 feet deep, contains the Falls of Measach which plunge 150 feet. Suspension bridge viewpoint.

218 CORRIMONY CAIRN 2H9

At Glen Urquhart, 8m W of Drumnadrochit, Loch Ness. All times. Free. (AM) Tel: 031-226 2570.

This neolithic chambered cairn is surrounded by a slab kerb, outside which is a circle of standing stones.

219 CORRYVRECKAN WHIRLPOOL 4D4

Between the islands of Jura and Scarba.

This treacherous tide-race, very dangerous for small craft, covers an extensive area and may be seen from the north end of Jura or from Craignish Point. The noise can be heard from a considerable distance.

220 COULTER MOTTE 5B6

Off A72, 2m N of Coulter, 1½m SW of Biggar (A702). Opening standard. Free. (AM) Tel: 031-226 2570.

Early medieval castle mound, originally moated and probably surrounded by a palisade enclosing a timber tower.

221   **'COUNTESS FIONA'**   **4G4**

Cruising on Loch Lomond from Balloch pier. (Sailing times) Apr-Sep, daily 1015; also 28 Jun-30 Aug 1545. Adult: £6.50, OAP/child: £3.25 (Low Season only). Group rates: discount of 10% on party bookings of over 20 persons. (Alloa Brewery Ltd). Tel: 041-226 4271.

The only traditional type cruise ship now on Loch Lomond. Covered observation lounge, ample seated deck area. Full 5-hour (approx) cruise from Balloch calls at Luss, Rowardennan, Tarbet and Inversnaid. Licensed bar and self-service snack bar.

222   **CRAIG CASTLE**   **3E9**

B9002 off A97, 12m SSW of Huntly (signposted). Open summer, by appointment only (contact Baroness of Craig, tel: Lumsden (046 48) 202). Admission: 50p.

The oldest part of the castle is the keep, 60 feet high, which bears the date 1528, though possibly earlier. Of special interest are the courthouse and the coat of arms.

223   **CRAIGCLEUCH SCOTTISH EXPLORERS' MUSEUM**   **5D9**

2m NW of Langholm on B709. Easter, 1 May-30 Sep, daily 1000-1700, or by arrangement. Adult/OAP: £1.00, child: 50p. (Mr David Young). Tel: Langholm (0541) 80137.

Baronial Scottish mansion house, with exhibition of beautiful carvings in coral, jade, ivory, wood, oriental paintings and hundreds of outstanding historic tribal sculptures. Includes rare objects as may have been seen by Scottish explorers Mungo Park (on the Niger), David Livingstone (on the Zambezi) and George Young (on Canada's North West Coast). House has panoramic views, woodland walks.

224   **CRAIGELLACHIE BRIDGE**   **3D8**

Near A941, just N of Craigellachie, 12m SSE of Elgin.

One of Thomas Telford's most beautiful bridges. Opened in 1814, it carried the main road till 1973 when a new bridge was built alongside. It has a 152-feet main span of iron, cast in Wales, and two ornamental stone towers at each end.

Craigievar Castle

225 CRAIGIEVAR CASTLE 3F10

On A980, 6m S of Alford, 26m W of Aberdeen. Castle: 1 May-30 Sep, daily 1400-1800 (last tour 1715). Adult: £1.40, child: 70p; group rates. Grounds: open all year 0930-sunset. (NTS) Tel: Lumphanan (033 983) 635.

This masterpiece of Scottish baronial architecture stands on the Braes of Leochel-Cushnie in the midst of 100 acres of farm and parkland. Completed in 1626 for William Forbes (Willie the Merchant or Danzig Willie), it stands today virtually as the builders left it—a fairytale castle of turrets, chimney stacks, corbelling and gables. Famous for magnificent original plaster ceilings, carved panelling and all family contents. Picnic area, woodland walk.

226 CRAIGNETHAN CASTLE 5A6

2½m W of A72 at Crossford, 5m NW of Lanark. Opening standard. Adult: 50p, OAP/child: 25p. Group rates: 10% discount for parties of 11 or more visitors. (AM) Tel: 031-226 2570.

This extensive and well-preserved ruin, chief stronghold of the Hamiltons who were supporters of Mary, Queen of Scots, was repeatedly assailed by the Protestant party and partly dismantled by them in 1579. The oldest, central portion is a large tower house of unusual and ornate design. Recent excavations have revealed possibly the earliest example in Britain of a *caponier*, a covered gun-looped passageway across a defensive ditch.

227 CRAIGSTON CASTLE 3G8

Off B9105, 10m SE of Banff. By arrangement. (Mr Bruce Urquhart). Tel: King Edward (08885) 228.

Seat of the Urquhart family since its building 1604-07. Can be seen from the Aberdeen to Banff road. Adjacent woodlands of interesting species, etc. Parking.

228 CRAIL MUSEUM AND HERITAGE CENTRE 6H3

62 Marketgate, Crail. Easter (2 weeks), Jun-Sep. Adult: 50p, OAP/child: 20p. Group rates by arrangement. Tel: Crail (0333) 50869.

Exhibits include relics of the Royal Burgh, the Collegiate Church, local architecture, the old harbour, crafts and Crail past and prtesent. Heritage Centre and Information Office.

229 CRAIL TOLBOOTH 6H3

Marketgate, Crail. 9m SE of St Andrews.

The Tolbooth dates from the early 16th century, displaying a fish weather vane, and a coat of arms dated 1602. In the striking Dutch Tower is a bell dated 1520, cast in Holland. There have been 18th and 19th century additions. Elsewhere in this picturesque fishing village which is the oldest Royal Burgh in the East neuk of Fife, see the Collegiate Church dating back to the 13th century, the Mercat Cross topped by a unicorn, the harbour and the crowstepped, red-tiled houses. The Tolbooth is a library and Town Hall.

230 CRARAE GLEN GARDEN 3F11

A83, 10m SW of Inveraray. All year, daily 0900-1800. Adult: £1.00, child: free. (Crarae Garden Charitable Trust). Tel: Minard (0546) 86633.

Among the loveliest open to the public in Scotland, these gardens of Crarae Lodge, beside Loch Fyne and set in a Highland glen, are noted for rhododendrons, azaleas, conifers and ornamental shrubs.

231 CRATHES CASTLE AND GARDENS   3F11

♿
P
T

Off A93, 3½m E of Banchory. Castle: 28-31 Mar and 1 May-30 Sep, Mon-Sat 1100-1800, Sun 1400-1800 (last admission 1715). Garden and grounds: all year, daily 0930-sunset. Visitor Centre, shop and restaurant: 28-31 Mar and 1 May-30 Sep, Mon-Sat 1100-1800, Sun 1400-1800 (last admission 1715). Admission: castle only, adult: £1.40, child: 70p; garden only, adult: 80p, child: 40p; grounds only, adult: 50p, child: 25p. (Easter and May-Sep only, other times by donation.) Combined tickets, adult: £1.80, child: 90p. Group rates. No dogs in garden, please. Tel: Crathes (033044) 525.

The double square tower of the castle dates from 1533 and the building, an outstanding example of a Scottish tower house, was completed in 1660. The notable interior includes the fascinating painted ceilings, dating from 1599, in the Chamber of the Nine Nobles, the Chamber of the Nine Muses and the Green Lady's Room. The Queen Anne and Victoria wings were destroyed by fire in 1966. The Queen Anne wing only was rebuilt and opened in 1972. Yew hedges dating from 1702 enclose a series of small gardens with fine collections of trees and shrubs. Nature trails designed for wheelchair users. Shop, licensed restaurant and snack bar; formal gardens, grounds with 7½ miles of wayfaring trails, visitor centre with exhibition rooms and field study centre. Ample parking, cars and coaches.

232 CRATHIE CHURCH   3D11

♿

Crathie, 8m W of Ballater. Daily 0930-1730, Sun 1400-1800 (services held at 1130, Sun). Free. Tel: Crathie (03384) 208.

This small church, built in 1895, is attended by the Royal Family when in residence at Balmoral. (see No 71)

233 CRAWFORD CENTRE FOR THE ARTS   6G2

♿
A

93 North Street, St Andrews. Gallery. All year. Mon-Sat 1000-1700, Sun 1400-1700. Gallery free. Tel: St Andrews (0334) 76161, ext 591.

Arts Centre with exhibition galleries and Drama Studio open throughout the summer; drama workshops and summer theatre are a feature of the programme and the galleries have changing exhibitions often of local interest. Coffee available in gallery

**234 CREETOWN GEM ROCK MUSEUM
AND GALLERY**   4H10

♿
T

Approach by A75 to Creetown, turn up opposite clock tower. Daily, summer 0930-1900, winter 0930-1700. Adult: 65p, OAP: 45p, child: 20p. Group rates: 40p for large parties. Tel: Creetown (0671 82) 357.

A beautiful collection of gems and minerals from around the world. This large collection has taken over 50 years in collecting and is recognised as being one of the most comprehensive collection of its type, and shows the many fascinating mineral forms created by nature. Tearoom, gift shop and custom gemstone cutting workshop.

235 CRICHTON CASTLE   6F7

B6367, 7m SE of Dalkeith. Opening standard, except Oct-Mar, Sat and Sun only. Adult: 50p, OAP/child: 25p. Group rates: 10% discount for parties of 11 or more persons. (AM) Tel: 031-226 2570.

The keep dates from the 14th century, although today's ruins are mostly 15th/17th century. This castle, elaborate in style, has an arcaded range, the upper frontage of which is wrought with faceted stonework, erected by the Earl of Bothwell in the 16th century. The little Collegiate Church, ½m north, dating from 1499 and still in use, is notable for its tower and barrel vaulting.

236 CRINAN CANAL 4E4

Crinan to Ardrishaig, by Lochgilphead. Tel: Ardrishaig (0546) 3210.

Constructed between 1793 and 1801 to carry ships from Loch Fyne to the Atlantic without rounding Kintyre. The 9-mile stretch of water with 15 locks is now almost entirely used by pleasure craft. The towing path provides a very pleasant, easy walk with the interest of canal activity and magnificent views to the River Add and Loch Crinan.

237 CROICK CHURCH 2H6

On unclassified road up Strathcarron, 10m W of Ardgay. All reasonable times. Free.

A small Highland church, built by Telford, with remarkable inscriptions on the windows by crofters evicted in 1845.

238 CROMBIE COUNTRY PARK 5E1

  ፈ
  A
  P

On B961, 3½m NE of Newbigging. All year, 1000-dusk. Free. Car park charge. Buses by appointment. (Tayside Regional Council). Tel: Carmyllie (024 16) 360.

Victorian reservoir with the appearance of a natural loch. Extensive conifer woodland and some broadleaf and specimen trees in 250 acres of land. Wildlife hides, trails, display and interpretation centre. Ranger Centre with environmental displays, woodland and lochside walks. Guided walks, talks, picnic and barbecue areas, children's play park and conservation areas.

239 CROSS KIRK 5C6

Peebles. Opening standard. Key from custodian in nearby house. Free. (AM) Tel: 031-226 2570.

The remains of a Trinitarian Friary, consisting of a nave and west tower. The foundations of the cloistered building have been laid bare.

Crossraguel Abbey

240 CROSSRAGUEL ABBEY 4G8

A77, 2m SW of Maybole. Opening standard, except closed Thu afternoon and Fri. Adult: 50p, OAP/child: 25p. Group rates: 10% discount for parties of 11 or more persons. (AM) Tel: 031-226 2570.

A Cluniac monastery built in 1244 by the Earl of Carrick during the reign of Alexander II. The Abbey was inhabited by Benedictine monks from 1244 until the end of the 16th century, and the extensive remains are of high architectural distinction.

Croy Brae: see No 399.

241 CRUACHAN PUMPED STORAGE POWER STATION 4F2

&
A
P

Off A85, 18m E of Oban. Easter-Oct, daily 0900-1700. Adult: £1.00, child (10-15 years): 50p. (North of Scotland Hydro-Electric Board). Tel: Cruachan (086 62) 673.

In a vast cavern inside Ben Cruachan is a 400,000 kilowatt pumped storage power station which utilises water pumped from Loch Awe to a reservoir 1,200 feet up the mountain. Visitor Centre, guided minibus tour, picnic area and snack bar. Car park.

242 CRUGGLETON CHURCH AND CASTLE 4H11

Off B7063, 9m SSE of Wigtown. Summer months, any time. Church: keys from nearby farmer, Mr Fisher. Free.

The little church, just off the road, is Norman; the chancel arch doors and windows are 12th century. An arch, the only remains of the castle, lies near the shore.

243 CULCREUCH CASTLE AND COUNTRY PARK 5A4

At Fintry, 6m E of Killearn on B818, junction with B822. All year, Mon-Fri 1030-1600, Sun 1200-1730. 60p admission to grounds on Sun. Conducted tours: adult: £1.00, child: 50p. Group rates: 25% discount on castle tours. (Baron of Culcreuch). Tel: Fintry (036 086) 228.

A splendid and typical example of a clan castle built in the 14th and 15th centuries by the Galbraith Clan. In excellent condition and still the home of the Laird of Culcreuch. Contains a bottle dungeon, secret passages and rooms, and a master bedroom with handpainted wallpaper of 1723, preserved by its 6-feet thick walls. Conducted tours available. 1,600 acres parkland gardens. Coffee shop, restaurant, bar, souvenir shop, closed Oct-April.

244 CULLERLIE STONE CIRCLE 3G10

Off A974, 1m S of Garlogie, 13m W of Aberdeen. All times. Free. (AM) Tel: 031-226 2570.

The stone circle of eight undressed boulders encloses an area on which eight small cairns were later constructed, probably of late second millennium BC.

245 CULLODEN MOOR 3B8

&
T

B9006, 5m E of Inverness. Site open all year. Visitor Centre: 28 Mar-31 May and 1-26 Oct, daily 0930-1750; 1 June-30 Sep, daily 0900-1930. Visitor Centre (including audio-visual): adult: £1.10, child: 55p. Group rates—Adult parties: 90p, children: 45p. (NTS) Tel: Inverness (0463) 790607.

Here Prince Charles Edward's cause was finally crushed at the battle on 16 April 1746. The battle lasted only 40 minutes: the Prince's army lost some 1,200 men, and the King's army 310. Features of interest include the Graves of the Clans, communal burial places with simple headstones bearing individual clan names alongside the main road; the great memorial cairn, erected in 1881; the Well of the Dead, a single stone with the inscription 'The English were buried here'; Old Leanach farmhouse, now restored as a battle museum; and the huge Cumberland Stone from which the victorious Duke of Cumberland is said to have viewed the scene. Information available on cassette. Tearoom.

246 CULROSS ABBEY 6C5

7½m W of Dunfermline. All reasonable times. Free. Tel: 031-226 2570.

The remains of a 13th-century Cistercian Monastery. The choir of the Abbey Church is the present Parish Church.

---

247 CULROSS PALACE 6C5

Culross, 7½m W of Dunfermline. Opening standard. Adult: £1, OAP/child: 50p. Group rates: 10% discount for parties of 11 or more persons. (AM) Tel: 031-226 2570.

Culross, on the north shore of the River Forth, is a most remarkable example of a small town of the 16th and 17th centuries which has changed little in 300 years. The small 'palace' was built between 1597 and 1611 by Sir George Bruce, who developed the sea-going trade in salt and coal from Culross. With crow-stepped gables and pantiled roofs, the 'palace' also has outstanding painted ceilings. Other buildings which must be seen include the Study (No 919), the Town House (No 952), the Abbey (No 246), the Ark and the Nunnery.

---

248 CULSH EARTH HOUSE 3F10

Access by Culsh Farmhouse, near Tarland on B9119, 13m NE of Ballater. Opening standard. Free. (AM) Tel: 031-226 2570.

A well-preserved earth house of Iron Age date with roofing slabs intact over a large chamber and entrance.

---

249 CULZEAN CASTLE AND COUNTRY PARK 4G8

   T

A719, 12m SSW of Ayr. Castle: 28 Mar-30-Sep, daily 1000-1800; 1-31 Oct, daily 1200-1700. Adult: £1.60, child: 80p. Group rates (except in Jul and Aug). Country Park: grounds always open. Information Centre, auditorium and exhibition 28 Mar-30 Sep, daily 1000-1800; 1-31 Oct, daily 1200-1600. Pedestrians free, car and occupants: £2.00, minibuses and caravans: £3.50, coaches: £10.00 (these charges apply 24 Mar-31 Oct only; vehicles except school coaches free other times). (NTS; Strathclyde Regional Council; Kyle and Carrick, Cunninghame, Cumnock and Doon Valley District Councils). Tel: Kirkoswald (06556) 274.

The splendid castle, one of Robert Adam's most notable creations, although built around an ancient tower of the Kennedys, dates mainly from 1777. Special features are the Round Drawing Room, the fine plaster ceilings and magnificent oval staircase. The Eisenhower Presentation explains the General's association with Culzean.

In 1970 Culzean became the first country park in Scotland; in 1973 a Reception and Interpretation Centre with exhibition etc was opened in the farm buildings designed by Robert Adam. The 565-acre grounds include a walled garden established in 1783, aviary, swan pond, camelia house and orangery. Ranger naturalist service with guided walks, talks and films in summer. Licensed self-service restaurant.

---

250 CUWEEN HILL CAIRN 1B11

A965, ½m S of Finstown, which is 6m WNW of Kirkwall. All reasonable times. Apply to key-keeper at nearby farmhouse. Free. (AM) Tel: 031-226 2570.

A low mound covering a megalithic passage tomb. Contained bones of men, dogs and oxen when discovered. Probably mid third millennium BC.

251   DALKEITH PARK   6F7

*At E end of Dalkeith High Street, 7m S of Edinburgh on A68. Easter-
end Oct, daily; Nov, Sat & Sun 1100-1800. Adult: 65p, child: 65p.
Group rates: parties of 20 or more: 60p. (Duke of Buccleuch).
Tel: 031-663 5684 (1100-1800) or 031-663 4178 outwith these hours.*

Woodland walks beside the river in the extensive
grounds of Dalkeith Palace. Tunnel walk, adventure
woodland play area, nature trails, 18th-century bridge
and orangery.

Dalmeny House

252   DALMENY HOUSE   6D6

*By South Queensferry, 7m W of Edinburgh, take A90 then B294.
1 May-30 Sep, daily 1400-1730. Closed Fri and Sat. Adult: £1.70,
OAP: £1.40, children and students: £1.10. Group rates. (Earl of Rosebery).
Tel: 031-331 1888.*

The Primrose family, Earls of Rosebery, have lived
here for over 300 years. The present house dates from
1815, in Tudor Gothic style, built by William Wilkins.
Interior Gothic splendour of hammerbeamed hall,
vaulted corridors and classical main rooms.
Magnificent collection of 18th-century British
portraits, 18th-century French furniture, tapestries,
porcelain from the Rothschild Mentmore collection,
the Napoleon collection and other works of art.
Lovely grounds and 4½-mile shore walk from Cramond
to South Queensferry. Open all year. (See also No 337).

253   DALMENY KIRK   6D6

Off A90, 7m W of Edinburgh. All year, daily. Free. Tel: 031-331 1869.

An attractive Romanesque church, built in the middle
of the 12th century, with the Rosebery Aisle to the
north, built in 1671 by Sir Archibald Primrose.

254   DARNAWAY FARM VISITOR CENTRE   3C8

*Off A96, 3m W of Forres. Easter, May-Sep, daily 1000-1700.
Admission: 80p; group rates. (Moray Estates). Also available: tours to
Darnaway Castle (Jun-Aug, Wed & Sun, £1.00 per person); tour of estate
with countryside ranger (Tue & Thu, begins 1415, £1.00 per person).
Tel: Brodie (03094) 469.*

At the Visitor Centre, an exhibition of the farms and
forest of Moray Estates, with audio-visual programme.
Viewing platform to watch cows being milked.
Nature trails and woodland walks, picnic areas,
tearoom and play area.

255   DAVID MARSHALL LODGE   4H3

*Off A821, 1m N of Aberfoyle. Mid Mar-mid Oct, daily 1000-1800.
10p per car. (FC)*

Visitor Centre and starting point for walks in the
Queen Elizabeth Forest Park. It commands wide views
over the upper Forth Valley to the Menteith Hills,
Campsie Fells and Ben Lomond. (See also No 24).

256 DAWYCK BOTANIC GARDENS 5C6

&
T

*B712, 8m SW of Peebles. Apr-Sep inclusive, daily 1200-1700.
Admission: 50 per car. Group rates: coach parties 50p per every 4 persons.
Dogs on lead only. (Royal Botanic Garden, Edinburgh).
Tel: Peebles (0721) 6254.*

Rare trees, including many very fine conifers, shrubs,
rhododendrons and narcissi, among woodland walks.
In the woods is Dawyck Chapel, designed by William
Burn.

257 DEAN CASTLE 4H7

*Dean Road, off Glasgow Road, Kilmarnock. 12 May-22 Sep, Mon-Fri
1400-1700, Sat & Sun 1200-1700 (and by arrangement). Adult: 50p,
children and residents: free. Group rates: 1 person in every 10 free.
Tel: Kilmarnock (0563) 26401.*

14th-century fortified keep and 15th-century palace,
the ancestral home of the Boyd family. It contains an
outstanding collection of medieval arms, armour,
tapestries and musical instruments. Also Dean Castle
Country Park, open all year, free; 200 acres of
woodland and farmland extending over the old estates
of Dean and Assloss. Tearoom and riding centre.

258 THE DEAN'S HOUSE 6A4

&
P

*Cathedral Square, Dunblane. Jun-Sep, Mon-Sat 1030-1230, 1430-1630.
Free. Tel: Dunblane (0786) 822217.*

Former dwelling house, built 1624, of Dean James
Pearson, housing a cathedral museum and library.

259 DEER ABBEY 3H8

*At Old Deer, B9029, off A950, 10m W of Peterhead. Apr-Sep, Thu-Sat
0930-1900, Sun 1400-1900. Closed Oct-Mar. Adult: 50p,
OAP/child: 25p. Group rates: 10% discount for parties of 11 or more
persons. (AM) Tel: 031-226 2570.*

Rather scant remains of a Cistercian monastery
founded in 1219.

Deer Museum: see Nos 442 and 949.

Delgatie Castle

260 DELGATIE CASTLE 3G8

*Off A947, 2m E of Turriff. By previous arrangement.
(Capt Hay of Hayfield). Adult: £1.00, child: 50p.*

Tower house, home of the Hays of Delgatie, dating
back to the 12th century with additions up to the
17th century. Its contents include pictures and arms;
the notable painted ceilings were installed
c 1590. Mary, Queen of Scots stayed here for three
days in 1562; a portrait hangs in the room she used.
Turnpike stair of 97 steps.

261 DESKFORD CHURCH 3E8

*Off B9018, 4m S of Cullen. Opening standard. Free. (AM)
Tel: 031-226 2570.*

This ruined building includes a rich carving which
bears an inscription telling that *this present lovable work
of sacrament house* was provided by Alexander Ogilvy of
Deskford in 1551.

262 DEVIL'S BEEF TUB 5C8

A701, 6m N of Moffat. Tel: Moffat (0683) 20620.

A huge, spectacular hollow among the hills, at the head of Annandale. In the swirling mists of this out-of-the-way retreat Border reivers hid cattle 'lifted' in their raids.

Devorgilla's Bridge: see No 755.

263 JOHN DEWAR & SONS 6D2

Dunkeld Road, Inveralmond, Perth. All year except holidays. Tours: Mon-Wed 1015 & 1415, Thu & Fri 1015 & 1400. Free. (Mr R Keiller, visits organiser). Tel: Perth (0738) 21231.

During a conducted tour of 1½ hours visitors see the casks of matured whisky arriving for blending and follow the process through to bottling and despatch. Gift shop.

264 DICK INSTITUTE 4H7

Elmbank Avenue, off London Road, Kilmarnock. Apr-Sep, Mon, Tu, Thu, Fri 1000-2000, Wed & Sat 1000-1700; Oct-Mar, Mon-Sat 1000-1700. Free. Tel: Kilmarnock (0563) 26401.

The museum has an important collection of geological specimens, local archaeology, Scottish broadswords, firearms and natural history. The Art Gallery has frequently changing exhibitions.

265 DINGWALL TOWN HALL 3A8

Dingwall town centre. Apr-Oct. Admission charge. Tel: Dingwall (0349) 63461.

Museum of local history in the Town House, which dates from 1730. There is a special exhibit of General Sir Hector MacDonald (1853-1903), born near Dingwall, and recalling his distinguished military career.

Dirleton Castle

266 DIRLETON CASTLE 6G5

A198, 8m W of North Berwick. Opening standard. Adult: £1.00, OAP/child: 50p. Group rates: 10% discount for parties of 11 or more persons. Tel: 031-226 2570.

Near the wide village green of Dirleton, these beautiful ruins date back to 1225 with 15th/17th-century additions. The castle had an eventful history from its first siege by Edward I in 1298 until its destruction in 1650. The 'clustered' donjon dates from the 13th century and the garden encloses a 17th-century bowling green surrounded by yews.

267 DOGTON STONE 6E4

Off B922, 5m NW of Kirkcaldy. All reasonable times. Free. Entry by Dogton Farmhouse. (AM) Tel: 031-226 2570.

An ancient Celtic Cross with traces of animal and figure sculpture.

268 DORNOCH CATHEDRAL 3B6

In Dornoch. All year. 0900-dusk. Free.

Founded in 1224 by Gilbert, Archdeacon of Moray
and Bishop of Caithness, this little cathedral was
partially destroyed by fire in 1570, restored in the 17th
century, in 1835-37, and again in 1924. The fine 13th-
century stonework is still to be seen.

269 DORNOCH CRAFT CENTRE 3B6

P
T
*Town Jail. All year. Summer, Mon-Sat 0930-1700, Sun 1200-1700;
Winter, Mon-Fri 0930-1700. Free. Tel: Dornoch (0862) 810555.*

Weaving of tartans on Saurgr power looms, kilt
making and soft toy making. Small exhibition in Jail
cells. Coffee room (Apr-Sep).

Doune Castle

270 DOUNE CASTLE 5A3

*Off A84 at Doune, 8m NW of Stirling. Opening standard. Adult:
£1.00, OAP/child: 50p. Group rates: 10% discount for parties of 11 or
more persons. (AM) Tel: 031-226 2570.*

Splendid ruins of one of the best preserved medieval
castles in Scotland, built late 14th or early 15th
century by the Regent Albany. After his execution in
1424 it came into the hands of the Stuarts of Doune,
Earls of Moray, in the 16th century, and the 'Bonnie
Earl of Moray' lived here before his murder in 1592.
The bridge in the village was built in 1535 by Robert
Spittal, James IV's tailor, to spite the ferryman who
had refused him a passage.

271 DOUNE MOTOR MUSEUM 5A3

A
T
*At Doune on A84, 8m NW of Stirling. Apr-Oct, daily 1000-1700.
Adult: £1.50, OAP: 90p, child: 75p. (Earl of Moray).
Tel: Doune (0786) 841 203.*

The Earl of Moray's collection of vintage and post-
vintage cars, including examples of Hispano Suiza,
Bentley, Jaguar, Aston Martin, Lagonda and the
second oldest Rolls Royce in the world. Cafeteria.

**272 DOUNREAY NUCLEAR POWER
DEVELOPMENT ESTABLISHMENT** 3C3

*Dounreay, 10m W of Thurso. May-Sep, daily 0900-1600. Free. No dogs.
Tours (free) by arrangement with Tourist Information Centre, Riverside,
Thurso, tel: Thurso (0847 62371; or through the exhibition, tel: Thurso
(0847) 62121, ext 656. (United Kingdom Atomic Energy Authority).*

An interesting exhibition giving visitors a general
conception of nuclear power and of the activities and
work taking place at the establishment. Conducted
tours of the prototype Fast Reactor every afternoon
(limited to those over 14 years). Picnic area.

273 DRUM CASTLE 3G10

     A P T

Off A93, 10m WSW of Aberdeen. 1 May-30 Sep, daily 1400-1800 (last admission 1715). Adult: £1.40, child: 70p; group rates. Grounds open all year, 0930-sunset. (NTS) Tel: (03308) 204.

A massive granite tower built towards the end of the 13th century adjoins a mansion of 1619. The Royal Forest of Drum was conferred in 1323 by Robert the Bruce on his armour-bearer and clerk-register, William de Irwin. The family connection remained unbroken until the death of Mr H Q Forbes Irvine in 1975. The house stands in pleasant grounds with lawns, rare trees and shrubs, and inside are antique furniture and silver, family portraits and relics. Coffee room, adventure playground and wayfaring course.

274 DRUMCOLTRAN TOWER 5B10

Off A711, 8m SW of Dumfries. Opening standard, apply key-keeper. Free. (AM) Tel: 031-226 2570.

Situated among farm buildings, this is a good example of a Scottish tower house of about the mid-16th century, simple and severe.

275 DRUMLANRIG CASTLE 5B8

     T

Off A76, 3m N of Thornhill, Dumfriesshire and 16m off A74 by A702. 1 May-25 Aug, daily except Fri, May, Jun 1330-1615, Sun 1400-1715; Jul-25 Aug 1100-1615, Sun 1400.1715. Adult: £2.00, OAP: £1.50, child: £1.00. Group rates:—parties of 20 or more, adult: £1.50, OAP: £1.50, child (under 16): 75p. Tel: Thornhill (0848) 30248.

Unique example of late 17th century Renaissance architecture in pink sandstone, built on the site of earlier Douglas strongholds. Set in parkland ringed by the wild Dumfriesshire hills. Louis XIV furniture, and paintings by Rembrandt, Holbein, Murillo, Ruysdael. Adventure woodland play area, nature trail, gift shop and tearoom. Guide dogs by prior arrangement. Lift available but unaccompanied.

276 DRUMMOND CASTLE GARDENS 6A3

Off A8022, 2½m S of Crieff. Apr, Sep, Wed, Sun 1400-1800, May-Aug daily 1400-1800 (last admission 1700). Adult: £1, OAP/child: 50p (Grimsthorpe and Drummond Castle Trust).

The oldest tower, now an armoury, dates from the 15th century, but most of the old castle once attacked by Cromwell was dismantled in 1745. There is a multiple sundial dated 1630 and notable formal Italian garden.

277 DRUMTRODDEN 4H11

Off 714, 8m SSW of Wigtown. All times. Free. (AM) Tel: 031-226 2570.

A group of cup-and-ring markings of Bronze Age date on a natural rock face. 400 yards south is an alignment of three adjacent stones.

278 DRYBURGH ABBEY 5E7

Off A68, 6m SE of Melrose. Opening standard. Adult: £1.00, OAP/child: 50p. Group rates: 10% discount for parties of 11 or more persons. (AM) Tel: 031-226 2570.

One of the four famous Border abbeys, founded in the reign of David I by Hugh de Morville, Constable of Scotland. Though little save the transepts has been spared of the church itself, the cloister buildings have survived in a more complete state than in any other Scottish monastery, except Iona and Inchcolm (see Nos 571 and 558). Much of the existing remains are 12th/13th century. Sir Walter Scott is buried in the church

279 DRYHOPE TOWER 5D7

Off A708 near St Mary's Loch, 15m W of Selkirk. All reasonable times. Free.

A stout little tower originally four storeys high, rebuilt c 1613. Birthplace of Mary Scott, *The Flower of Yarrow* who married the freebooter Auld Wat of Harden, 1576— ancestors Sir Walter Scott was proud to claim.

Duart Castle

280 DUART CASTLE 4E2

Off A849, on E point of Mull. May-Sep, daily 1030-1800. Adult: £1.50, OAP/child: 70p. (Lord Maclean KT). Tel: Craignure (068 02) 309.

The keep, dominating the Sound of Mull, was built in the 13th century. A royal charter of 1390 confirmed the lands, including Duart, to the Macleans. The clan supported the Stuarts and the castle, extended in 1633, was taken and ruined by the Duke of Argyll in 1691. During the 1745 Rising, Sir Hector Maclean of Duart was imprisoned in the Tower of London and his estate forfeited, not to be recovered until 1911 when Sir Fitzroy Maclean restored it. Tearoom.

281 DUFF HOUSE 3F7

At Banff. Apr-Sep, Mon-Fri 0930-1900, Sun 1400-1900; key-keeper Oct-Mar. Adult: 50p, OAP/child: 25p. Group rates: 10% discount for parties of 11 or more persons. (AM) Tel: 031-226 2570.

Although incomplete, William Adam's splendid and richly detailed mansion is among the finest works of Georgian baroque architecture in Britain. There is an interpretative exhibition.

282 DUFFTOWN MUSEUM 3E9

The Tower, The Square, Dufftown. May, Jun, Sep, Mon-Sat 0930-1730; Jul, Aug, Mon-Sat 0930-1830, Sun 1400-1830. Free. Tel: Forres (0309) 73701.

Exhibitions on local history themes, including Mortlach Church. Tourist Information Office.

283 DUFFUS CASTLE 3D7

Off B9012, 5m NW of Elgin. Opening standard. Free. (AM) Tel: 031-226 2570.

Massive ruins of a fine motte and bailey castle, surrounded by a moat still entire and water-filled. A fine 14th-century tower crowns the Norman motte. The original seat of the de Moravia family, the Murrays, now represented by the dukedoms of Atholl and Sutherland.

284 DUMBARTON CASTLE   4H5

Dumbarton, off A814 on Dumbarton Rock. Opening standard. Adult: 50p, OAP/child: 25p. Group rates: 10% discount for parties of 11 or more persons. (AM) Tel: 031-226 2570.

Though mainly modern barracks, a dungeon, a 12th-century gateway and a sundial gifted by Mary, Queen of Scots are preserved. It was from Dumbarton that Queen Mary left for France in 1548, at the age of five.

285 DUMFRIES MUSEUM   5B9

The Observatory, Dumfries. Apr-Sep, Mon-Sat 1000-1300, 1400-1700, Sun 1400-1700; Oct-Mar, Tues-Sat only 1000-1300, 1400-1700. Free. Discount for camera obscura. (Nithsdale District Council). Tel: Dumfries (0387) 53374.

This regional museum for the Solway area has recently been refurbished and contains a wide variety of interesting exhibits. It is based on an 18th-century windmill and has a camera obscura (admission charge).

286 DUN CARLOWAY BROCH   2C4

A858, 16m WNW of Stornoway, Isle of Lewis. Opening standard. Free. (AM) Tel: 031-226 2570.

One of the best presented Iron Age broch towers. Still standing about 30 feet high.

287 DUN DORNADILLA BROCH   2H4

20m N of Lairg. A836, then on Loch Hope road. All times. Free. (AM) Tel: 031-226 2570.

A notable example of a prehistoric brooch.

Dun Telve and Dun Troddan: see No 497.

288 DUNADD FORT   4E4

W of A816, 4m NNW of Lochgilphead. All reasonable times. Free. (AM) Tel: 031-226 2570.

On an isolated once-fortified hillock, Dunadd was one of the ancient capitals of Dalriada (c 5000-800), from which the Celtic Kingdom of Scotland sprang. Near its citadel is carved a fine figure of a boar and the sign of a footprint; this is probably where the early kings were invested with royal power.

289 DUNAVERTY ROCK   4D8

At Southend, dominating beach and golf course. All times. Free.

Formerly the site of Dunaverty Castle, a Macdonald stronghold. In 1647, about 300 people were put to death there by Covenanters under General Leslie. The rock is known locally as 'Blood Rock'.

290 DUNBLANE CATHEDRAL   6A4

In Dunblane, A9, 6m N of Stirling. Opening standard, except summer when 1400-1700 on Sunday. Free. (AM) Tel: 031-226 2570.

The existing building dates mainly from the 13th century but incorporates a 12th-century tower. The nave was unroofed after the Reformation but the whole building was restored in 1829-95.

Dunblane Cathedral Museum: see No 258.

**291 HENRY DUNCAN COTTAGE
MUSEUM**   **5C10**

*In Ruthwell, 6½m W of Annan. All year; custodian on call at all
reasonable times. Free (pre-booking preferred). (Trustee Savings Bank
Scotland). Tel: Clarencefield (038 787) 640.*

The cottage was the first Savings Bank, founded
by Dr Henry Duncan in 1810. The museum with its
interesting exhibition, is a mine of information about
the early days of the Savings bank movement.

---

292 DUNCANSBY HEAD   **3E2**

The NE point of mainland Scotland, 18m N of Wick. All times. Free.

The lighthouse on Duncansby Head commands a fine
view of Orkney, the Pentland Skerries and the
headlands of the east coast. A little to the south are
the three Duncansby Stacks, huge stone 'needles' in
the sea. The sandstone cliffs are severed by great deep
gashes (geos) running into the land. One of these is
bridged by a natural arch.

**293 DUNDEE, BARRACK STREET
MUSEUM**   **6F1**

*City centre. All year, Mon-Sat 1000-1700. Free (prior notice of groups
preferred). (City of Dundee District Council). Tel: Dundee (0382) 23141.*

Currently being developed as Dundee's museum of
natural history. Main displays on wildlife of Tayside,
including highlands. Also exotic wildlife and geology.
Some disruption of displays may occur during
redevelopment. Small shop, toilets.

**294 DUNDEE, BROUGHTY CASTLE
MUSEUM**   **6F1**

*Broughty Ferry, 4m E of city centre. Mon-Thu & Sat 1000-1300 and
1400-1700 (closed Fri). Sun, (Jul-Sep only) 1400-1700. Free. Booking
essential for large groups. (City of Dundee District Council).
Tel: Dundee (0382) 23141 or 76121.*

Former estuary fort, now museum. Local history
gallery includes sections on fishing, lifeboat, ferries and
growth of town. Important collection of relics from
Dundee's former whaling industry including
harpoons, knives and scrimshaw. Wildlife of sea-shore.
Display of arms and armour, and military history of
castle. Small shop.

---

295 DUNDEE, CAMPERDOWN   **6F1**

Off A923, near junction with A972, 3m NW of city centre.

A mansion of c 1829 for the 1st Earl of Camperdown,
son of Admiral Lord Duncan, victor of the Battle of
Camperdown, 1797. View from outside only. There is
a Field Study Centre and a wide range of outdoor
activities in the extensive parkland. (See also No 155).

---

296 DUNDEE, CLAYPOTTS CASTLE   **6F1**

*S of A92, 3m E of city centre. 1 Apr-30 Sep, Mon-Sat 0930-1900, Sun
1400-1900; closed winter. Adult: 50p, OAP/child: 25p. Group rates:
10% discount for parties of 11 or more persons. (AM) Tel: 031-226 2570.*

Now in suburban surroundings, this is one of the
most complete of tower houses, laid out on a Z-plan.
It bears the dates 1569 and 1588 and was built for the
Strachan family.

297 DUNDEE, HOWFF BURIAL GROUND   6F1

Meadowside. Daily, closes 1700. Tel: Dundee (0382) 23141.

Formerly the gardens of the Greyfriars' Monastery, the
Howff was granted to Dundee as a burial ground by
Mary, Queen of Scots. Used as a burial ground
between the 16th and 19th centuries, it contains many
finely carved tombstones. It was also used as a meeting
place by Dundee's Incorporated Trades until 1778,
hence the name 'howff'.

Dundee, Claypotts Castle

298 DUNDEE, McMANUS GALLERIES   6F1

& *Albert Square, city centre. All year, Mon-Sat 1000-1700. Free. (prior
T notice of groups preferred). (City of Dundee District Council).
Tel: Dundee (0382) 23141.*

Dundee's principal museum and art gallery. Local
history displays including major new galleries on trade
and industry, social and civic history. Archaeology
gallery under redevelopment. Art galleries contain
important collection of Scottish and Victorian
paintings; and silver, glass, ceramics, furniture.
Regular touring exhibitions. Shop.

299 DUNDEE, MILLS OBSERVATORY   6F1

& *Balgay Hill, north side of the city. Apr-Sep, Mon-Fri 1000-1700,
A Sat 1400-1700; Oct-Mar, Mon-Fri 1500-2200, Sat 1400-1700. Free
P (booking essential for large groups). (City of Dundee District Council).
Tel: Dundee (0382) 67138.*

A public astronomical observatory with telescopes,
displays on astronomy and space exploration, lecture
room with projection equipment, and small
planetarium. Viewing of sky subject to weather
conditions. Balcony with fine views over River Tay.
Audio-visual programme. Small shop and toilets.

300 DUNDEE REPERTORY THEATRE   6F1

& *Tay Square. All year. Tel: Dundee (0832) 27684.*
A

Theatre housed in award-winning, purpose-built
complex which includes exhibition gallery, bars and
restaurant.

Dundee, Unicorn

301 DUNDEE, UNICORN   6F1

♿

Victoria Dock, just E of Tay Road Bridge. Apr-Oct, Mon, Wed-Sat 1100-1300, 1400-1700; Sun 1400-1700. Adult: 50p, child: 25p. (The Unicorn Preservation Society). Tel: Dundee (0382) 21555.

The *Unicorn* is a 46-gun wooden frigate now in the course of restoration. She was launched at Chatham in 1824 and is Britain's oldest ship afloat. Displays on board of the history of the *Unicorn*, ship-building and the Royal Navy.

---

302 DUNDRENNAN ABBEY   5A11

A711, 7m SE of Kirkcudbright. Opening standard. Adult: 50p, OAP/child: 25p. Group rates: 10% discount for parties of 11 or more persons. (AM) Tel: 031-226 2570.

A Cistercian house founded in 1142 whose ruins include much late Norman and transitional work. Here it is believed Mary, Queen of Scots spent her last night in Scotland, 15 May 1568.

---

303 DUNFERMLINE ABBEY AND PALACE   6D5

Monastery Street, Dunfermline. Apr-Sep, Mon-Sat 0930-1200, 1300-1700, Sun 1400-1700; Oct-Mar, Mon-Sat 0930-1200, 1300-1600, Sun 1400-1600. Free. Tel: 031-226 2570.

This great Benedictine house owes its foundation to Queen Margaret, wife of Malcolm Canmore (1057-93) and the foundations of her modest church remain beneath the present nave, a splendid piece of late Norman work. At the east end are the remains of St Margaret's shrine, dating from the 13th century. Robert the Bruce is buried in the choir, his grave marked by a modern brass. Of the monastic buildings, the ruins of the refectory, pend and guest-house still remain. The guest-house was later reconstructed as a royal palace, and here Charles I was born.

---

304 DUNFERMLINE DISTRICT MUSEUM   6D5

♿
A
P

Viewfield Terrace, Dunfermline. All year. Mon-Sat 1100-1700. Free. (Dunfermline District Council). Tel: Dunfermline (0383) 721814.

The museum, housed in a Victorian villa, has an interesting local history collection, particularly of weaving and linen damask material, the industry that made Dunfermline famous. Special exhibitions are on show regularly.

---

305 DUNGLASS COLLEGIATE CHURCH   5F5

On estate road, W of A1 (signposted Bilsdean) 1m N of Cockburnspath. All reasonable times. (AM) Free. Tel: 031-226 2570.

Founded in 1450, the church consists of nave, choir, transepts, sacristy and a central tower; richly embellished interior, in an attractive estate setting.

306   DUNKELD BRIDGE   **5B1**

Over the River Tay at Dunkeld. All times. Free.

One of Thomas Telford's finest bridges, built in 1809.
An attractive riverside path leads from here
downstream to the famous *Birnam Oak*, last relic of
Macbeth's Birnam Wood, and then around the village
of Birnam. Best view is from riverside garden.
Wheelchair users should approach from the square
through the archway. Hotel and tearoom adjacent.

307   DUNKELD CATHEDRAL   **5B1**

*High Street, Dunkeld, 15m NNW of Perth. Opening standard. Free.
(AM) Tel: 031-226 2570.*

Refounded in the early 12th century on an ancient
ecclesiastical site, this cathedral has a beautiful setting
by the Tay. The choir has been restored and is in use as
the parish church. The nave and the great north-west
tower date from the 15th century.

308   DUNKELD LITTLE HOUSES   **5B1**

*Dunkeld, 15m NNW of Perth. Tourist Information Centre with
audio-visual presentation open 28 Mar-31 May, 1 Sep-23 Dec, Mon-Sat
1000-1300, 1400-1630. 1 Jun-31 Aug, Mon-Sat 1000-1800, Sun
1400-1700. Free. (NTS) Tel: Dunkeld (03502) 460.*

The houses date from the rebuilding of the town after
the Battle of Dunkeld, 1689. Charmingly restored by
NTS and Perth County Council, they are not open to
the public but may be seen from the outside and
information on them gained from the Visitor Centre
or from the National Trust for Scotland's
representative at the Ell shop.

309   DUNMORE PINEAPPLE   **6B5**

*N of Airth, 7m E of Stirling off A905, then B9124. Viewed from the
outside only. (NTS, leased to the Landmark Trust) Tel: 031-226 5922.*

This curious structure, built as a 'garden retreat' and
shaped like a pineapple, stands in the grounds of
Dunmore Park, and bears the date 1761. It is the focal
point of the garden and is available for holiday and
other short lets.

310   DUNNET HEAD   **3D2**

B855, 12m NE of Thurso.

This bold promontory of sandstone rising to 417 feet
is the northernmost point of the Scottish mainland
with magnificent views across the Pentland Firth to
Orkney and a great part of the north coast to Ben
Loyal and Ben Hope. The windows of the lighthouse
are sometimes broken by stones hurled up by the
winter seas.

Dunnottar Castle

311   DUNNOTTAR CASTLE   3G11

*Off A92, S of Stonehaven. All year. Mon-Sat 0900-1800, Sun
1400-1700. Closed Fri, Oct-Apr. Adult: 55p, child: 30p; group rates.
Tel: Lyne of Skene (033 06) 62173.*

An impressive ruined fortress on a rocky cliff 160 feet
above the sea, a stronghold of the Earls Marischal of
Scotland from the 14th century. Montrose besieged it
in 1645. During the Commonwealth wars, the
Scottish regalia were hidden here for safety.
Cromwell's troops occupied the castle but in 1652 this
treasure was smuggled out by the wife of the minister
at Kinneff, 7 miles south, and hidden under the pulpit
in his church. (See also No 600).

312   DUNROBIN CASTLE   3B6

*Off A9, 12½m NNE of Dornoch. 1 June-15 Sep, Mon-Sat 1030-1730,
Sun 1300-1730. Adult: £1.80, OAP: £1.40, child: 90p. Group rates—
Adult: £1.60, OAP: £1.20, child: 80p. Open to groups all year by prior
arrangement. (Countess of Sutherland)
Tel: Golspie (04083) 3177 or 3268.*

Magnificently set in a great park and formal gardens,
overlooking the sea, Dunrobin Castle was originally a
square keep built about 1275 by Robert, Earl of
Sutherland, from whom it got its name Dun Robin.
For centuries this has been the seat of the Earls and
Dukes of Sutherland. The present outward appearance
results from extensive changes made 1845-50. Fine
paintings, furniture and a steam-powered fire engine
are among the miscellany of items to be seen. Beach
and tearoom.

313   DUNSGIATH CASTLE   2E10

*At Tokavaig, on unclassified road 20m SSW of Broadford, Isle of Skye.
All reasonable times. Free.*

Well-preserved ruins of a former Macdonald
stronghold.

**314   DUNSTAFFNAGE CASTLE AND
        CHAPEL**   4E2

*Off A85, 4m N of Oban. Opening standard, Oct-Mar, closed Thu
afternoon and Fri. Adult: 50p, OAP/child: 15p. Group rates: 10%
discount for parties of 11 or more persons. (AM) Tel: 031-226 2570.*

A fine, well-preserved example of a 13th-century castle
with curtain wall and round towers. The ruins of a
chapel of exceptional architectural refinement are
nearby.

315   DUNVEGAN CASTLE   2C9

*Dunvegan, Isle of Skye. Easter-mid Oct 1400-1700 (Mid-May to Sep
1030-1700). Closed Sun. Adult: £1.90, child: £1. Group rates (under
review). (J Macleod of Macleod) Tel: Dunvegan (047 022) 206.*

Historic stronghold of the Clan Macleod, set on the
sea loch of Dunvegan, still the home after 700 years of
the chiefs of Macleod. Possessions on view, books,
pictures, arms and treasured relics, trace the history of
the family and clan from the days of their Norse
ancestry through thirty generations to the present day.
Boat trips from the castle jetty to the seal colony.
Restaurant and shops.

316   DURNESS OLD CHURCH   2H3

*At Balnakeil, ½m W of Durness, near Craft Village. All reasonable
times. Free.*

Built in 1619, now a ruin.

317 DWARFIE STANE   1A12

On island of Hoy, Orkney. All times. Free. (AM) Tel: 031-226 2570.

A huge block of sandstone in which a burial chamber has been quarried. No other tomb of this type is known in the British Isles. Probably third millenium BC.

---

318 DYCE SYMBOL STONES   3G10

At Dyce Old Church, 5m NW of Aberdeen. All reasonable times. Free. (AM) Tel: 031-226 2570.

Two fine examples of Pictish symbol stones.

---

319 EAGLE STONE   3A8

♻ *By A834 on east side of village of Strathpeffer. All reasonable times. Free.*

A Pictish stone which has two symbols etched into its surface. One is the shape of a horseshoe and the other is of an eagle. Several theories as to the stone's origin exist — one of which is that it is a marriage stone.

Earl Patrick's Palace and Bishop's Palace

320 EARL PATRICK'S PALACE AND BISHOP'S PALACE   1B11

Kirkwall, Orkney. (Both) Opening standard, except Oct-Mar closed Fri afternoon and Sat. Adult: 50p, OAP/child: 25p. Group rates: 10% discount for parties of 11 or more persons. (AM) Tel: 031-226 2570.

Earl Patrick's Palace has been described as *the most mature and accomplished piece of Renaissance architecture left in Scotland*; it was built in 1607. The Bishop's Palace nearby dates back to the 13th century, with a 16th-century round tower.

Earl's Palace, Birsay

321 EARL'S PALACE, BIRSAY   1A10

At Birsay, N end of Mainland, 11m N of Stromness, Orkney. All times. (AM) Tel: 031-226 2570.

The impressive remains of the palace built in the 16th century by the Earls of Orkney.

Earlshall Castle and Gardens

322 EARLSHALL CASTLE AND GARDENS   6G2

1m E of Leuchars, 6 miles from St Andrews. Open Easter, Sat, Sun, Mon, thereafter Thu-Sun 1400-1800; closes last Sun in Sep. Adult: £1.50, OAP/child: £1.00. Group rates: £1.25 per person. Tel: Leuchars (033483) 205.

Earlshall is a fine example of a 16th-century Scottish castle, very strongly built with 5-feet-thick walls, battlements and gun loops. Richly fitted main rooms, including the gallery with its magnificent painted ceiling and wealth of old timber panelling. Still a family home with permanent display of Scottish weapons. Yew topiary gardens, tearoom, gift shop, picnic facilities, nature trail, gardens. Free car and coach park.

---

323 EAS COUL AULIN   2H5

At the head of Loch Glencoul, 3m W of A894.

The tallest waterfall in Britain, dropping 658 feet (200 metres). There are occasional cruises to the waterfall.

---

324 EASDALE ISLAND FOLK MUSEUM   4E3

Easdale Island, 16m S of Oban, take B844 then ferry. Apr-Oct, Mon-Sat 1030-1730, Sun 1030-1700, or by arrangement. Adult: 60p, student/child: 20p. Tel: Balvicar (05823) 382.

A pictorial history of life on the Slate islands in the 1800s, showing the industrial and domestic life of the villagers. Scenic walks around the island and panoramic views from the hill. Restaurant and lounge bar.

---

325 EASSIE SCULPTURED STONE   5D1

In Eassie Kirkyard, 7m WSW of Forfar. All reasonable times. Free. (AM) Tel: 031-226 2570.

A fine example of an early Christian monument, elaborately carved.

---

326 EDEN CASTLE   3F8

Off A947, 5½m S of Banff. All reasonable times. Free.

The ruin of the family home (built 1676) of the Nicholases. A reputed reason for its downfall is that the wife of a tenant asked the laird to control her wayward son, which he did by drowning him in the nearby river, and was subsequently cursed.

327 EDEN COURT THEATRE 3B8

&
P
T

Bishops Road, Inverness. Concession for parties of 20 or more persons (depends on show). Tel: Inverness (0463) 239841 or 221718.

An 800-seat, multi-purpose theatre, conference centre and art gallery, completed in 1976, on the banks of the River Ness. Part of the complex is the 19th-century house built by Robert Eden. There is a wide variety of shows, films and exhibitions throughout the year. Restaurant.

328 EDINBURGH, ACHESON HOUSE 6E6

&
P

Canongate, Royal Mile. All year, Mon-Sat 1000-1730. Free. Tel: 031-556 8136/7370.

A mansion of 1633-343 entered through a small courtyard, now the Scottish Craft Centre. It shows and sells the work of Scotland's leading craft workers, including pottery, weaving, silver, woodwork, textiles, glass and jewellery.

329 EDINBURGH, BRAIDWOOD AND RUSHBROOK FIRE MUISEUM 6E6

&
A

McDonald Road, off Leith Walk. Visits by arrangement with Fire Brigade Headquarters. Free. (Lothian & Borders Fire Brigade) Tel: 031-228 2401.

Guided tours round the museum, with its collection of old uniforms, equipment and engines, subject to the availability of a Fireman Guide.

330 EDINBURGH BRASS RUBBING CENTRE 6E6

&
A

Canongate Tolbooth, Royal Mile. Jun-Sep, weekdays 1000-1800; Oct-May, weekdays 1000-1700; Suns during Festival 1400-1700. Free. A charge is made for every rubbing, which includes cost of materials and a royalty to the churches where applicable. Tel: 031-225 2424, ext 6638/6689.

Rubbings of the brass commemorating Robert the Bruce and the Burghead Bull, a Pictish incised stone c AD 700 are among the selection available. Instruction and materials supplied.

331 EDINBURGH BUTTERFLY FARM 6E6

&
T

6m S of Edinburgh on A7 towards Dalkeith. Apr-Oct (incl), Mon-Fri 1000-1800, Sat & Sun 1000-1530 (closes 1700 Sep and Oct). Adult: £1.75, OAP/child: £1.00. Group rates: reductions on booking application. (Dobbies Garden Centre). Tel: 031-663 4932.

The farm, housed in a large greenhouse with lush tropical plants, cascading waterfalls and lily ponds, provides the setting for butterflies from all over the world to fly freely around. Exotic insects, photographic displays, tearoom, garden centre, tropical fish shop, children's playground and picnic area. Free car parking.

Edinburgh, Calton Hill

332 EDINBURGH, CALTON HILL   6E6

Off Regent Road at E end of city centre. All times. Free.
Monument: Apr-Sep, Tues, Sat 1000-1800, Mon 1300-1800;
Oct-Mar 1000-1500. Admission 40p. (Edinburgh District Council).
Tel: 031-225 2424.

A city centre hill, 350 feet above sea level, with
magnificent views over Edinburgh and the Firth of
Forth. The monumental collection on top includes a
part reproduction of the Parthenon, intended to
commemorate the Scottish dead in the Napoleonic
Wars; it was begun in 1824 but ran out of funds and
was never completed. The 102 feet high Nelson
Monument (completed 1815) improves the view from
its high parapets.

The buildings of the Royal Observatory (1744 and
1818) are open on application to: The Custodian, City
Observatory, Calton Hill, Edinburgh.

Edinburgh, Camera Obscura: see No 364.

---

333 EDINBURGH, CANONGATE KIRK   6E6

On the Canongate, Royal Mile. If closed apply the Manse, Reid's Court,
near the church.

The church, built by order of James VII in 1688, is the
Parish Church of the Canongate and also the Kirk of
Holyroodhouse and Edinburgh Castle. The church
silver dates from 1611. Restored in 1951, the church
contains much heraldry. The burial ground contains
the graves of Adam Smith, the economist, 'Clarinda',
friend of Robert Burns, and Robert Fergusson, the
poet.

---

334 EDINBURGH, CANONGATE
TOLBOOTH   6E6

Canongate, Royal Mile. Jun-Sep, weekdays 1000-1800; Oct-May,
weekdays 1000-1700; Sun during Festival 1400-1700. Free.
Tel: 031-225 2424, ext 6638/6689.

Built in 1591 with outside stair and a turreted tower.
Temporary exhibitions are held throughout the year.
Edinburgh Brass Rubbing Centre at street level.

---

335 EDINBURGH CASTLE   6E6

Castle Rock, top of the Royal Mile. Apr-Sep, Mon-Sat 0930-1705, Sun
1100-1705; Oct-Mar, Mon-Sat 0930-1620, Sun 1230-1535. Adult:
£2.00, OAP/child: £1.00, family: £4.00. (AM) Tel: 031-226 2570.

One of the most famous castles in the world, whose
battlements overlook the Esplanade where the floodlit
Military Tattoo is staged each year, late August to early
September. The castle stands on a rock which has been
a fortress from time immemorial. The oldest part of
the buildings which make up the castle is the
12th-century chapel dedicated to St Margaret. In
addition to the Great Hall built by James IV, with fine
timbered roof, and the Old Palace, which houses the
Regalia of Scotland and the Military Museum; the
castle also holds the Scottish National War Memorial,
opened in 1927.

336   EDINBURGH, CRAIGMILLAR CASTLE   6E6

A68, 3½m SW of city centre. Opening standard (closed Thu (pm) and Fri). Adult: 50p, OAP/child: 25p. Group rates: 10% discount for parties of 11 or more persons. (AM) Tel: 031-226 2570.

Imposing ruins of massive 14th-century keep enclosed in the early 15th century by an embattled curtain wall; within are the remains of the stately ranges of apartments dating from the 16th and 17th centuries. The castle was burnt by Hertford in 1544. There are strong connections with Mary, Queen of Scots, who frequently stayed here. While she was in residence in 1566 the plot to murder Darnley was forged.

337   EDINBURGH, CRAMOND   6E6

&   *5m NW of city centre, on the shores of the Firth of Forth.*
A   *Tel: 031-336 6034*
P

This picturesque 18th-century village is situated at the mouth of the River Almond. See particularly the Roman fort and medieval tower, the kirk, kirkyard and manse, the old schoolhouse and the iron mills. Conducted walks around the village start from Cramond Kirk, Jun-Sep, Sun 1500, free. Exhibition at The Maltings, Cramond Village, Jun-Sep, Sat & Sun 1400-1800, free.

**338   EDINBURGH CRYSTAL
VISITOR CENTRE   6E7**

&   *Eastfield, Penicuik, 10m S of Edinburgh. By arrangement. All year,*
T   *Mon-Fri (not holidays) 0900-1530. Admission charge (except for disabled). Tel: Penicuik (0968) 75128.*

Conducted tours are available, unveiling every aspect of the glassmaker's craft. Children under 10 years not admitted on factory tours. No photography. Audio-visual presentations Mon-Sat, 0900-1630. Licensed cafeteria, children's play area and picnic facilities.

Edinburgh, Dean Village

339   EDINBURGH, DEAN VILLAGE   6E6

&   *Bell's Brae, off Queensferry Street, on Water of Leith. Tel: 01-332 2368.*
A   There was grain milling in this notable village of Edinburgh for over 800 years. The view downstream through the high arches of Dean Bridge is among the most picturesque in the city. A walk along the waterside leads to St Bernard's Well, an old mineral source (open by arrangement).

340 EDINBURGH, RICHARD DEMARCO GALLERY 6E6

10 Jeffrey Street (off Royal Mile). All year, Tues-Sat 1000-1800. Free except during Edinburgh Festival. (Richard Demarco). Tel: 031-557 0707.

An international communications centre for artists and those interested in contemporary visual arts, as well as theatre, music and art education. It is concerned with Scotland's celtic and prehistoric cultures in relation to Europe. The Gallery opened in 1966 and has presented over 900 exhibitions and 250 related events.

341 EDINBURGH, FOUNTAIN BREWERY 6E6

Scottish & Newcastle Breweries plc, Gilmore Park. By arrangement. Free. Tel: 031-229 9377 (ext 3015 between 1000-1400).

A tour of the complete brewing process and high-speed canning line, in the most fully automated brewery in Europe.

342 EDINBURGH, FRUIT MARKET GALLERY 6E6

29 Market Street. Oct-10 Sep, Mon-Sat 1030-1730. Free. (City of Edinburgh). Tel: 031-225 2383

The gallery is a non-profit-making organisation which presents a changing programme of exhibitions of contemporary art, architecture and design.

343 EDINBURGH, GEORGIAN HOUSE 6E6

No 7 Charlotte Square. 28 Mar-31 Oct, Mon-Sat 1000-1700, Sun 1400-1700; 1-30 Nov, Sat 1000-1630, Sun 1400-1630. Last admission 1½ hours before closing. Adult: £1.20, child: 60p. (NTS) Tel: 031-225 2160.

The lower floors have been furnished as they might have been by their first owners, showing the domestic surroundings and reflecting the social conditions of that age. Charlotte Square itself was built at the end of the 18th century and is one of the most outstanding examples of its period in Europe. Bute House is the official residence of the Secretary of State for Scotland. The west side of the square is dominated by the green dome of St George's Church, now West Register House. (See No 390).

344 EDINBURGH, GLADSTONE'S LAND 6E6

Lawnmarket, Royal Mile. 1 Apr-31 Oct, Mon-Sat 1000-1700, Sun 1400-1700; 1 Nov-9 Dec, Sat 1000-1630, Sun 1400-1630. Adult: £1.00, child: 50p. (NTS) Tel: 031-226 5922.

Completed in 1620, the six-storey tenement contains remarkable painted ceilings, and has been refurbished as a typical home of the period.

345 EDINBURGH, GREYFRIARS BOBBY 6E6

Corner of George IV Bridge and Candlemaker Row. All times. Free.

Statue of Greyfriars Bobby, the Skye terrier who, after his master's death in 1858, watched over his grave in the nearby Greyfriars Churchyard for 14 years. (See No 351).

346 EDINBURGH, GEORGE HERIOT'S   6E6
SCHOOL

Lauriston Place. May be viewed from the grounds. Gates close 1630.
Tel: 031-229 7263 (Trust Office).

Now a school, the splendid building was begun in
1628, endowed by George Heriot, goldsmith and
jeweller to James VI and I, the 'Jingling Geordie' of
Scott's novel *Fortunes of Nigel*.

347 EDINBURGH, HIGH KIRK OF ST GILES   6E6
(St Giles' Cathedral, The High Kirk of Edinburgh)

  ♿ *On the Royal Mile. Mon-Sat 0900-1700 (1900 in summer), Sun (pm).*
  A *Free. (Thistle Chapel, adult: 30p, child: 5p). Tel: 031-225 4363.*

There has been a church here since the 9th century. Of
the present building, the tower is late 15th century. At
one time, there were four churches here, and yet
another served as a prison. See also the exquisite
Thistle Chapel. In the street outside the west door is
the Heart of Midlothian, a heart-shaped design in the
cobblestones. It marks the site of the Old Tolbooth,
built 1466, which was stormed in the 1736 Porteous
Riots and demolished in 1817. Restaurant.

348 EDINBURGH, HILLEND   6E6
  ⛷ *Biggar Road, S outskirts of Edinburgh. Charge for chairlift: Adult: 80p,*
child: 40p. Session tickets for skiers are also available. (Lothian Regional
Council). Tel: 031-445 4433.

The largest artificial ski slope in Britain. Facilities
include chairlift, drag lift, ski-hire, tuition, showers
and changing rooms. Grass ski-ing available May to
September. Fine views from top of chairlift (available
to non-skiers) of the Pentland Hills, over Edinburgh
and beyond. Refreshments and picnic area.

349 EDINBURGH, HUNTLY HOUSE   6E6
  ♿ *Canongate, Royal Mile. Jun-Sep, weekdays 1000-1800; Oct-May,*
  P *weekdays 1000-1700; Sun during Festival 1400-1700. Free.*
Tel: 031-225 2424, ext 6629.

Built in 1570, this fine house was later associated with
members of the Huntly family. It is now a city
museum illustrating Edinburgh life down the ages,
and contains important collections of Edinburgh silver
and glass and Scottish pottery.

350 EDINBURGH, KING'S THEATRE   6E6
  ♿ *2 Leven Street. Tel: 031-229 1201*
  A
  P Opened 1906. A memorial stone laid by Andrew
  T Carnegie and a plaque commemorating the occasion
may be seen in the theatre. Completely restored in
1985 to original design and colour scheme.

351 EDINBURGH, KIRK OF THE   6E6
GREYFRIARS

  ♿ *Greyfriars Place, S end of George IV Bridge. Easter-Sep, Mon-Fri*
  T *1000-1600, Sat 1000-1200. Free. Guided tour of Kirk and Kirkyard last*
Sun each month, Apr-Sep 1430. Free. Tel: 031-225 1900.

The Kirk, dedicated on Christmas Day, 1620, was the
scene of the adoption and Signing of the National
Covenant on 28 February 1638. The kirkyard,
inaugurated in 1562, is on the site of a 15th century
Franciscan Friary. In 1679, 1,400 Covenanters were
imprisoned in the kirkyard. Various literature available.
(See No 345.)

352

EDINBURGH, JOHN KNOX'S HOUSE   6E6

*45 High Street, Royal Mile. All year, Mon-Sat 1000-1700. Adult: £1.00,
child/OAP: 60p, group rates. Tel: 031-556 6961*

A picturesque house, said to be the only 15th century
house in Scotland, having traditional connections with
John Knox, the famous Scottish reformer. The recent
restoration programme has revealed the original walls,
fireplaces and painted ceiling. There is also a 10-minute
video film of John Knox's life in Geneva and Scotland.

---

353   ### EDINBURGH, LAMB'S HOUSE   6E6

*Burgess Street, Leith. All year, daily 0900-1700. Free (NTS)
Tel: 031-554 3131.*

The restored residence and warehouse of Andrew
Lamb, a prosperous merchant of the 17th century.
Now an old people's day centre.

---

354   ### EDINBURGH, LAURISTON CASTLE   6E6

*N of A90 at Cramond Road South, 4m WNW of city centre. Apr-Oct,
daily except Fri 1100-1300, 1400-1700; Nov-Mar, Sat and Sun only,
1400-1600. Adult: 80p, child: 40p: group rates.
Tel: 031-336 2060/225 2424, ext 6689.*

The original 16th-century tower, built by Sir
Archibald Napier, father of the inventor of logarithms,
has been much extended to become a gracious house
with paintings and old furniture. John Law
(1671-1729), founder of the first Bank of France and
author of the disastrous 'Mississippi Scheme' of
1717-20, spent his early years in this castle, now
administered by the City of Edinburgh. The grounds
include gardens and croquet lawns. Car park.

---

355   ### EDINBURGH, MAGDALEN CHAPEL   6E6

*Cowgate, off the Grassmarket. By arrangement. Free. (Scottish
Reformation Society). Tel: 031-225 1836.*

This 16th-century chapel, temporarily the chaplaincy
for Heriot-Watt University, is notable for its stained-
glass windows.

356   EDINBURGH, MEADOWBANK STADIUM 6E6

193 London Road. Tel: 031-661 5351.

Sports complex, opened in 1970, was the venue for the Commonwealth Games of that year, and is now used for a wide variety of major sporting events throughout the year, with facilities for over 30 sports. Temporary membership is available to visitors on application to the Sports Centre. The Centre will also be host to the Commonwealth Games in 1986.

Edinburgh: Mercat Cross: see No 365.

Edinburgh, Museum of Childhood

357   EDINBURGH, MUSEUM OF CHILDHOOD 6E6

High Street, Royal Mile. Opening times and admission subject to review. Tel: 031-225 2424, ext 6638/6652.

This unique museum has a fine collection of toys, dolls, dolls' houses, costumes and nursery equipment. The museum is presently being extended and is due to reopen in 1986. A temporary (free) display is at the Canongate Tolbooth (see No 334).

358   EDINBURGH, NATIONAL GALLERY OF SCOTLAND 6E6

& *The Mound, Mon-Sat 1000-1700 (extended hours during Festival); Sun*
T *1400-1700. Free. Tel: 031-556 8921.*

One of the most distinguished of the smaller galleries of Europe, the National Gallery of Scotland contains a comprehensive collection of old masters, impressionist and Scottish paintings. This includes masterpieces by Raphael, El Greco, Rembrandt, Constable, Titian, Velasquez, Raeburn, Van Gogh and Gauguin. Drawings, watercolours and original prints (Turner, Goya, Blake etc) are shown on request (Mon-Fri 1000-1230, 1400-1630).

359   EDINBURGH, NATIONAL LIBRARY OF SCOTLAND 6E6

George IV Bridge. All year. (Reading Room) Mon-Fri 0930-2030, Sat 0930-1300. (Exhibition) Mon-Fri 0930-1700 (0930-2030 during Festival), Sat 0930-1300, (Apr-Sep) Sun 1400-1700. Free. Tel: 031-226 4531.

Founded in 1682, this is one of the four largest libraries in Great Britain. The Map Room annexe at 137 Causewayside (tel: 031-667 7848) is open Mon-Fri 0930-1700, Sat 0930-1300.

360 EDINBURGH, NATIONAL MUSEUMS OF SCOTLAND, CHAMBERS STREET 6E6 (formerly Royal Scottish Museum)

Mon-Sat 1000-1700, Sun 1400-1700. Free. Tel: 031-225 7534.

Part of the Royal Museum of Scotland in a fine Victorian building. Houses the national collections of decorative arts of the world, archaeology and ethnography, natural history, geology, technology and science. Special exhibitions, lectures, gallery talks, films and other activities for adults and children. Tearoom.

361 EDINBURGH, NATIONAL MUSEUMS OF SCOTLAND, QUEEN STREET 6E6 (formerly the National Museum of Antiquities of Scotland)

All year, Mon-Fri 1000-1700 (Festival period 1000-1800); Sun 1400-1700 (Festival period 1100-1800). Charge for temporary exhibitions. Tel: 031-557 3550.

An intriguing and comprehensive collection of the history and everyday life of Scotland from the Stone Age to modern times.

Edinburgh, Nelson Monument: see No 332.

362 EDINBURGH, NETHERBOW ARTS CENTRE 6E6

&
A
P

43 High Street. All year, Tue-Sat 1000-1600 (also in evenings for theatre). Free. (Church of Scotland Dept of Home Mission). Tel: 031-556 9579.

A modern three-storey building in the style of a medieval town house, with three barrel-vaulted arches and open courtyard, offering a wide variety of exhibitions, theatre and concerts. Restaurant.

363 EDINBURGH, NEW TOWN CONSERVATION CENTRE 6E6

13A Dundas Street. All year. Mon-Fri. 0900-1300, 1400-1700. Free. Tel: 031-556 7054.

Headquarters of committee which administers grants for the conservation of the Georgian 'New Town'. There is a display of work in progress and a conservation reference library. Publications are on sale. There are guided walks from June to September and at other times by arrangement; walks on Wednesday evenings include house visits and wine. Particulars from Conservation Centre.

364 EDINBURGH, OUTLOOK TOWER AND CAMERA OBSCURA 6E6

&

Castle Hill, between the Castle and Lawnmarket. All year, daily, Apr-Oct, Mon-Fri 0930-1730, Sat & Sun 1000-1800; Nov-Mar, Mon-Fri 0930-1700, Sat & Sun 1030-1630. Adult: £1.25, student: £1.00, OAP/child: 60p; group rates on application. (Landmark). Tel: 031-226 3709.

This unique Victorian optical device projects a spectacular live image of the surrounding city onto a viewing table high in the Outlook Tower. Also rooftop terrace, and related optical displays including 'Holography', a permanent public collection of 3D laser images; pin-hole photography; space photography.

Edinburgh, Palace of Holyroodhouse

365 EDINBURGH, PALACE OF HOLYROODHOUSE 6E6

Foot of the Royal Mile. Apr-Oct 0930-1715, Sun 1030-1630; Nov-Mar 0930-1545 (not Sun). The Palace is also closed during Royal and State Visits, and for periods before and after visits; check dates in May to July. Adult: £1.40, child: 70p.

The Palace of Holyroodhouse is the official residence of the Queen in Scotland. The oldest part is built against the monastic nave of Holyrood Abbey, little of which remains. The rest of the palace was reconstructed by the architect Sir William Bruce for Charles II. Here Mary Queen of Scots lived for six years; here she met John Knox; here Rizzio was murdered, and here Prince Charles Edward Stuart held court in 1745. State apartments, house tapestries and paintings; the picture gallery has portraits of over 70 Scottish kings, painted by De Wet in 1684-86.

366 EDINBURGH, PARLIAMENT HOUSE 6E6

Parliament Square, behind the High Kirk of St Giles, Royal Mile. All year, Tue-Fri 1000-1600. Free. Tel: 031-225 2595, ext 223.

Built 1632-39 this was the seat of Scottish government until 1707, when the governments of Scotland and England were united. Now the Supreme Law Courts of Scotland. See the Parliament Hall with fine hammer beam roof and portraits by Raeburn and other major Scottish artists. Access (free) to the splendid Signet Library on an upper floor is by prior written request only, to: The Librarian, Signet Library, Parliament House, Edinburgh. Outside is the medieval Mercat Cross, which was restored in 1885 by W E Gladstone. Royal proclamations are still read from its platform. Restaurant.

367 EDINBURGH, PHILATELIC BUREAU 6E6

In the Post Office, Waterloo Place. Mon-Thu 0900-1630, Fri 0900-1600. Free. Tel: 031-550 8370.

Display of British stamps and historic relics of postal services.

368 EDINBURGH, REGISTER HOUSE 6E6

E end of Princes Street. all year, Mon-Fri. Search rooms: 0900-1645, Exhibitions: 1000-1600. Free. Tel: 031-556 6585.

This fine Robert Adam building, founded 1774, is the headquarters of the Scottish Record Office and the home of the national archives of Scotland. There is a branch repository at West Register House in Charlotte Square (see No 390). In front is a notable statue of the Duke of Wellington (1852).No guide dogs.

Edinburgh, Royal Botanic Gardens

**369 EDINBURGH, ROYAL BOTANIC
GARDEN** 6E6

  ♿
T

*Inverleith Row; Arboretum Road (car parking). Daily 0900 (Sun 1100) to
one hour before sunset, summer; 0900-dusk, winter. Free. Plant houses
1000 (Sun 1100) to 1700, summer; 1000 (Sun 1100) to dusk, winter.
During Festival, opens at 1000 on Sun. Free. Tel: 031-552 7171.*

The Royal Botanic Garden has a world famous rock
garden and probably the biggest collection of
rhododendrons in the world. The unique exhibition
plant houses show a great range of exotic plants
displayed as indoor landscapes and a plant exhibition
hall displays many aspects of botany and horticulture.
Tearoom and publications counter.

**370 EDINBURGH, ROYAL LYCEUM
THEATRE** 6E6

  ♿
P
T

Grindlay Street. All year. Group rates. Tel: 031-229 9697.

A fine Victorian theatre, recently renovated, offering a
wide variety of plays and entertainment. Refreshments
available. Induction loop in stalls. L'Aperitif restaurant.

371 EDINBURGH, ROYAL OBSERVATORY 6E6

  ♿
P
T

*Blackford Hill. (Visitor Centre) All year, daily, Mon-Fri 1000-1600, Sat,
Sun & public holidays 1200-1700. Adult: 65p, OAP/child: 35p;
group rates. Tel: 031-667 3321.*

Situated at the home of the Royal Observatory and
University Department of Astronomy, the Visitor
Centre demonstrates the work of astronomers,
especially with telescopes in Australia and Hawaii.
Also on show is the largest telescope in Scotland.
Wide ranging bookshop, fine views of Edinburgh
from hill. Alternative entrance for wheelchairs.

**372 EDINBURGH, ROYAL SCOTTISH
ACADEMY** 6E6

  ♿

*At the foot of the Mound, on Princes Street. Open for its Annual
Exhibition late Apr-Jul, and for Festival exhibitions; Mon-Sat 1000-2100,
Sun 1400-1700. Adult: £1.20, concession: 50p. Tel: 031-225 6671.*

Ramped wheelchair entrance at side.

**373 EDINBURGH, ROYAL SCOTS DRAGOON
GUARDS DISPLAY ROOM** 6E6

The Castle. All year, daily, Mon-Fri 0930-1615. Free.

Display of pictures, badges, brassware and other
historical relics of the regiment. Souvenir shop.

374 EDINBURGH, ST CECILIA'S HALL   6E6

& *The Cowgate, off the Grassmarket. Wed 1400-1700, Sat 1400-1700. 25p*
A *(University of Edinburgh). Tel: 031-667 1011, ext 4577/4415.*

The elegant Georgian hall, built in 1726 by Robert
Milne, originally the concert hall for the Edinburgh
Music Society, contains the Russell collection of early
keyboard instruments, many of which are unique. (See
also No 388).

**375 EDINBURGH, ST CUTHBERT'S
       CHURCH**   6E6

& *Lothian Road. Open with guides Jun-Sep, Mon-Fri 1100-1600; other
times by arrangement. Free. Tel: 031-229 1142.*

An ancient church, the 'West Kirk', rebuilt by
Hippolyte Blanc in 1894. The tower is 18th century,
and there is a monument to Napier of Merchiston,
inventor of logarithms. Thomas de Quincey is buried
in the churchyard. Coffee served Tuesday mornings.

Edinburgh, St Giles' Cathedral: see No 347.

---

376 EDINBURGH, ST JOHN'S CHURCH   6E6

& *W end of Princes Street. All reasonable times. Free. Tel: 031-227 7565.*
T
An impressive 19th-century church, the nave of which
was built in 1817 by William Burn. There is a fine
collection of Victorian stained glass. SPCK bookshop,
Peace and Justice Resource Centre, One World Shop
and Corner Stone.

---

377 EDINBURGH, ST MARY'S CATHEDRAL 6E6

& *In Palmerston Place, West End. Tel: 031-225 6293.*

Built 1879, with the western towers added in 1917.
The central spire is 276 feet high and the interior is
impressive. Nearby is the charming Easter Coates
House, built in the late 17th century with some stones
filched from the old town; it is now St Mary's Music
School. Gardens with seats.

---

378 EDINBURGH, ST TRIDUANA'S CHAPEL 6E6

*At Restalrig Church, in Restalrig district, 1½m E of city centre. Opening
standard. Free. (AM) Tel: 031-226 2570.*

From the late 15th century the shrine of St Triduana
was situated in the lower chamber of the King's
Chapel built by James III, adjacent to Restalrig
Church. The design, a two storey vaulted hexagon, is
unique. The lower chapel of St Triduana survives
intact but the upper chamber was demolished in 1560.

**379 EDINBURGH, SCOTLAND'S CLAN
       TARTAN CENTRE**   6E6

& *70-74 Bangor Road, Leith, Edinburgh. Daily, 0900-1730. Free.*
T *Tel: 031-553 5100 (0900-1800).*

Exhibition, reference library and audio-visual display.
Computerised tracing of clan links, extensive range of
tartan accessories and clan crests. Full Highland dress.
Restaurant, large free car park and free courtesy bus
(phone for details).

**380 EDINBURGH, SCOTMID TRANSPORT
       COLLECTION**   6E6

*Grove Street, off Dundee Street. By written request to Transport Manager,
Mon-Fri 1300-1700. Free.*

An extensive collection of horse-drawn carriages.

Edinburgh, Scott Monument

381 EDINBURGH, SCOTT MONUMENT   6E6

In Princes Street. Apr-Sep, Mon-Fri 0900-1800; Oct-Mar, Mon-Fri 0900-1500. Adult/child: 45p. Tel: 031-225 2424, ext 6596/6689

Completed in 1844, a statue of Sir Walter Scott and his dog Maida, under a canopy and spire 200 feet high, with 64 statuettes of Scott characters. Fine view of the city from the top.

382 EDINBURGH, SCOTTISH AGRICULTURAL MUSEUM   6E6

Ingliston. May-Sept, Mon-Fri 1000-1600, Sun 1200-1700. Free. Open to groups outside normal hours/season. (National Museum of Antiquities of Scotland). Tel: 031-557 3550, ext 267 or 263.

Scotland's national rural life collection, built up over the last 200 years and now housed in a purpose-built museum. Displays cover farming, crafts, buildings, home life and social life. Special commendation in European Museum of the Year Award. Shop, light refreshments and picnic area.

Edinburgh, Scottish Craft Centre: see No 328.

383 EDINBURGH, SCOTTISH NATIONAL GALLERY OF MODERN ART   6E6

Belford Road. All year, Mon-Sat 1000-1700, Sun 1400-1700 (extended hours during Festival). Free. Tel: 031-556 8921.

Scotland's collection of 20th-century painting, sculpture and graphic art, with masterpieces by Derain, Matisse, Braque, Hepworth, Picasso and Giacometti; and work by Hockney, Caulfield and Sol Le Witt. Also Scottish School. Café.

384 EDINBURGH, SCOTTISH NATIONAL PORTRAIT GALLERY   6E6

E end of Queen Street. Weekdays 1000-1700 (extended hours during Festival), Sun 1400-1700. Free. Tel: 031-556 8921.

Illustrates the history of Scotland through portraits of the famous men and women who contributed to it in all fields of activity from the 16th century to the present day, such as Mary, Queen of Scots, James VI and I, Flora Macdonald, Robert Burns, Sir Walter Scott, David Hume and Ramsay MacDonald. The artists include Raeburn, Ramsay, Reynolds and Gainsborough. Reference section of engravings and photographs including calotypes by Hill and Adamson.

385 EDINBURGH, LADY STAIR'S HOUSE 6E6

Off Lawnmarket, Royal Mile. Jun-Sep, weekdays 1000-1800; Oct-May, weekdays 1000-1700; Sun during Festival 1400-1700. Free.

Built in 1622, this is now a museum of Burns, Scott and Stevenson.

---

386 EDINBURGH, TALBOT RICE ART CENTRE 6E6

♿ P

University of Edinburgh, Old College, South Bridge. Mon-Sat 1000-1700. Free. Tel: 031-667 1011, ext 4308.

Edinburgh University's Torrie Collection and changing exhibitions are on public display in this fine building, part of the University of Edinburgh, begun by Robert Adam in 1789 and completed by William Playfair around 1830. Visitors are invited to view the fine architecture of Robert Adam and William Playfair in the Old College building. Wheelchair access by arrangement.

---

387 EDINBURGH, TRAVERSE THEATRE 6E6

112 West Bow, Grassmarket. All year. Group rates available on request. Tel: 031-226 2633 for details of events.

One of Britain's best-known centre for new plays, complete with a restaurant and bar, housed in a building over 200 years old just off the Grassmarket. Two theatres and exhibition area.

---

388 EDINBURGH UNIVERSITY COLLECTION OF HISTORIC MUSICAL INSTRUMENTS 6E6

♿ A T

Reid Concert Hall, Bristo Square. All year, Wed 1500-1700, Sat 1000-1300. Free. Tel: 031-441 3133 or 031-667 1011, ext 2573.

The collection now consists of over 1,000 instruments and is maintained by the University for the purposes of research, performance and support for teaching. Some 350 are woodwind, over 150 are brass, about 250 stringed and the rest percussion, bagpipes, ethnographic and acoustical instruments. Study room by arrangement. (See also No 374).

---

389 EDINBURGH, WAX MUSEUM 6E6

High Street, Royal Mile. 1 Apr-30 Sep 1000-1900, 1 Oct-31 Mar 1000-1700. Admission charge; group rates. Tel: 031-226 4445.

Models of prominent figures in Scottish history, including Mary, Queen of Scots, Bonnie Prince Charlie, Robert Burns and William Wallace. Also a Chamber of Horrors, featuring such characters as Burke and Hare, and Deacon Brodie; as well as a 'Never, Never Land' with fairy tale characters.

---

390 EDINBURGH, WEST REGISTER HOUSE 6E6

♿ A P

W side of Charlotte Square. Mon-Fri. Exhibitions: 1000-1600. Search Room: 0900-1645. Free. Tel: 031-556 6585.

Formerly St George's Church, 1811, this now holds the more modern documents of the Scottish Record Office (see No 368). Permanent exhibition on many aspects of Scottish history, including the Declaration of Arbroath, 1320. No guide dogs.

391 EDINBURGH, WHITE HORSE CLOSE   6E6

♿ A

Off Canongate, Royal Mile.

A restored group of 17th-century buildings off the High Street. The coaches to London left from White Horse Inn (named after Queen Mary's Palfrey), and there are Jacobite links.

392 EDINBURGH ZOO   6E6

♿ T

Entrance from Corstorphine Road (A8), 4m W of city centre. All year, daily, summer 0900-1800, winter 0900-1700 (or dusk if earlier). Sun opening 0930. Adult: £2.40, OAP/child/UB40s: £1.20. Group rates: 20% discount for pre-booked parties of 10 or more persons. Tel: 031-334 9171.

Established in 1913 by the Royal Zoological Society of Scotland, this is one of Britain's leading zoos, with a large and varied collection of mammals, birds and reptiles in extensive grounds on Corstorphine Hill. Edinburgh Zoo is world famous for its large breeding colony of Antarctic Penguins. Restaurants, bars, adventure playground and shops.

393 EDINSHALL BROCH   5F5

On the NE slope of Cockburn Law, off A6112 4m N of Duns. All times. Free. (AM) Tel: 031-226 2570.

Listed among the ten Iron Age brochs known in lowland Scotland, its dimensions are exceptionally large. The site was occupied into Roman times.

394 EDROM NORMAN ARCH   5F5

Off A6105, 3m ENE of Duns. All reasonable times. Free. (AM)
Tel: 031-226 2570.

Fine Norman chancel arch from church built by Thor
Longus c 1105, now standing behind recent parish
church.

---

395 EDZELL CASTLE AND GARDEN   3F12

Off B966, 6m N of Brechin. Opening standard, except closed Tue and
Thu mornings. Adult: 50p, OAP/child: 25p. Group rates: 10% discount
for parties of 11 or more persons. (AM) Tel: 031-226 2570.

The beautiful pleasance, a walled garden, was built by
Sir David Lindsay in 1604; the heraldic and symbolic
sculptures are unique in Scotland, and the flower-
filled recesses in the walls add to the outstanding
formal garden, which also has a turreted garden house.
The castle itself, an impressive ruin, dates from the
early 16th century, with a large courtyard mansion of
1580.

---

396 EGLINTON CASTLE   4G6

2m N of Irvine. Open from dawn to dusk. Free.

Built in 1796, with a central tower 100 feet high, the
castle was the site of the Eglinton tournament in 1839.
The gardens are also open.

Eilean Donan Castle

397 EILEAN DONAN CASTLE   2F10

Off A87, 9m E of Kyle of Lochalsh. Easter-Sep, daily 1000-1230,
1400-1800. Admission: £1.00. (Mr J D H MacRae).
Tel: Kyle (0599) 85 202.

On an islet (now connected by a causeway) in Loch
Duich, this picturesque castle dates back to 1220. It
passed into the hands of the Mackenzies of Kintail
who became Earls of Seaforth. In 1719 it was
garrisoned by Spanish Jacobite troops and was blown
up by an English man o'war. Now completely
restored, it incorporates a war memorial to the Clan
Macrae, who held it as hereditary Constables on behalf
of the Mackenzies. Gift shop.

---

398 ELCHO CASTLE   6D2

On River Tay, 4m SE of Perth. Opening standard. Adult: 50p,
OAP/child: 25p. Group rates: 10% discount for parties of 11 or more
persons. (AM) Tel: 031-226 2570.

A preserved fortified mansion notable for its tower-
like jambs or wings and for the wrought-iron grills
protecting its windows. An ancestral seat of the Earls
of Wemyss; another castle, on or very near the site,
was a favourite hide-out of William Wallace.

399 ELECTRIC BRAE   4G8

A719 9m S of Ayr (also known as Croy Brae). All times. Free.

An optical illusion is created so that a car appears to be going down the hill when it is in fact going up.

Elgin Cathedral

400 ELGIN CATHEDRAL   3D8

North College Street, Elgin. Opening standard. Adult: 50p, OAP: 25p, child: 25p. Group rates: 10% discount for parties of 11 or more persons. (AM) Tel: 031-226 2570.

When entire, this was perhaps the most beautiful of Scottish cathedrals, known as the Lantern of the North. It was founded in 1224, but in 1390 it was burned by the Wolf of Badenoch. It did not fall into ruin until after the Reformation. Much 13th-century work still remains; the nave and chapter house are 15th-century. There is a 6th-century Pictish slab in the choir.

401 ELGIN MUSEUM   3D8

High Street, Elgin. Apr-mid Sep, Mon-Fri 1000-1600, Sat 1000-1200. Adult: 25p, child/OAP/student: 10p. Tel: Elgin (0343) 3675

An award-winning museum housing a world famous collection of Old Red Sandstone, Permian and Triassic fossils. Also exhibited are items ranging from pre-historic to modern times and natural history specimens of the area.

402 ANDREW ELLIOT   5A7

Forest Mill, Selkirk. Mon-Fri 0900-1700, evenings and weekends by arrangement. Free. (Andrew Elliot). Tel: Selkirk (0750) 20412.

The weaving of woollen tie, dress and skirt fabrics and a display of rugs and upholstery tweeds. Due to working machinery, small groups only. No coach parties.

403 ELLISLAND FARM   5B9

  ♿
A
Off A76, 6½m NNW of Dumfries. All reasonable times, but intending visitors are advised to phone in advance. Free. (Ellisland Trust). Tel: Dumfries (0387) 74 426.

Robert Burns took over this farm in June 1788, built the farmhouse, and tried to introduce new farming methods. Unsuccessful, he became an Exciseman in September 1789; in August 1791 the stock was auctioned, and he moved to Dumfries in November 1791. Some of the poet's most famous works were written at Ellisland, including *Tam o'Shanter* and *Auld Lang Syne*. The Granary houses a display showing Burns as a farmer. Farmhouse with museum room; granary building with Burns display; riverside walk.

404 EXHIBITION OF THE SCOTTISH HIGHLANDER 3B8

4/9 Huntly Street, Inverness. 1 Apr-30 Sep, daily 0900-2100.
Adult: 80p, OAP: 70p, child: 35p, student: 70p; group rates.
Tel: Inverness (0463) 222781.

A comprehensive exhibition of the history of the
Scottish Highlander. Includes the Picts, the Kings, the
Chiefs, the battles, the rise of the Highland regiments,
the clearances, the Celtic revival, the story of whisky,
the history of the bagpipes and the costumes of the clans.

405 EYEMOUTH MUSEUM 5G5

*Market Place, Eyemouth. Easter, May-Oct, Mon-Sat 1000-1800, Sun
1400-1800. Adult: 70p, OAP/child: 35p; group rates. (Eyemouth
Museum Trust). Tel: Eyemouth (0390) 50678.*

Opened in 1981 to commemorate the Great East
Coast Fishing Disaster in which 189 fishermen were
lost, 129 of them from Eyemouth. Displays include
Eyemouth tapestry, and the wheelhouse of a modern
fishing boat. Museum reflects the fishing and farming
history of East Berwickshire.

406 EYNHALLOW CHURCH 1B10

On island of Eynhallow. Orkney. All reasonable times. Free. (AM)
Tel: 031-226 2570.

A 12th-century church, now largely in ruins. Close by
is a group of domestic buildings, also ruined.

407 FAIR ISLE 1F8

*Most isolated inhabited island in Britain, halfway between Orkney and
Shetland. Twice-weekly mailboat sailings in summer from Shetland and
scheduled and charter flights from Shetland. (NTS)*
Tel: Fair Isle (035 12) 258

Home of internationally-famous Bird Observatory,
open March to October. Important breeding ground
for great and Arctic skuas, storm petrel, fulmar,
razorbill, puffin, etc. The Observatory, on main bird
migration routes, notes some 300 species. The island
itself is notable for Fair Isle knitwear in intricate
colourful patterns, a traditional skill of the
womenfolk.

408 FAIR MAID'S HOUSE GALLERY 6D2

*North Port, Perth. All year, Mon-Fri 1100-1600, Sat 1100-1700. Gallery
closed Jan, Aug; Craft Shop open all year. Free. Tel: Perth (0738) 25976.*

One of the oldest buildings in Perth, now housing
contemporary Scottish crafts and a gallery. Exhibition
changes each month, covering painting, embroidery,
tapestry, sculpture, etching and print-making.

409 FALCONER MUSEUM 3C8

*Tolbooth Street, Forres, 12m W of Elgin. May, Jun, Sep, Mon-Sat
0930-1730; Jul, Aug, Mon-Sat 0930-1830, Sun 1400-1830; Oct-Apr,
Mon-Fri, 1000-1630. Free. Tel: Forres (0309) 73701.*

Displays on local history, natural history, fossils and
temporary exhibitions. Shop, Tourist Information
Office (open May-Sep).

410 FALKIRK MUSEUM 6B6

15 Orchard Street, Falkirk. All year, Mon-Sat 1000-1230, 1330-1700.
Free. Tel: Falkirk (0324) 24911, ext 2472.

Permanent displays on the archaeology of the district,
Dunmore Pottery, 19th-century foundry products and
natural history.

Falkland Palace and Gardens

411 FALKLAND PALACE AND GARDENS 6E3

&. P

A912, 11m N of Kirkcaldy. 28 Mar-30 Sep, Mon-Sat 1000-1800, Sun 1400-1800; 1-31 Oct, Sat 1000-1800, Sun 1400-1800, last admission 1715. (Palace and gardens) Adult: £1.40, child: 70p. (Gardens only) Adult: 80p, child: 40p. Group rates, Adult party: £1.10. (NTS) Tel: Falkland (033 757) 397.

A lovely Royal Palace in a picturesque little town. The buildings of the Palace, in Renaissance style, date from 1501-41. This was a favourite seat of James V, who died here in 1542, and of his daughter Mary, Queen of Scots. The Royal Tennis Court of 1539 is still played on. The gardens are small but charming.

412 FALLS OF CLYDE CENTRE 5B6

&. P

New Lanark. Easter-Oct, Mon-Fri 1100-1700, Sat-Sun 1200-1700; Oct-Easter, Sat-Sun 1200-dusk, weekdays by prior arrangement. Adult: 50p, OAP/child: 25p. Group rates, Family: £1.50; 15p per person for booked parties of children, 25p for adults. (Scottish Wildlife Trust). Tel: New Lanark (0555) 65262.

Visitor Centre, in the old dyeworks building in New Lanark (see No 740), for the nature reserve and nearby waterfalls.

413 FALLS OF GLOMACH 2G10

Unclassified road off A87, 18m E of Kyle of Lochalsh. (NTS) Tel: 031-226 5922.

One of the highest falls in Britain, 370 feet, above wild Glen Elchaig. From Croe Bridge on Loch Duich, an 8-mile round trip on a long-distance walkers' path through the hills via Dorusdain. Stout footwear essential.

Falls of Measach: see No 217.

414 FALLS OF SHIN 3A6

A836, 5m N of Bonar Bridge.

Spectacular falls through a rocky gorge famous for salmon leaping.

Farr Church: see No 911.

415 FARIGAIG FOREST CENTRE 3A9

Off B862 at Inverfarigaig, 17m S of Inverness. Easter mid-Oct 0930-1900. Free. (FC) Tel: Drumnadrochit (04563) 249.

A Forestry Commission interpretation centre in a converted stone stable, showing the development of the forest environment in the Great Glen. Forest walks.

416 FASQUE 3F12

&. P T

Approx 1m N of Fettercairn on the Edzell-Banchory road (B974). May-Sep, daily (not Fri) 1330-1730 and evenings for parties by arrangement, tel: Fettercairn 201. Adult: £1.40, child: 70p. Tel: Fettercairn (05614) 201.

Castle home of the Gladstones including Victorian Prime Minister W E Gladstone. Built in 1809. Impressive public rooms also with extraordinary complete 'downstairs' quarters and articles. Large deer park and deer farm.

417 FAST CASTLE 5F5

Off A1107, 4m NW of Coldingham.

The scant, but impressive remains of a Home stronghold, perched on a cliff above the sea. Care should be taken on the cliffs.

418 M.V. "FERRY QUEEN" 4H5

Easter-Sep, Sat, Sun afternoons and public holidays; Mon afternoons at 1330 and 1530. Adult: £1.50, OAP: £1.00, child: 50p (under fives free). Group rates by arrangement. Tel: 041-772 1620.

The M.V. "Ferry Queen" is a restored Clyde Ferry Boat which cruises on the Forth & Clyde Canal between the Stables Inn and Bishopbriggs.

419 FETTERCAIRN ARCH 3F12

In Fettercairn. On B9120, 4m W of Laurencekirk. All times. Free.

Stone arch built to commemorate the visit by Queen Victoria and the Prince Consort in 1861.

420 FIFE FOLK MUSEUM 6F3

  &
A
P

At Ceres, 3m SE of Cupar. Apr-Oct, Mon-Sat (except Tue) 1400-1700, Sun 1430-1730. Adult: 50p, child: 20p. Group rates, Adult: 40p, child: 20p. (Central & North Fife Preservation Society). Tel: Ceres (033 482) 380.

Situated in the 17th-century Weigh House, near an old bridge in an attractive village, this museum is a growing collection in a unique setting, showing the domestic and agricultural past of Fife. New countryside annexe opened in 1983. Nearby is the attractive Ceres Church (1806) with a horse-shoe gallery. Alternative wheelchair entrance.

421 FINAVON DOOCOT 5D1

Off A94, 5m NE of Forfar, opposite Finavon Doocot Shop. May-Sep, daily. Adult: 50p, child: 25p. (Angus Historic Building Society)

A two-chamber lean-to doocot containing over 2,100 nesting boxes (still occupied), the largest in Scotland. In one chamber there is an exhibition of the 66 doocots in Angus.

Fingal's Cave

422 FINGAL'S CAVE 1C2

  &
A
P

On the uninhabited island of Staffa, 8m off the W coast of Mull. Seen by steamer and boat trips from Oban and Mull. Group rates: 10% reduction on groups of over 20. Tel: Oban (0631) 63122.

A huge cave, 227 feet long and some 66 feet high from sea level, flanked by black pillared walls and columns. The basaltic rock formations of Staffa, where there are other curious caves, are famous. Fingal's Cave inspired Mendelssohn's *The Hebrides* overture. Catering/bar facilities on Caledonian MacBrayne steamer; depending on tour taken there is access to refreshments en route

423 FINLAYSTONE

1H5

&

P

*By A8 W of Langbank, 17m W of Glasgow. Mon-Sat 0900-1700, Sun
1400-1700. (Woods and Gardens) Adult: 60p, child: 40p. (House) Apr-
Aug, Sun afternoon, or by arrangement. (Mr George MacMillan).
Tel: Langbank (047 554) 285 (1230-1300 or evenings).*

Country estate with woodland walks, nursery gardens,
formal gardens, adventure playgrounds and pony-
trekking. Countryside Ranger Service. The house has
some fine rooms, Victorian relics, flower prints and an
international collection of dolls shown in the billiard
room. Historical connections with John Knox and
Robert Burns. Afternoon teas (Apr-Sep).

424 FLODDEN MONUMENT

5E7

&

Town Centre, Selkirk. All times. Free.

The monument was erected in 1913 on the 400th
anniversary of the battle and is inscribed 'O Flodden
Field'.

425 FLOORS CASTLE

5F6

*B6089, 2m NW of Kelso. (Castle and grounds) 27 Apr-30 Sep, daily
except Fri & Sat; Jul, Aug, daily except Sat, 1130-1730. Adult: £1.80,
child: £1.20, OAP: £1.60. Group rates to be arranged. (Garden centre)
All year, daily 0930-1700. (Duke and Duchess of Roxburghe).
Tel: Kelso (0573) 23333.*

A large and impressive mansion, built by William
Adam in 1721, with additions in the 1840s by William
Playfair. A holly tree in the grounds is said to mark
the spot where James II was killed by the bursting of a
cannon in 1460. Location of the film 'Greystoke'.

426 FOCHABERS FOLK MUSEUM

3E8

&

P

*Fochabers. All year, daily 0900-1300, 1400-1730. Adult: 40p,
OAP/child: 20p. (Christies (Fochabers) Ltd).
Tel: Fochabers (0343) 820362.*

An interesting conversion of an old church housing a
large collection of horse-drawn carts on the top floor,
and on the ground floor a varied collection of local
items, giving the history of Fochabers over the past
200 years.

427 FOGO CHURCH

5F6

Off B6460 3m SW of Duns. All reasonable times.

The attractive church has an outside staircase giving
access to the private laird's loft dating from 1671.

428 FORDYCE

3F7

Unclassified road off A98, 4m SE of Cullen.

A tiny village built round a small 16th-century castle.
Adjacent are the remains of the old church with an
interesting belfry.

429 FORFAR MUSEUM AND ART GALLERY 5D1

&

A

P

*Meffan Institute, Forfar. Mon, Tues, Wed, Fri 0930-1900;
Thu, Sat 0930-1700. Free. Tel: Forfar (0307) 63468.*

Housed in the Meffan Institute, there are collections of
burgh's civic and industrial history, folk life and
archaeology, displays of local fossils and works by local
artists. Entrance by request at library issue desk.

430 FORT CHARLOTTE   1G4

Lerwick, Shetland. Opening standard. Free. (AM) Tel: 031-226 2570.

A fort roughly pentagonal in shape with high walls containing gun ports pointing seawards. Designed by John Mylne and begun in 1665 to protect the Sound of Bressay, it was burned in 1673 with the town of Lerwick by the Dutch, but repaired in 1781.

431 FORT GEORGE   3B8

B9039, off A96 W of Nairn, Opening standard. Adult: 50p, OAP/child: 25p. Group rates: 10% discount for parties of 11 or more persons. (AM) Tel: 031-226 2570.

Begun in 1748 as a result of the Jacobite rebellion, this is one of the finest late artillery fortifications in Europe. There is also the Regimental Museum of the Queen's Own Highlanders. (See No 796).

432 FORTH BRIDGES   6D6

Queensferry, 10m W of Edinburgh.

For over 800 years travellers were ferried across the Firth of Forth. Queensferry was named from Queen Margaret who regularly used this passage between Dunfermline and Edinburgh in the 11th century. The ferry ceased in 1964 when the Queen opened the Forth Road Bridge, a suspension bridge then the longest of its kind in Europe (1,993 yards). Also here is the rail bridge of 1883-90, one of the greatest engineering feats of its time. It is 2,765 yards long.

433 FORTH/CLYDE CANAL   6A6

Tel: 041-332 6936.

Opened in 1790, the Canal linked industrial towns of West Central Scotland with the east coast at Grangemouth. When the Union Canal opened this link was extended via Falkirk to the heart of Edinburgh. The route of the Canal is close to that of the Antonine Wall. Although closed to navigation in 1963 the Canal is beginning to enjoy a renaissance through recreation activity. The towing path provides delightful walks through town and country and excursions by canal boat are available from the Stables Inn, Glasgow Road, near Kirkintilloch. A restaurant barge sails from Ratho, near Edinburgh. (See No 418).

434 FORTINGALL YEW   5A1

& *Fortingall, 9m W of Aberfeldy.*

The great yew in an enclosure in the churchyard is over 3,000 years old, perhaps the oldest tree in Britain. The attractive village, which was rebuilt in 1900 with many thatched cottages, is claimed to be the birthplace of Pontius Pilate.

Fortrose Cathedral

435 FORTROSE CATHEDRAL   3B8

At Fortrose, 8m SSW of Cromarty. Opening standard. Free. (AM) Tel: 031-226 2570.

The surviving portions of this 14th century cathedral include the south aisle with its vaulting and much fine detail.

---

436 FOULDEN TITHE BARN   5G5

A6105, 5m NW of Berwick-upon-Tweed. May be viewed from the roadside. (AM) Tel: 031-226 2570.

A two-storeyed tithe barn, with outside stair and crow-stepped gables.

---

437 FOWLSHEUGH NATURE RESERVE   3G11

Access along cliff-top path north from small car park at Crawton, signposted from A92, 3m S of Stonehaven. All times. Free. (RSPB) Tel: 031-556 5624.

Large and spectacular seabird colony, best seen April- July.

---

438 FYRISH MONUMENT   3A7

Above village of Evanton on Fyrish Hill, off A9. All times. Free.

Curious monument erected in 1782 by Sir Hector Munro who rose from the ranks and distinguished himself at the relief of Seringapatam. The monument is a replica of the Indian gateway and was built to provide work at a time of poverty and unemployment in the Evanton area.

---

439 FYVIE CASTLE   3G9

P
T

Off A947, 8m SE of Turriff and 25m NW of Aberdeen. 1 May-30 Sep, daily 1400-1800 (last tour 1715). Adult: £1.40, OAP/child: 70p. Group rates: £1.10 for pre-booked parties of 20 or more. (National Trust for Scotland). Tel: Fyvie (065 16) 266.

The five towers of Fyvie Castle enshrine five centuries of Scottish history, each being built by the five families who owned the castle. The oldest part dates from the 13th century and it is now one of the grandest examples of Scottish baronial architecture. Apart from the great wheel stair, the finest in Scotland, and the 17th-century morning room, with its contemporary panelling and plaster ceiling, the interior as created by the 1st Lord Leith of Fyvie reflects the opulence of the Edwardian era. There is an exceptionally important collection of portraits including works by Batoni, Raeburn, Ramsay. Gainsborough, Opie and Hoppner. In addition, there are arms and armour and 16th-century tapestries. Tearoom, grounds including loch.

---

440 FYVIE CHURCH   3G9

Off A947, 7m NW of Oldmeldrum. By arrangement. (The Manse). Free. Tel: Fyvie (065 16) 230 or 498.

An attractive church with notable stained glass, Celtic stones and 17th-century panelling inside. 'Mill of Tifty's Annie' is buried in the churchyard, and nearby a cross marks the site of a 12th-century monastery. Restaurant facilities nearby.

---

441 GAIRLOCH HERITAGE MUSEUM   2F7

T

In Gairloch, on A832. Easter-end Sep, Mon-Sat 1000-1700. Adult: 30p, OAP: 30p, child: 10p. Tel: Badachro (044 583) 243.

Award-winning museum with displays of all aspects of the past life of the West Highland area from prehistoric times to the present day. Licensed restaurant attached.

442   **GALLOWAY DEER MUSEUM**   **4H10**

  On A712, by Clatteringshaws Loch, 6m W of New Galloway. Apr-Sep, daily 1000-1800. Free. (FC) Tel: New Galloway (064 42) 285.

The museum, in a converted farm steading, has a live trout exhibit as well as many features on deer and other aspects of Galloway wildlife, geology and history. Bruce's Stone (See No 121) on Raploch Moss is a short walk away.

443   **GALLOWAY FOREST PARK**   **4H9**

Off A714, 10m NW of Newton Stewart. Free. (FC) Tel: Newton Stewart (0671) 2420.

250 square miles of magnificent countryside in Central Galloway, including Merrick (2,765 feet) the highest hill in southern Scotland. The land is owned by the Forestry Commission and there is a wide variety of leisure facilities including forest trails, fishing, a red deer range, a wild goat park, a forest drive (see No 80), and a deer museum (see No. 442). Murray's Monument dominates a hillside off the A712. It was erected to commemorate the son of a local shepherd who became a Professor at Edinburgh University.

444   **GALLOWAY HOUSE GARDENS**   **4H11**

At Garlieston, 8m S of Wigtown. All year, daily, all reasonable times. Admission by collection box, in aid of Scotland's Garden Scheme and Sorbie Church Organ Fund. Tel: Garlieston (098 86) 225.

Galloway House was built in 1740 by Lord Garlies, eldest son of the 7th Earl of Galloway, and later enlarged by Burn, and the hall decorated by Lorimer. Not open to the public.

The grounds cover some 30 acres and go down to the sea and sandy beach. There are fine old trees, and as a speciality in May/June there is a well-grown handkerchief tree. In season there are many snowdrops, pretty old-fashioned daffodills and a good collection of rhododendrons and azaleas. Also a walled garden with greenhouses and a camellia house. Home-baked teas are available in Garlieston village.

445   **GARGUNNOCK GARDEN**   **5A4**

Gargunnock, off A811, 6m W of Stirling. Apr-Oct, Wed 1300-1700. Admission by donation, minimum 50p. (Miss Stirling of Gargunnock). Tel: Gargunnock (078 686) 202.

Small shrub and flower garden beside 16th-18th century house (not open). Drive and small woodland walk. Narcissi, azaleas, rhododendrons, flowering shrubs and trees, autumn colours. Gargunnock House open by written arrangement only.

446   **GARTMORN DAM COUNTRY PARK AND NATURE RESERVE**   **6C5**

By Sauchie, 2m NE of Alloa off A908. (Park) All year at all times. (Visitor Centre) Apr-Sep, Mon-Wed 1000-1645, Sat 1330-1700, Sun 1400-1845; Oct-Mar, Wed 1000-1600, Sun 1400-1600. Free. (Clackmannan District Council)

The oldest dam in Scotland, with reservoir. The park is an important winter roost for migratory duck, there are pleasant walks and fishing is available. Visitor Centre has exhibits and information and through the ranger service slide shows, talks and escorted walks can be arranged.

447 GARVAMORE BRIDGE 3A11

  ♿ *6m W of Laggan Bridge, on unclassified road, 17m SW of Newtonmore. All times. Free.*

This two-arched bridge at the south side of the Corrieyarick Pass was built by General Wade in 1735.

Gifford: see No 999.

---

448 GILNOCKIE TOWER 5D9·

A7, 5m S of Langholm. All reasonable times. Free.
Tel: Langholm (0541) 80976.

Also known as Holehouse, the tower dates from the 16th century and has walls 6 feet thick. It was once the home of the 16th-century Border freebooter, Johnny Armstrong.

449 GLADSTONE COURT STREET MUSEUM

A702 North Back Road, Biggar, 26m from Edinburgh, 12m from A74 (South). Easter-Oct, daily 1000-1230, 1400-1700; Sun 1400-1700; other times by arrangement. Adult: 80p, child: 40p. Group rates: Less 10%. (Biggar Museum Trust). Tel: Biggar (0899) 21050.

An indoor street museum of shops and windows. Grocers, photographer, dressmaker, bank, school, library, ironmonger, chemist, china merchant, telephone exchange, etc. Reduced price for joint admission to Greenhill Covenanters' House. (See No 519).

Glamis Castle

450 GLAMIS CASTLE 5D1

  ♿
  P
  T
A928, 5m SW of Forfar. Easter, 1 May-1 Oct, daily (not Sat) 1300-1700, other times by prior arrangement only. Adult: £2.00, child: £1. Group rates: 20p off quoted prices. (Earl of Strathmore and Kinghorne). Tel: Glamis (030 784) 242.

This famous Scottish castle, childhood home of Her Majesty Queen Elizabeth The Queen Mother and birthplace of The Princess Margaret, owes its present aspect to the period 1675-87. Portions of the high square tower, with walls 15 feet thick, are much older. There has been a building on the site from very early times and Malcolm II is said to have died there in 1034. The oldest part of today's castle is Duncan's Hall, legendary setting for Shakespeare's famous play 'Macbeth'. There are also fine collections of china, tapestry and furniture. Gift shop, gallery shop (selling pictures, prints and antiques); garden produce stall, self-service tearoom (with a range of home-baked items).

451 GLASGOW, ART GALLERY AND MUSEUM 4H5

  In Kelvingrove Park. All year, weekdays 1000-1700, Sun 1400-1700.
T *Free. (Glasgow Museums and Art Galleries). Tel: 041-357 3929.*

This fine municipal art collection has outstanding Flemish, Dutch and Italian canvases, including magnificent works by Giorgione and Rembrandt, as well as a wide range of French Impressionist and British pictures. Other areas include sculpture, furniture designed by Charles Rennie Mackintosh and his contemporaries, silver, pottery, glass and porcelain, an important collection of European arms and armour and displays of archaeological, historical and ethnographic material.
The natural history displays illustrate geology, with minerals, dinosaurs and other fossils. There is a comprehensive collection of British birds. The natural history of Scotland is treated in depth in a developing new gallery. Alternative entrance for wheelchairs.

452 GLASGOW, THE BARRAS 4H5

  ¼m E of Glasgow Cross. All year, Sat and Sun 0900-1700. Free.
T *Tel: 041-552 7258 (Wed-Sun 1000-1600).*

Glasgow's world famous weekend market, with an amazing variety of stalls and shops. Founded one hundred years ago, the Barras is now home to over 800 traders each weekend. Look out for the Barras archways, children's creche and buskers. Numerous licensed premises and cafes. All markets are covered.

453 GLASGOW BOTANIC GARDENS 4H5

  Entrance from Great Western Road (A82). Gardens 0700-dusk; Kibble
T *Palace 1000-1645; Main Range 1300 (Sun 1200)-1645. Closes 1615 Oct-Mar. Free. Tel: 041-334 2422*

The glasshouses contain a wide range of tropical plants including an internationally recognised collection of orchids and the 'National Collection' of begonias. The Kibble Palace, an outstanding Victorian glasshouse, has a unique collection of tree ferns and other plants from temperate areas of the world. Outside features include a Systematic Garden, a Herb Garden and a Chronological Border.

454 GLASGOW, THE BURRELL COLLECTION 4H5

  Pollok Country Park. All year, weekdays 1000-1700, Sun 1400-1700.
T *Free. (Glasgow Museums and Art Galleries). Tel: 041-649 7151.*

Housed in a new building opened in 1983, a world famous collection of textiles, furniture, ceramics, stained glass, art objects and pictures (especially 19th century French) gifted to Glasgow by Sir William and Lady Burrell. Restaurant and bar, parking and facilities for handicapped.

455 GLASGOW, CATHCART CASTLE 4H5

  In Linn Park. All reasonable times. Free.
T

Sparse ruins of a 15th-century castle now in a city park. Nearby is the Queen's Knowe, associated with Mary, Queen of Scots.

456 GLASGOW CATHEDRAL   **4H5**

At E end of Cathedral Street. Opening standard. Free. (AM)
Tel: 031-226 2670.

The Cathedral, dedicated to St Mungo, is the most
complete survivor of the great Gothic churches of
south Scotland. A fragment dates from the late 12th
century, though several periods (mainly 13th century)
are represented in its architecture. The splendid crypt
of the mid-13th century is the chief glory of the
cathedral, which is now the Parish Church of
Glasgow.

457 GLASGOW, CITIZENS' THEATRE   **4H5**

&
A
T

Gorbals. Sep-May. Concessions for OAPs, unemployed and students.
Tel: 041-429 0022 (1000-2000, box office), 041-429 5561 (admin).

Opened in 1878 originally as a Music Hall and now a
listed building. Stalls, upper and dress circle bars,
confectionery and coffee available during performances.
Alternative wheelchair entrance.

458 GLASGOW, CITY CHAMBERS   **4H5**

George Square, Mon-Fri, guided tours at 1030 and 1430 or by
arrangement. Sometimes restricted owing to Council functions. Free.
Tel: 041-227 4017/8.

Built in Italian Renaissance style, and opend in 1888
by Queen Victoria. The interiors, particularly the
function suites and the staircases, reflect all the
opulence of Victorian Glasgow.

459 GLASGOW, COLLINS GALLERY   **4H5**

&

University of Strathclyde, Richmond Street, off George Street. Open
during exhibitions, Mon-Fri 1000-1700, Sat 1200-1600. Free.
Tel: 041-552 4400, ext 2682/2416.

Modern gallery which presents a varied programme of
historical and contemporary visual art exhibitions and
other related events.

460 GLASGOW, CROOKSTON CASTLE   **4H5**

4m SW of city centre. Opening standard, except Oct-Mar closed Wed
afternoon and Fri. Adult: 50p, OAP/child: 25p. Group rates:
10% discount for parties of 11 or more persons. (AM) Tel: 031-226 2570.

On the site of a castle built by Robert Croc in the
mid-12th century, the present tower house dates from
the early 15th century. Darnley and Mary Queen of
Scots stayed here after their marriage in 1565.

461 GLASGOW, CUSTOM HOUSE QUAY   **4H5**

N shore of the Clyde, between Glasgow Bridge and Victoria Bridge.

The Quay is part of the Clyde Walkway, an ambitious
project to give new life to the riverside. By Victoria
Bridge is moored the *Carrick* (1864) and there is a fine
view of Carlton Place on the opposite bank.

Glasgow, Fossil Grove: see No 491.

462 GLASGOW, GEORGE SQUARE   **4H5**

The heart of Glasgow with the City Chambers
(see No 458) and statues of Sir Walter Scott, Queen
Victoria, Prince Albert, Robert Burns, Sir John
Moore, Lord Clyde, Thomas Campbell, Dr Thomas
Graham, James Oswald, James Watt, William
Gladstone and Sir Robert Peel.

463 GLASGOW, GREENBANK GARDEN 4H5

&
T

Flenders Road, Clarkston, Glasgow (6m S of city centre), off Mearns Road (B761) off A726. All year, daily 0930-sunset. Adult: 65p, child: 30p. Group rates: children's party 25p per person. (NTS) Tel: 041-552 8391.

Two and a half acres of walled garden and 13 acres of policies surround an elegant Georgian house (not open to the public). Now a Gardening Advice Centre, especially suitable for the owners of small gardens. Gardening classes are held regularly, the syllabus being available at Greenbank; also garden advice given (Thu 1400-1700) at the garden. Dogs on leash. Disabled visitors' facilities including special garden and tuition. Gardening advice classes (monthly). Shop and refreshments in season.

---

464 GLASGOW, HAGGS CASTLE 4H5

&
P

100 St Andrew's Drive. All year, Mon-Sat 1000-1700, Sun 1400-1700. Free. (Glasgow Museums and Art Galleries). Tel: 041-427 2725

Built in 1585 by John Maxwell of Pollok, the castle was acquired by the city in 1972, and, after restoration, was developed as a museum of history for children. As well as the exhibitions, there are workshops where every Saturday, there are museum-based activities for children. The gardens have been landscaped and include herb and vegetable plots and a knot garden. Shop and workshop.

---

465 GLASGOW, HUNTERIAN ART GALLERY 4H5

&
P
T

Glasgow University, Hillhead Street, 2m NW of city centre. All year, Mon-Fri 1000-1700, Sat 0930-1300. Free. Tel: 041-339 8855, ext 7431.

Unrivalled collections of work by Charles Rennie Mackintosh, including reconstructed interiors of the architect's house, and by J M Whistler. Works by Rembrandt, Chardin, Stubbs, Reynolds, Pissarro, Sisley, Rodin, plus Scottish painting from the 18th century to the present. Sculpture Courtyard. Varied programme of temporary exhibitions from 16th century to present. Sales point, university refectory nearby. Alternative wheelchair entrance.

---

466 GLASGOW, HUNTERIAN MUSEUM 4H5

&
P
T

Glasgow University, 2m NW of city centre. All year, Mon-Fri 0930-1700, Sat 0930-1300. Free. Tel: 041-339 8855, ext 4221.

Glasgow's oldest museum, opened in 1807. Exhibits include geological, archaeological and ethnological material; new coin gallery and exhibition on history of Glasgow University. Scottish Museum of the Year Award 1983 and 1984. Temporary exhibitions of scientific instruments are exhibited in the Natural Philosophy Building. The anatomical and zoological collections, and manuscripts and early printed books, can be seen on application. Bookstall and small coffee-house in 18th-century style. Alternative wheelchair entrance (via lift), please telephone.

467 GLASGOW, HUTCHESONS' HALL   4H5

&
P
T

158 Ingram Street, near SE corner of George Square. All year, Mon-Fri 0900-1700, Sat 1000-1600. Shop: Mon-Sat 1000-1600. Free. (NTS) Tel: 041-552 8391.

Described as one of the most elegant buildings in Glasgow's city centre, Hutchesons' Hall was built in 1802-5 to a design by David Hamilton and includes a handsome meeting hall introduced by James Baird II in 1876. It incorporates on its frontage the statues of the founders, George and Thomas Hutcheson, from an earlier building. It is now used as a visitor centre, gift shop and the Trust's regional offices.

468 GLASGOW, KING'S THEATRE   4H5

Bath Street, Glasgow.

This 1,800 seat theatre dates back to 1904 and preserves the style and elegance of the Edwardian period. Now carefully modernised, it has become one of the best equipped civic theatres in Scotland.

469 GLASGOW, CHARLES RENNIE MACKINTOSH SOCIETY   4H5

&
P

Queens Cross, 870 Garscube Road (enter by Springbank Street). All year, Tue, Thu, Fri 1200-1730, Sun 1430-1700, and by arrangement. Free. Tel: 041-946 6600 or (0360) 50595.

Queens Cross, a Mackintosh church, and now the international headquarters of the Charles Rennie Mackintosh Society. Reference library and small exhibition area, bookstall and tearoom.

470 GLASGOW, MERCHANTS' HOUSE   4H5

&
A
P

W side of George Square. May-Sep, Mon-Fri 1400-1600. Free. The hall and ante-rooms may be seen by arrangement. (The Merchants' House of Glasgow). Tel: 041-221 8272.

This handsome building occupies one of the best sites in the city. Built in 1874 by John Burnet, it contains the Glasgow Chamber of Commerce, the oldest in Britain, the fine Merchants' Hall, with ancient relics and good stained-glass windows, and the House's own offices. Tour and commentary on history of Merchants' House.

471 GLASGOW, THE MITCHELL LIBRARY   4H5

&
T

North Street. Mon-Fri 0930-2100, Sat 0930-1700. Free. (Glasgow District Council). Tel: 041-221 7030.

Founded in 1874, this is the largest public reference library in Scotland, with stock of over one million volumes. Its many collections include probably the largest on Robert Burns in the world. Coffee room (1030-1630).

Glasgow, Museum of Transport

472 GLASGOW, MUSEUM OF TRANSPORT   4H5

25 Albert Drive. All year, weekdays 1000-1700, Sun 1400-1700. Free.
(Glasgow Museums and Art Galleries). Tel: 041-423 8000.

The museum presents a large collection of trams,
buses, motor cars (including the oldest car in
Scotland), horse drawn vehicles, railway locomotives,
fire engines and bicycles, in addition to a wealth of
special displays and models, including a working
model railway. Of particular note is the gallery
housing a fine collection of ship models. Self-service
tearoom and shop.

473 GLASGOW, NECROPOLIS   4H5

Behind Glasgow Cathedral.

Remarkable and extensive burial ground laid out in
1833, with numerous elaborate tombs of 19th-century
illustrious Glaswegians and others; see particularly the
Menteith Mausoleum of 1842.

474 GLASGOW, PEOPLE'S PALACE   4H5

In Glasgow Green. All year, weekdays 1000-1700, Sun 1400-1700. Free.
(Glasgow Museums and Art Galleries). Tel: 041-554 0223.

Opened in 1898, contains important collections
relating to the tobacco and other industries, Glasgow
stained glass, ceramics, and political and social
movements including temperance, co-operation,
women's suffrage and socialism. Wholefood snack
bar/tearoom in Winter Gardens and shop. Alternative
wheelchair entrance at west door (Winter Gardens).

475 GLASGOW, POLLOK HOUSE   4H5

2060 Pollokshaws Road (A736). All year, weekdays 1000-1700, Sun
1400-1700. Free. (Glasgow Museums and Art Galleries)
Tel: 041-632 0274.

Built c 1750, with additions 1890-1908 designed by Sir
Robert Rowand Anderson. It houses the Stirling
Maxwell collection of Spanish and other European
paintings. Also displays of furniture, ceramics, glass
and silver (mostly 18th century). Tearoom, gardens
and shop. Alternative wheelchair entrance to tearoom.

476 GLASGOW, PROVAN HALL   4H5

At Auchinlea Road (B806), Easterhouse, off M8, 4m E of city centre.
(NTS) Tel: 041-552 7941.

Built in the 15th century, this is probably the most
perfect example of a pre-Reformation house in
Scotland. Now part of Auchinlea Park. The property
is leased to the City of Glasgow District Council and
while the old hall is closed at present, visitors may
view the surrounding garden and parkland. Situated in
Auchinlea Park, Easterhouse.

477 GLASGOW, PROVAND'S LORDSHIP 4H5

  ♿
  P

Castle Street, opposite the Cathedral. Free. (Glasgow Museums and Art Galleries). Tel: 041-552 8819.

The only surviving medieval building in Glasgow apart from the Cathedral. Built 1471 as the manse for the chaplain of the Hospital of St Nicholas by Bishop Andrew Muirhead. Period house displays, 1500-1900.

478 GLASGOW, REGIMENTAL HEADQUARTERS OF THE ROYAL HIGHLAND FUSILIERS 4H5

  ♿

518 Sauchiehall Street, Glasgow. Mon-Thu 0900-1630, Fri 0900-1600. Free. Tel: 041-332 0961.

The exhibits in this regimental museum include medals, badges, uniforms and records which illustrate the histories of The Royal Scots Fusiliers, The Highland Light Infantry and The Royal Highland Fusiliers.

479 GLASGOW, ROUKEN GLEN 4H5

Thornliebank. All reasonable times. Free.

One of Glasgow's most attractive parks with lovely shaded walks and a waterfall.

480 GLASGOW, ST ANDREW'S PARISH CHURCH 4H5

  ♿
  A
  P

St Andrew's Square, Saltmarket, Glasgow. Wed, Fri and Sun 1100-1200, or by arrangement. Free. Tel: 041-560 3280.

Extremely fine Georgian church, built in 1756 by Tobacco Lords. Magnificent interior plaster work and mahogany gallery fronts.

481 GLASGOW, ST DAVID'S 'RAMSHORN' CHURCH 4H5

Ingram Street. All reasonable times. Free. Tel: 041-552 4400.

Impressive church built in 1824 with a graveyard containing the graves of many notable citizens including David Dale, creator of New Lanark.

482 GLASGOW, ST VINCENT STREET CHURCH 4H5

  ♿
  A
  P

St Vincent Street. All reasonable times, but prior letter to Church Officer appreciated. Free. Tel: 041-221 1937.

Church by Alexander 'Greek' Thomson of varied styles high on a plinth. There is an open air theatre feature on the south side.

Glasgow School of Art

483 GLASGOW SCHOOL OF ART 4H5

  ♿
  A
  P

In Renfrew Street. Mon-Fri 1000-1200, 1400-1600 and by arrangement. Tel: 041-332 9797.

A fine example of the work of Charles Rennie Mackintosh, designed in 1896, and built between 1897 and 1909.

484 GLASGOW, SCOTTISH DESIGN CENTRE 4H5

St Vincent Street. Mon-Fri 0930-1700, Sat 0900-1700. Free. Tel: 041-221 6121.

On show here are an average of 500 items selected from the Design Centre selection of British manufactured consumer and other products. Shop and coffee shop.

485 GLASGOW, STIRLING'S LIBRARY 4H5

Queen Street. All reasonable times. Closed Wed. Free. Tel: 041-221 1876.

Formerly known as the Royal Exchange, and before that the Cunningham Mansion, the present building, used as a library, was designed in 1827 and has a particularly rich interior.

486 GLASGOW, THE STOCK EXCHANGE—SCOTTISH 4H5

St George's Place. All year, Mon-Fri 1000-1245, 1400-1530. Free. Tel: 041-221 7060

A 'French Venetian' building of 1877, with Visitor's Gallery.

487 GLASGOW, TEMPLETON'S CARPET FACTORY 4H5

Off Glasgow Green. View from outside only. Free.

Victorian factory built to copy the design of the Doge's Palace in Venice with ornate decoration of coloured glazed brick, battlements, arches and pointed windows.

488 GLASGOW, THE TENEMENT HOUSE 4H5

145 Buccleuch Street, Garnethill, N of Charing Cross. 28 Mar-31 Oct, daily 1400-1700; 1 Nov-31 Mar, Sat, Sun 1400-1600. Adult: 90p, child: 45p; group rates. (NTS) Tel: 041-333 0183 (1000-1230 and 1400-1700).

A first-floor Victorian flat in a red sandstone tenement, with the furniture, furnishings and ephemera of the family who lived there for more than 50 years. Of great social significance, reflecting the inherent character of the City of Glasgow.

489 GLASGOW, THEATRE ROYAL 4H5

Hope Street. Booking office Mon-Sat 1000-1930. Group rates for parties of 15 or more persons. Tel: 041-331 1234.

A fine Victorian theatre, now elegantly restored as the home of Scottish Opera. Performances also by Scottish Ballet, Scottish Theatre Company, national visiting companies and major concert artists. Licensed bars, buffets during performances.

490 GLASGOW, THIRD EYE CENTRE 4H5

350 Sauchiehall Street. Tue-Sat 1000-1730, Sun 1400-1700. Free. Tel: 041-332 7521 (Tues-Sat 1000-1730).

Changing programme of exhibitions, drama, music, children's shows, poetry readings and other events; induction loop system. Also bar, cafe and bookshop.

491 GLASGOW, VICTORIA PARK AND FOSSIL GROVE   4H5

Victoria Park Drive North, facing Airthrey Avenue. Mon-Sat 0800-dusk; Sun 1000-dusk. Fossil Grove open by arrangement. Free.

Cornish elms, lime trees, formal flower garden and arboretum. Within the park is the famous Fossil Grove, with fossil stumps and roots of trees which grew here 230 million years ago.

492 GLASGOW ZOO   5A5

6m SE of city centre on M74 (Glasgow/Carlisle). All year, daily 1000-1800. Adult: £1.70, OAP/student/child: £1.00. Group rates, Adult: £1.20, child: 60p. Tel: 041-771 1185/6.

A medium sized but developing open plan collection, taking in 25 hectares, with another 25 more being developed. Many rare animals, most of them breeding. Speciality cats, reptiles; also education department. Long walks, picnic areas, children's showground and car park.

493 GLENCOE AND DALNESS   4F1

A82, 10m N of Tyndrum, runs through the glen. (Visitor Centre) 28 Mar-31 May, 1 Sep-26 Oct, daily 1000-1730; 1 Jun-31 Aug, daily 0900-1830. Adult: 30p, child: 15p (incl parking). (NTS) Tel: Ballachulish (085 52) 307.

The finest and perhaps the most famous glen in Scotland through which a main road runs. Scene of the Massacre of Glencoe, 1692, and centre for some of the best mountaineering in the country (not to be attempted by the unskilled). Noted for wildlife which includes red deer, wildcat, golden eagle, ptarmigan. NTS owns 14,200 acres of Glencoe and Dalness. Ski centre, chairlift and ski tows (weekends and New Year and Easter holiday periods only, other times by charter arrangement) at White Corries (see No   ). Visitor centre gives general information, particularly on walks. Visitor Centre, special presentation, Ranger Service, walks and trails, shop, picnic area and tea bar.

494 GLENCOE AND NORTH LORN FOLK MUSEUM   4F1

In Glencoe village, off A82, on S shore of Loch Leven. May-Sep, Mon- Sat 1000-1730. Adult: 30p, child: 10p.

Clan and Jacobite relics, also domestic implements, weapons, costumes, photographs, dolls' houses and dolls, agricultural tools, dairy and slate quarrying equipment are included in this museum housed in a number of thatched cottages.

495 GLENCOE CHAIRLIFT   4G1

Off A82 by Kingshouse. Jan-Apr, weekends and Easter 0930-1730; Jun-Sep, daily 1000-1700. Adult: £1.75, child: £1.25. Tel: Kingshouse (08556) 203.

Chairlift to 2,100 feet offers magnificent views of the areas around Glencoe and Rannoch Moor. Summer: access chairlift, snack bar, car park, toilets. Winter: two chairlifts.and three tows for ski-ing, car park, toilets and snack bars.

496 GLENDRONACH DISTILLERY   3F8

On B9001, between Huntly and Aberchirder, 19m N of Inverurie. All year, Mon-Fri 1000 or 1400 (by arrangement only). Free. Tel: Forgue (046682) 202 (0830-1630).

Visitor Centre and guided tour around malt whisky distillery dating from 1826.

Glenelg Brochs

497   GLENELG BROCHS   2F10
*Unclassified road from Eilanreach, 12m W of Shiel Bridge. All times.
Free. (AM) Tel: 031-226 2570.*

Two Iron Age brochs, Dun Telve and Dun Troddan,
have walls still over 30 feet high.

---

498   GLENESK FOLK MUSEUM   3F12
& *16m NNW of Brechin. Easter weekend and Sun from Easter; daily
Jun- Sep 1400-1800. Adult: 50p, child: 20p. Tel: (035 67) 236/254.*

A series of displays shows everyday life in Glenesk from
c 1800 to the present day. Tearoom.

---

499   GLENFARCLAS DISTILLERY   3D9
&   *Off A95, 17m WSW of Keith and 17m NE of Grantown-on-Spey.*
A   *All year. Mon-Fri 0900-1630; Jul, Aug, Sep, Sat 1000-1600.*
P   *Closed Christmas, New Year. Free. Groups by arrangement.
Tel: Ballindalloch (08072) 257.*

Tours of a well-known malt whisky distillery, visual
exhibition and museum of old illicit distilling
equipment in Reception Centre.

---

500   GLENFIDDICH DISTILLERY   3E9
&   *Just N of Dufftown on A941, 16m S of Elgin. All year (except between*
A   *Christmas and New Year) Mon-Fri 0930-1630; mid May-mid Oct, Sat
0930-1630, Sun 1200-1630. Free. Tel: Dufftown (0340) 20373.*

After an audio-visual programme available in six
languages, visitors are shown around the distillery and
bottling hall and are then offered a complimentary
dram. Picnic area, gift shop at car park.

---

501   GLENFINNAN MONUMENT   2F12
&   *A830, 18½m W of Fort William. 28 Mar-30 Jun, 1 Sep-26 Oct, daily*
P   *1000-1730; 1 Jul-31 Aug, daily 0900-1830. Adult: 55p, child: 25p.*
T   *(NTS) Tel: (039783) 250.*

The monument commemorates the raising of Prince
Charles Edward Stuart's standard at Glenfinnan on
19 August 1745. It was erected by Macdonald of
Glenaladale in 1815; a figure of a Highlander
surmounts the tower. The Visitor Centre tells of the
Prince's campaign from Glenfinnan to Derby and back
to the final defeat at Culloden. Audio-visual
programme, snack bar and viewpoint.

---

502   GLENGARIOCH DISTILLERY   3G9
*15m NW of Aberdeen at Oldmeldrum. Adult: £1. By arrangement.
Tel: Oldmeldrum (065 12) 2706/7/8 (Mon-Fri 1430 and 1930).*

Display of the whole process of producing single malt
Scotch whisky. 1¾ acres of greenhouse, growing
tomatoes, pot plants, utilising hot water from
distillery condensers. Reception Centre and gift shop.

503 GLENGOULANDIE DEER PARK 5A1

   9m from Aberfeldy on B846 to Kinloch Rannoch. Daily, 0900-one hour
A *before sunset. Per car: £2, individuals on foot: 40p; group rates.*
P *Tel: Kenmore (08873) 509.*

Native animals housed in a natural environment.
Many endangered species are kept, and there are fine
herds of red deer and Highland cattle. No guide dogs.

504 GLENGOYNE DISTILLERY 4H4

   By Dumgoyne, 1½m SE of Killearn. Conducted tours Apr-Oct, Mon-Fri
   1030, 1115, 1400, 1515. Free. Groups by arrangement. (Lang Bros Ltd).
   Tel: 041-332 6361.

Scottish Highland malt whisky distillery, first recorded
in 1833. Waterfalls and views of Campsie Hills and
Ben Lomond. Ladies are recommended not to wear
high heels.

505 GLEN GRANT DISTILLERY 3D8

   Rothes. Late Apr-end Sep, Mon-Fri 1000-1600. Free. Coach parties by
P *arrangement. Tel: Rothes (034 03) 413.*

Tours of distillery, with Reception Centre and whisky
sample. Children under 8 not admitted to production
areas but welcome in Reception Centre.

506 THE GLENLIVET DISTILLERY
VISITOR CENTRE 3D9

   B9008, 10m N of Tomintoul. Easter-end Oct, Mon-Sat 1000-1600. Free.
P *Coach parties by arrangement. Tel: Glenlivet (08073) 427 (during season)*
T *and Rothes (03403) 413 (during winter).*

Guided tours of distillery. Exhibits of ancient whisky
tools and artefacts and life-size reproduction of
Landseer's painting 'The Highland Whisky Still'. Free
whisky sample. Children under 8 not admitted to
production areas but welcome in Reception Centre.

Glenluce Abbey

507 GLENLUCE ABBEY 4G10

   Off A75, 2m N of Glenluce. Opening standard, closed Mon-Fri
   Oct-Mar. Adult: 50p, OAP/child: 25p. Group rates: 10% discount for
   parties of 11 or more persons. (AM) Tel: 031-226 2570.

Founded in 1192 by Roland, Earl of Galloway, for the
Cistercian order. A fine vaulted chapter house is of
architectural interest.

508 GLENMORE FOREST PARK   3C10

7m E of Aviemore, off A951. Open all year. (FC)
Tel: Kincraig (05404) 223.

Over 12,000 acres of pine and spruce woods and
mountainside on the north-west slopes of the
Cairngorms, with Loch Morlich as its centre. This is
probably the finest area in Britain for wildlife,
including red deer, reindeer, wildcat, golden eagle,
ptarmigan, capercailzie, etc. Remnants of old
Caledonian pinewoods. Well-equipped caravan sites
and hostels open all year, canoeing, sailing, fishing,
swimming, forest trails and hillwalking, and an
Information Centre. Campsite, forest walks, toilets,
picnic area, shop, café and wayfaring trail.

**509 GLENRUTHVEN WEAVING MILL AND
HERITAGE CENTRE**   6B3

& *Abbey Road, Auchterarder, ¼m SE of A9. Open daily 1000-1500.*
T *Admission by donation. Tel: Auchterarder (07646) 2079.*

Textile heritage centre, with only working steam
textile engine in Scotland. Museum, textile displays.
Mill shop and river bank grass area.

510 GLENSHEE CHAIRLIFT   4D12

Off A93, 10m S of Braemar. Daily, 0900-1700. Charge for chairlift.
Tel: Braemar (033 83) 320.

Ascends the Cairnwell mountain (3,059 feet) from the
summit of the highest main road pass in Britain (2,199
feet). Restaurant.

511 GLENTURRET DISTILLERY   6A2

& *From Crieff take A85 to Comrie for 1m, then turn right at crossroads for*
P *¼m. Mar-Oct, Mon-Fri 1000-1600; Jul and Aug, Mon-Sat 0930-1630.*
T *Nov-Dec 1400-1600. Free. Large parties by arrangement.*
Tel: Crieff (0764) 2424.

Scotland's oldest distillery, with guided tour and free
taste. Award-winning heritage centre, audio-visual and
3-D exhibition museum. Good facilities for blind
visitors.

512 GLOBE INN   5B9

Off High Street, Dumfries. Open licensed hours.
Tel: Dumfries (0387) 52335.

Burns' favourite howff (pub) where his chair, inscribed
window pane and other relics can still be seen and
enjoyed in a convivial atmosphere. Restaurant

513 GOATFELL   4F6

3½m NNW of Brodick, Arran.

At 2,866 feet this is the highest peak on Arran. NTS
property includes Glen Rosa and Cir Mhor, with
grand walking and climbing. The golden eagle may
occasionally be seen, along with hawks, harriers, etc.

514 GOSFORD HOUSE, LONGNIDDRY   6F6

Jun and Jul, Wed, Sat & Sun 1400-1700. Adult: £1.00, OAP: 75p,
child: 50p. Group rates by arrangement. (Earl of Wemyss.)
Tel: Aberlady (087 57) 201.

In fine setting on the Firth of Forth. Central part of
the house by Robert Adam, 1800. North and south
wings by William Young, 1890. South wing contains
celebrated marble hall, 1891. Ornamental waters with
wildlife including (for last four years) nesting wild geese.

515 GRANGEMOUTH MUSEUM   6B6

Victoria Library, Bo'ness Road, Grangemouth. All year Mon-Sat 1000-1700. Free. (Falkirk District Council) Grangemouth (0324) 471853.

This display concentrates on Central Scotland canals, including canal tools and a model lock. Also exhibits relating to *Charlotte Dundas*, the world's first practical steamship, and to modern Grangemouth.

516 GRAIN EARTH HOUSES   1B11

Hatson, Kirkwall, Orkney. Opening standard, on application to key keeper. Free. (AM) Tel: 031-226 2570.

An Iron Age souterrain; an entrance stair leads to an underground passage and chamber.

517 GRAMPIAN TRANSPORT MUSEUM   3F10

T

At Alford, 27m W of Aberdeen on A944. 1 Apr-30 Sep, daily 1030-1700. Adult: £1.00, OAP/child: 50p. Group rates variable but basic reduction is to Adult: 80p, child: 40p. Tel: Alford (0336) 2292.

A large independent transport museum, opened in April 1983. Extensive collection of road vehicles, including horse drawn, steam, commercial and vintage motor cars. Pedal cycles and motorcycles also well represented. Highland rail transport is described in the railway museum in Alford's former railway station.

518 GREAT GLEN (HIGHLAND HERITAGE) EXHIBITION   2H10

Centre of Fort Augustus beside the canal. Apr-Oct, daily 0930-1700. Free, but donations welcome. Tel: Fort Augustus (0320) 6341.

Visitor centre for those wishing to take in the atmosphere of the history of Scotland's 'Great Glen'. All aspects of Highland Heritage are covered with further exhibits planned for the future. Garden area with picnic tables.

519 GREENHILL COVENANTERS' HOUSE   5B6

A
P

In Biggar on A702, 26m from Edinburgh, A74 (South) 12m. Easter-mid Oct, daily 1400-1700. Adult: 60p, child: 30p. Group rate: less 10%. (Biggar Museum Trust). Tel: Biggar (0899) 21050.

Burn Braes Farmhouse, rescued in ruinous condition and rebuilt at Biggar, ten miles from the original site. Exhibits include relics of local Covenanters, Donald Cargill's bed (1681), 17th century furnishings, costume dolls, rare breeds of animals and poultry. Reduced price for joint admission to Gladstone Court Street Museum. Audio-visual programme. (See No 449).

520 GREENKNOWE TOWER   5E6

½m W of Gordon on A6089, 9m NW of Kelso. Opening standard. Apply custodian. Free. Tel: (AM) 031-226 2570.

A fine turreted tower house of 1581, still retaining its iron yett (gate).

521 GREY CAIRNS OF CAMSTER   3D4

6m N of Lybster on Watten Road, off A9. All reasonable times. Free. (AM) Tel: 031-226 2570.

Two megalithic cairns: a round cairn and a long cairn containing chambers, probably 4th millenium BC.

Gretna Green Smithies: see No 754.

Grey Mare's Tail

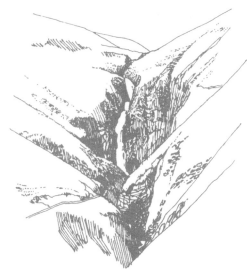

522 GREY MARE'S TAIL   5C7

Off A708, 10m NE of Moffat. (NTS) Tel: 031-226 5922.

A spectacular 200-feet waterfall formed by the Tail
Burn dropping from Loch Skene. The area is rich in
wild flowers and there is a herd of wild goats.
NB. Visitors should keep to the path to the foot of the
falls: there have been serious accidents to people
scrambling up and care should be exercised.

---

523 GROAM HOUSE MUSEUM   3B8

*High Street, Rosemarkie. 1 Jun-mid Sep, Mon-Sat 1030-1230 and
1430-1630, Sun 1430-1630. Adult/OAP: 30p, child: 15p. (Fortrose and
Rosemarkie Community Council). Tel: Fortrose (0381) 20924.*

This small museum contains a splendid pictish symbol
stone c 750 AD, and other fragments, all found in
Rosemarkie. Also audio-visual programmes on the
Black Isle and Brahan Seer with a selection of
photographs and other local items.

---

524 GUILDHALL   6A5

*St John Street, Stirling. May-Sep, Mon-Fri 0930-1730; Oct-Apr, Mon-Fri
0930-1630. Free.*

The Guildhall, or Cowane's Hospital, was built
between 1634 and 1649 as an almshouse for elderly
members of the Guild of Merchants. It contains
portraits of former Deans of Guild, weights and
measures and an old scaffold.

---

525 GURNESS BROCH   1B10

*Off A966 at Aikerness, about 4m NW of Kirkwall, Orkney. Opening
standard. Adult: 50p, OAP/child: 25p. Group rates: 10% discount for
parties of 11 or more persons. (AM) Tel: 031-226 2570.*

An Iron Age broch still over 10 feet high, surrounded
by stone huts and a deep ditch. Later inhabited in
Dark Age and Viking times.

---

526 GYLEN CASTLE   4E2

*On the island Kerrera, 1m W of Oban. Passenger ferry 2m S of Oban,
2m walk from ferry terminal. All reasonable times. Free.
Tel: Oban (0631) 63122.*

The castle, dating from c 1582 and once a MacDougall
stronghold, is now in ruins.

527 HADDINGTON   6G6

17m E of Edinburgh.

One of the best-conserved towns in the country,
Haddington preserves a very complete medieval street
plan and 284 of its buildings are scheduled as of special
architectural or historic interest. A 'Walk around
Haddington' (booklet available locally) includes the
Town House (1748) designed by William Adam; the
17th-century Nungate Bridge; 18th-century Poldrate
Mill; St Mary's Parish Church, late 14th and 15th-
century; Jane Welsh Carlyle's birthplace; and Museum
(open Apr-Oct); and the High Street, with its
attractive facades and shop fronts. (See also No 848).

528 HADDINGTON MUSEUM   6G6

*In Haddington Library, Newton Port. Mon, Tue, Thu and Fri
1000-1300, 1400-1900; Sat 1000-1300. Free.
Tel: Haddington (062 082) 4161, ext 346.*

An interesting display of local historical items in a
small room in the 19th-century former meeting house,
now used as a local public library.

529 HADDO HOUSE   3G9

T
*Off B999, 4m N of Pitmedden, 19m N of Aberdeen. (House)
1 May-30 Sep, daily 1400-1800 (last tour 1715). (Closed 10, 11 May).
Adult: £1.40, child: 70p; group rates.*

Designed in 1731 by William Adam, a pupil of Sir
William Bruce and father of the Adam brothers, for
William, second Earl of Aberdeen, Haddo House
replaced the old House of Kellie, home of the Gordons
of Methlick for centuries. Much of the interior is
'Adam Revival' carried out about 1880 for John,
seventh Earl and first Marquess of Aberdeen and his
Countess, Ishbel. Garden, Trust shop and tearoom.

Hailes Castle

530 HAILES CASTLE   6H6

*Off A1, 5m E of Haddington. Opening standard. Adult: 50p,
OAP/child: 25p. Group rates: 10% discount for parties of 11 or more
persons. (AM) Tel: 031-226 2570.*

These extensive ruins date from the 13th/15th
century. There is a fine 16th-century chapel. Here
Bothwell brought Mary, Queen of Scots on their
flight from Borthwick Castle in 1567.

531 HALLIWELL'S HOUSE MUSEUM AND GALLERY 5E7

Off main square, town centre, Selkirk. Apr-Oct, Mon-Sat 1000-1700, Sun 1400-1700. Adult: 50p, child/OAP/UB40s: 25p. Group rates: Nov-Dec, Mon-Fri 1400-1630. Free. (Ettrick and Lauderdale District Council). Tel: Selkirk (0750) 20096/20054.

This row of 18th-century dwelling houses has recently been extensively renovated and now houses an attractive and lively museum dealing with Selkirk's long and rich history. The building's history and its long link with the ironmongery trade are thoughtfully re-created. The Robson Gallery has constantly changing exhibitions. Listening post in ironmongers shop, and video in upstairs gallery.

532 HAMILTON DISTRICT MUSEUM 5A6

½m SW of M74 at A7283 interchange. All year, Mon-Sat 1000-1700. Free. Tel: Hamilton (0698) 283981.

Local history museum housed in a 17th-century coaching inn complete with original stable and 18th century Assembly Room. Displays include costume, art, archaeology, natural history, transport and a reconstructed Victorian kitchen. Also regular temporary exhibition programme. Museum shop with a wide range of publications and souvenirs.

Hamilton Mausoleum: see No 719.

533 HANDA ISLAND NATURE RESERVE 2G4

Handa Island, 3m NW of Scourie. Access: day visits by local boatmen from Tarbet. Apr-mid Sep, Mon-Sat 1000-1700. Adult: 30p, child: 15p. Accommodation in well-equipped bothy available to members of RSPB only (contact RSPB, 17 Regent Terrace, Edinburgh). Warden on island. (RSPB) Tel: 031-556 5624.

An island seabird sanctuary with vast numbers of fulmars, shags, gulls, kittiwakes and auks. Arctic and great skuas on moorland. Shelter for visitors with displays.

534 HARBOUR COTTAGE GALLERY 3F7

Kirkcudbright. Mar-Dec, Mon-Sat 1030-1230, 1400-1700, certain Suns 1400-1700. Adult: 25p, OAP: 15p, child: 5p. (Harbour Cottage Trust)

Exhibitions of paintings and sometimes crafts in a picturesque whitewashed building beside the River Dee.

535 KEIR HARDIE STATUE 4H7

Cumnock town centre. All times. Free.

Bust outside the Town Hall to commemorate James Keir Hardie (1856-1915), an early socialist leader, and founder of the Independent Labour Party in 1893.

536 JOHN HASTIE MUSEUM 5A6

Strathaven. May-Sep, Mon-Fri 1400-1700 (Thu 1630), Sat 1400-1900. Free. Tel: Strathaven (0357) 21257 or East Kilbride (035 52) 43652.

Museum of local history set in Strathaven Park.

537 HAWICK MUSEUM 5E7

In Wilton Lodge Park, on western outskirts of Hawick. Apr-Sep, Mon-Sat 1000-1200 and 1300-1700, Sun 1400-1700; Oct-Mar, Mon-Fri 1300-1600, closed Sat, Sun 1400-1600. Adult: 45p, OAP/Student/child/UB40s: 25p. Group rates: 5% discount for parties of over 20 persons. (Roxburgh District Council). Tel: Hawick (0450) 73457.

In the ancestral home of the Langlands of that Ilk, an unrivalled collection of local and Scottish Border relics, natural history, art gallery, etc. Situated in 107-acre Wilton Lodge Park, open at all times: riverside walks, gardens, greenhouses, recreations and playing fields. Small cafe.

538 THE HAYLIE CHAMBERED TOMB 4G6

Off A78 and through Douglas Park, Largs. All times. Free. Tel: Largs (0475) 673731.

Chambered tomb of Clyde-Solway group once covered by large cairn.

539 HEATHERBANK MUSEUM AND LIBRARY OF SOCIAL WORK TRUST 4H5

163 Mugdock Road, Milngavie, 8m NW of Glasgow. All year, by arrangement. Free. Tel: 041-956 2687 and Dumbarton 65151, ext 98.

The only museum of social work in the world. There are 2500 slides of the 19th and early 20th century and 5000 volumes in the reference library.

540 THE HECKLING SHOP AND GLASGOW VENNEL 4G6

Glasgow Vennel, between High Street and Townhead, Irvine. All year. Mon-Sat 1000-1600. Tel: Irvine (0294) 75059.

Shop with audio-visual display, an introduction to this recently restored street where Burns lived and worked, 1781-84.

541 THE HERITAGE OF GOLF 6G5

West Links Road, Gullane, 14m ENE of Edinburgh. Open by appointment. Free. Tel: Aberlady (2277) 277.

The exhibition shows how the game of golf developed after it arrived in Scotland from Holland in the 15th century. The visitor can see the simple origins, the natural materials and the skill of the early makers; and the development of golf from early days to the present.

542 THE HERMITAGE 5B1

Off A9, 2m W of Dunkeld. All reasonable times. Car park 20p. (NTS) Tel: 031-226 5922.

A picturesque folly, built in 1758 and restored in 1952. It is set above the wooded gorge of the River Bran. There are nature trails in the area.

543 HERMITAGE CASTLE 5E8

Off B6399, 16m NE of Langholm. Opening standard. Adult: 50p, OAP/child: 25p. Group rates: 10% discount for parties of 11 or more persons. (AM) Tel: 031-226 2570.

This grim 13th-century castle was a stronghold of the de Soulis family and, after 1341, of the Douglases. It has had a vivid, sometimes cruel history; to here Mary Queen of Scots made her exhausting ride from Jedburgh in 1566 to meet Bothwell, a journey which almost cost her her life. The building consists of four towers and connecting walls, outwardly almost perfect.

544 HIGHLAND FOLK MUSEUM 3B11

       A9 at Kingussie, 12m SW of Aviemore. All year, Apr-Oct, Mon-Sat 1000-1800, Sun 1400-1800; Nov-Mar, Mon-Fri 1000-1500. Adult: £1.00, child: 50p. Group rates: 20% discount for all groups of over 10 persons. 40% educational visits. (Highland Regional Council). Tel: Kingussie (054 02) 307.

The open air museum includes an 18th-century shooting lodge, a 'Black House' from Lewis, a Clack Mill, a turf-walled house from the Central Highlands and exhibits of farming equipment. Indoors, the farming museum has fine displays of a barn, dairy, stable and an exhibition of Highland tinkers; and there are special features on weapons, costume, musical instruments and Highland furniture. Picnic garden. Special events Easter-September.

545 HIGHLAND MARY'S MONUMENT 4H7

At Failford, on A758 3m W of Mauchline. All times. Free.

The monument commemorates the place where, it is said, Robert Burns parted from his 'Highland Mary', Mary Campbell. They exchanged vows, but she died the following autumn.

546 HIGHLAND MARY'S STATUE 4F5

Dunoon, near pier. All times. Free.

The statue of Burns' Highland Mary at the foot of the Castle Hill. Mary Campbell was born on a farm in Dunoon, and consented to become Burns' wife before he married Jean Armour.

547 HIGHLAND WILDLIFE PARK 3B10

       Off A9 (B9152), 7m S of Aviemore. Open daily 1000-1700 (closing times vary during spring and autumn); Jun-Aug 1000-1800, closed winter season. Car and passengers £5.50 (1985 prices). Tel: Kincraig (084 04) 270. Office open 0900-1700.

This notable wildlife park features breeding groups of Highland animals and birds in a beautiful natural setting. Drive-through section has red deer herd, bison, Highland cattle, etc. Aviaries display capercailzie, eagles; also wolves, wildcats and nearly 60 other species. There is an exhibition on 'Man and Fauna in the Highlands', and a children's animal park. Also souvenir shop, cafeteria and picnic area.

548 THE HILL HOUSE 4G4

       Upper Colquhoun Street, Helensburgh. All year, daily, 1300-1700. Adult: £1.00, child/OAP/student: 50p. (NTS) Tel: Helensburgh (0436) 3900.

Designed and built for W W Blackie Esq in 1902-03 by Charles Rennie Mackintosh with Mackintosh furniture and other items.

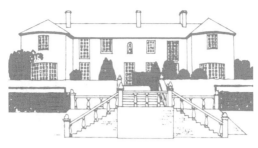

Hill of Tarvit

549   HILL OF TARVIT   **6F3**

&
P
T

A916, 2m S of Cupar. House: open weekends during Easter weekend,
Apr & Oct, 1400-1800; 1 May-30 Sep, daily 1400-1800 (last admission
1730). Garden: grounds open all year, 1000-sunset. House and Gardens—
adult: £1.40, child 70p; group rates. Gardens and grounds only—
adult: 60p, child: 30p. (NTS) Tel: Cupar (0334) 53127.

An Edwardian country house designed by Sir Robert
Lorimer for Mr Frederick Boner Sharp, an art collector
of note. Fine collection of furniture, paintings,
tapestries, chinese porcelain and bronzes. Tearoom
(weekends only, Apr, May, Jun, Sep, Oct and daily
July, Aug). Lovely gardens, woodland walk to hilltop
viewpoint.

**550   THE HIRSEL, HOMESTEAD MUSEUM,
CRAFT CENTRE AND GROUNDS**   **5F6**

&
A
T

On A697, immediately W of Coldstream. All reasonable daylight hours
every day of the year. Entrance by donation. Groups by arrangement.
(Lord Home of the Hirsel, KT). Tel: Coldstream (0890) 2834.

Museum housed in old farmstead buildings (with
integrated Craft Centre) with history of estate, old
tools, natural history. Walks in Leet Valley, round the
grounds of Hirsel House (not open to the public).
Famous rhododendron wood. Tearoom open Sun and
bank holiday afternoons, and for groups by
arrangement.

551   HJALTASTEYN   **1G4**

At Whiteness, 9m W of Lerwick, Shetland. (Workshop) Mon-Fri
1100-1230, 1430-1600. (Showroom) Mon-Fri 0930-1300, 1400-1700.
Free. (Tearoom, Mon-Sat 1030-1630, Sun 1430-1700).

Stone polishing workshop, producing gemstones from
local raw materials in hand-wrought silver settings.
Tearoom with home baking.

552   JAMES HOGG MONUMENT   **5D7**

&

By Ettrick 1m W of B7009. All times. Free.

A monument on the site of the birthplace of James
Hogg (1770-1835), known as 'The Ettrick Shepherd',
friend of Scott. His grave is in the nearby church.
(See No 847).

553 HOPETOUN HOUSE 6D6

&
A
P
T

W of South Queensferry, May-Sep, daily 1100-1700. Adult: £2.00, child: £1. Group rate: £1.80 per person.(Marquess of Linlithgow) Tel: 031-331 2451 (0900-1700).

This great Adam mansion is the home of the Hope family, Earls of Hopetoun and later Marquesses of Linlithgow. Started in 1699 to the designs of Sir William Bruce, it was enlarged between 1721-54 by William Adam and his son, Robert. Notable portraits include Rubens, Rembrandt and Canaletto. The extensive grounds include deer parks with fallow and red deer and St Kilda sheep. Also sea walk, formal rose garden, educational day centre and stables museum featuring 'Horse and Man in Lowland Scotland'. Nature trail, licensed restaurant. Family museum, rooftop viewing platform. Free parking.

The House of the Binns

554 THE HOUSE OF THE BINNS 6D6

&
P

Off A904, 4m E of Linlithgow. 29-31 Mar, 1 May-Sep, daily (except Fri) 1400-1700. (Park) 1000-1900. Adult: £1.20, child: 60p; group rates. (NTS) Tel: Linlithgow (050683) 4255.

Occupied for more than 350 years, The Binns dates largely from the time of General Tam Dalyell, 1615-1685, and his father, and reflects the early 17th-century transition in Scottish architecture from fortified stronghold to gracious mansion. There are magnificent plaster ceilings, fine views across the Forth and a visitor trail.

Huntingtower Castle

555 HUNTINGTOWER CASTLE 6C2

Off A85, 3m WNW of Perth. Opening standard. Adult: 50p, OAP/child: 25p. Group rates: 10% discount for parties of 11 or more persons. (AM) Tel: 031-226 2570.

A 15th-century castellated mansion until 1600 known as Ruthven Castle. This was the scene of the Raid of Ruthven in 1582; James VI, then 16, accepted an invitation from the Earl of Gowrie to his hunting seat and found himself in the hands of nobles who demanded the dismissal of the royal favourites. When the king tried to escape, his way was barred by the Master of Glamis. The Ruthven conspirators held power for some months, but the Earl was beheaded in 1584. There are fine painted ceilings.

556 HUNTLY CASTLE 3F9

Castle Street, Huntly. Opening standard. Adult: 50p, OAP/child: 25p.
Group rates: 10% discount for parties of 11 or more persons. (AM)
Tel: 031-226 2570.

An imposing ruin which replaced medieval
Strathbogie Castle which, until 1544, was the seat of
the Gay Gordons, the Marquesses of Huntly, the most
powerful family in the north until the mid-16th
century. There are elaborate heraldic adornments on
the castle walls. The castle, now in a wooded park,
was destroyed by Moray in 1452, rebuilt, then rebuilt
again in 1551-54, burned 40 years later and again
rebuilt in 1602.

557 HUNTLY MUSEUM 3F9

& *In the Library, Main Square. All year, Tues-Sat 1000-1200, 1400-1600.*
A *Free. (North East of Scotland Museums Service).*
Tel: Peterhead (0779) 77778.

Permanent local history exhibitions and temporary
thematic exhibitions twice a year.

Inchcolm Abbey

558 INCHCOLM ABBEY 6D5

On Inchcolm Island in the Firth of Forth; check at Aberdour or South
Queensferry for boat trips or hire. Opening standard, except closed Wed
afternoon and Thu. Adult: £1.00, OAP/child: 50p. Group rates: 10%
discount for parties of 11 or more persons; 20% discount on Barrie's ferry
for Scotrail ticket holders and Friends of Scottish Monuments. (AM)
Tel: 031-226 2570.

The monastic buildings, which include a fine 13th
century octagonal chapter house, are the best preserved
in Scotland.

559 INCHMAHOME PRIORY 4H4

On an island in the Lake of Menteith, A81, 4m E of Aberfoyle. Access by
boat from lakeside, Port of Menteith. Opening standard, except closed
Oct-Mar. Admission free. Ferry charge: adult: £1, OAP/child: 50p;
tel: Stirling (0786) 62421.) (AM) Tel: 031-226 2570.

The ruins of an Augustinian house, founded in 1238,
where the infant Mary Queen of Scots was sent for
refuge in 1547.

560 INGASETTER 3F11

& *North Deeside Road, Banchory. All year, Mon-Fri 0900-1230,*
T *1330-1700; also Jul and Aug, Mon-Fri 0900-1700, Sat 1000-1630. Free.*
Tel: Banchory (03302) 2600.

Film and tour explaining the growing and distilling of
lavender and the manufacture of other toilet
preparations.

561 INNERPEFFRAY LIBRARY 6B2

B8062, 4m SE of Crieff. All year. Mon-Sat 1000-1245, 1400-1645, Sun 1400-1600. Closed all day Thu. Adult: 50p, child: 10p. Tel: Crieff (0764) 2819.

The oldest library still in existence in Scotland, founded 1691, housed in a late 18th-century building. The nearby church was built in 1508.

562 INNES HOUSE GARDENS 3D7

3m N of Lhanbryde, 4m NE of Elgin. May-Oct, Mon-Fri 0900-1700. 30p per person, car: 20p. (I M Tennant). Tel: Lhanbryde (034 384) 2410.

Walled garden of a 17th-century house, together with park and 'tree walk'. Herbaceous borders, rhododendrons, azaleas.

563 INVERARAY BELL TOWER 4F3

In Inveraray. Late May-late Sep, Mon-Sat 1000-1300, 1400-1700; Sun 1500-1800. Adult: 50p, OAP/child: 25p, to ascend the tower. Exhibition free. (Scottish Episcopal Church of All Saints). Tel: Inveraray (0499) 2433.

The 126-feet high granite tower houses Scotland's finest ring of bells and the world's third-heaviest ring of ten bells, which are rung regularly. Excellent views, pleasant grounds.

Inveraray Castle

564 INVERARAY CASTLE 4F3

½m N of Inveraray. Apr-Jun, Sep-mid Oct, Mon-Sat (not Fri) 1000-1230, 1400-1730, Sun 1300-1730; Jul-Aug, Mon-Sat 1000-1730, Sun 1300-1730. Adult: £2.00, OAP: £1.50, child: £1.00, family ticket: £5.50. Group rates: 20% discount on parties of 20 or more persons. (Argyll Estates). Tel: Inveraray (0499) 2203.

Inveraray has been the seat of the chiefs of Clan Campbell, Dukes of Argyll, for centuries. The present castle was started in 1743 when the third Duke engaged Roger Morris to build it. Subsequently the Adam family, father and sons, were also involved. The magnificent interior decoration was commissioned by the fifth Duke from Robert Mylne. In addition to many historic relics, there are portraits by Gainsborough, Ramsay and Raeburn. Tearoom and craft shop. Gardens open on selected weekends.

565 INVERESK LODGE GARDEN **6F6**

S of Musselburgh, A6124, 7m E of Edinburgh. All year, Mon, Wed, Fri 1000-1630, Sun 1400-1700 when house occupied. Adult: 40p, child: 20p. (NTS) Tel: 031-226 5922.

This garden of a 17th-century house (not open to the public) displays a range of plants suitable for the small garden. Good shrub rose border and selection of climbing roses.

566 INVEREWE GARDENS **2F7**

On A832, 6m NE of Gairloch. (Gardens) All year, daily 0930-sunset. (Visitor Centre and Shop) 28 Mar-5 May and 8 Sep-26 Oct. Mon-Sat 1000-1700, Sun 1230-1700; 6 May-7 Sep, Mon-Sat 1000-1830, Sun 1200-1830. Restaurant: 28 Mar-5 May and 8 Sep-14 Oct, Mon-Sat 1030-1630, Sun 1200-1630; 6 May-7 Sep, Mon-Sat 1000-1700, Sun 1200-1700. Adult: £1.50, child: 75p. Group rates: educational £1.20. Car Park: 10p. (NTS) Tel: Poolewe (044 586) 229.

Plants from many countries flourish in this garden created by Osgood Mackenzie over 120 years ago, giving an almost continuous display of colour throughout the year. Eucalyptus, rhododendron, and many Chilean and South American plants are represented in great variety, together with Himalayan lilies and giant forget-me-nots from the South Pacific. Garden for disabled, shop, restaurant, caravan and camp site, petrol, plant sales. Groups of disabled visitors welcome.

567 INVERKEITHING MUSEUM **6D5**

1m N of Forth Road Bridge. All year, Wed-Sat 1000-1230, 1430-1700, Sun 1200-1700. Closed Mon & Tues. Free. (Dunfermline District Council). Tel: Inverkeithing (0383) 413344 (Wed-Fri, museum Hours).

The museum is housed in the Old Friary, founded 1384; it shows the history of the Old Royal Burgh, with religious, military, industrial and domestic items.

568 INVERNESS MUSEUM AND ART GALLERY **3B8**

Castle Wynd, Inverness. Weekdays 0900-1700. Free. (Inverness District Council). Tel: Inverness (0463) 237114.

The museum interprets the social and natural history, archaeology and culture of the Highlands, with fine collections of Highland silver, bagpipes, and Jacobite relics. Special exhibitions, performances and talks. Coffee shop.

569 INVERPOLLY NATIONAL NATURE RESERVE **2G6**

Off A835, 12m NNE of Ullapool (Information Centre) May-Sep, Mon- Fri 1000-1730. Free. (NCC) Tel: Elphin (085 484) 234.

A remote, almost uninhabited area of bog, moorland, woodland, cliffs and summits. Car park, nature/geological trail and Information Centre at Knockan Cliff, 12m N of Ullapool; geological and wildlife interest.

570 INVERURIE MUSEUM **3G9**

Inverurie. All year, Mon-Fri 1400-1700, Sat 1000-1200. Free. (North East of Scotland Museums Service). Tel: Peterhead (0779) 77778.

Permanent display of local archaeology and thematic exhibitions three times a year. Just outside the town, on B993, is a 60 foot high motte, the Bass.

Iona

571 IONA 4B3

  ♿ *Off the SW tip of Mull; take A849 to Fionnphort, then ferry. Also*
  A *steamer trips from Oban. Tel: Iona (06817) 404.*
  P

In 563 St Columba with 12 followers came to this
little island to found a monastery from which his
monks travelled over much of Scotland preaching
Christianity to the Picts. The monastery, often
attacked up to the 9th century by Norse raiders, was
replaced in 1203 but, along with the cathedral, fell
into decay. Restoration started early this century. The
monastery is the home of the Iona Community,
founded by Dr George Macleod in 1938, who have
done much restoration of the Cathedral, which has a
beautiful interior and interesting carvings. For
centuries Iona was the burial place of Scottish kings
and chiefs. The oldest surviving building is St Oran's
Chapel, c 1080 (restored). The remains of the 13th-
century nunnery can be seen and outside the
Cathedral is 10th-century St Martin's Cross, 14 feet
high and elaborately carved. Abbey gift and bookshop
open 1000-1630 daily. Abbey coffee house open
1000-1630 daily except Sundays.

572 ISLE OF ARRAN HERITAGE MUSEUM 4F7

  ♿ *Rosaburn, Brodick, Isle of Arran. Mid-May to end Sep, Mon-Fri-*
  T *1030-1300 and 1400-1630. Adult: 60p, child: 30p. Group rates: Adult:*
    50p, child: 25p. Tel: Brodick (0770) 2636.

A group of old buildings which were originally an
18th-century croft farm on the edge of the village.
Smithy, cottage furnished in late 19th-century style,
stable block with displays of local history, archaeology
and geology. Demonstrations of spinning and other
hand crafts arranged periodically. Picnic area and
tearoom.

573 ITALIAN CHAPEL 1B12

*Lambholm, Orkney. All times. Free. (POW Chapel Preservation
Committee).*

Using a Nissen hut, Italian prisoners-of-war in 1943
created this beautiful little chapel out of scrap metal,
concrete and other materials.

Jail Museum: see No 172.

574 JARLSHOF 1G6

Sumburgh Head, approx 22m S of Lerwick, Shetland. Opening standard, except closed Tue and Wed afternoon. Adult: 50p, OAP/child: 25p. Group rates: 10% discount for parties of 11 or more persons. (AM) Tel: 031-226 2570.

One of the most remarkable archaeological sites in Europe with the remains of three extensive village settlements occupied from Bronze Age to Viking times, together with a medieval farmstead and the 16th-century house of the Earls Robert and Patrick Stewart.

575 JEDBURGH ABBEY 5E7

High Street, Jedburgh. Opening standard, except Oct-Mar closed Thu afternoon and Fri. Adult: 50p, OAP/child: 25p. Group rates: 10% discount for parties of 11 or more persons. (AM) Tel: 031-226 2570.

Perhaps the most impressive of the four great Border Abbeys founded by David I, dating from c 1118. The noble remains are extensive, the west front has a fine rose window, known as St Catherine's Wheel, and there is a richly carved Norman doorway. Remains of other domestic buildings have been recovered recently.

576 KAILZIE GARDENS 5D6

  T

2m E of Peebles on B7062. Daily 1100-1730. Adult: 90p, child: 40p. Group rates: Adult: 60p, child: 30p. (Mrs M A Richard) Tel: Peebles (0721) 20007.

17 acres of garden surrounded by mature timber. Walled garden dated 1812 with extensive greenhouses, laburnum alley, shrub borders and collection of shrub roses. Woodland and burnside walks. Also collection of owls, pheasants and waterfowl. Gift shop, art gallery and licensed tearoom.

Kay Park Museum: see No 138.

577 KEITH STATUE 3H8

Peterhead town centre. All times. Free.

Statue of James Keith, Earl Marischal and brother of George Keith, founder of Peterhead (1593). James became a marshal in the army of Frederick the Great of Prussia. The statue was presented in 1868 by William I of Prussia.

578 KELBURN COUNTRY CENTRE 4G6

  T

Off A78 between Largs and Fairlie. Easter-Sep (incl), daily 1000-1800. Adult: £1.50, OAP/child: £1.00; group rates. (Earl of Glasgow). Tel: Fairlie (047556) 685.

The historic estate of the Earls of Glasgow, famous for rare trees and the Kelburn Glen. Also waterfalls, gardens, nature trails, exhibitions, adventure course, Marine assault course, children's stockade, pets' corner and pony-trekking. The central, 18th-century farm buildings have been converted to form a village square with craft shop, workshops, display rooms and licensed cafe. Ranger Service. Car park.

Kellie Castle

579 KELLIE CASTLE AND GARDENS 6G3

Off A921, by Pittenweem, 10m S of St Andrews. (Castle) 28-31 Mar,
Apr and Oct, Sat, Sun 1400-1800; 1 May-30 Sep, daily 1400-1800
(last admission 1730). (Gardens) All year, daily, 1000-dusk. (Castle and
Gardens) Adult: £1.40, child: 70p; group rates. (Gardens) Adult: 60p,
child: 30p. (NTS) Tel: Arncroach (033 38) 271.

Fine domestic architecture of the 16th/17th centuries,
though the oldest part dates from c 1360. Owned by
the Oliphants for over 250 years, then by the Earls of
Mar and Kellie, it was restored nearly a century ago by
Professor James Lorimer. His grandson, the sculptor
Hew Lorimer, is resident custodian. Notable plaster
work and painted panelling. 4 acres of gardens.

580 KELSO ABBEY 5F6

Bridge Street, Kelso. Opening standard. Free. (AM) Tel: 031-226 2570.

This was the largest of the Border abbeys. One of the
earliest completed by David I, it was founded in 1128.
When the Earl of Hertford entered Kelso in 1545 the
abbey was garrisoned as a fortress and was taken only
at the point of the sword; the garrison of 100 men,
including 12 monks, was slaughtered, and the building
was almost entirely razed. The tower is part of the
original building.

581 KEMPOCK STONE 4G5

On the cliff side of Gourock. All reasonable times. Free.

Granny Kempock's stone, of grey schist six feet high,
was probably significant in prehistoric times. In past
centuries it was used by fishermen in rites to ensure
fair weather. Couples intending to wed used to
encircle the stone to get Granny's blessing.

582 KILBERRY SCULPTURED STONES 4D5

Off B8024, 20m SSW of Lochgilphead. All reasonable times. Free.
(AM) Tel: 031-226 2570.

A fine collection of late medieval sculptured stones.

583 KILCHURN CASTLE 4F2

N tip of Loch Awe, 21m E of Oban. Not open to the public, but may be
viewed from the outside. (AM) Tel: 031-226 2570.

The keep was built in 1440 by Sir Colin Campbell of
Glenorchy, founder of the Breadalbane family. The
north and south sides of the building were erected in
1693 by Ian, Earl of Breadalbane, whose arms and
those of his wife are over the gateway. Occupied by
the Breadalbanes until 1740, in 1746 it was taken by
Hanoverian troops. A gale in 1879 toppled one of its
towers.

584 KILDALTON CROSSES 4C6

7½m NE of Port Ellen, Isle of Islay. All reasonable times. Free. (AM)
Tel: 031-226 2570.

Two of the finest Celtic crosses in Scotland, and
sculptured slabs, are in Kildalton churchyard.

Kildrummy Castle

585 KILDRUMMY CASTLE 3E10

A97, 10m W of Alford. Opening standard. Adult: 50p, OAP/child: 25p. Group rates: 10% discount for parties of 11 or more persons. (AM) Tel: 031-226 2570.

The most extensive example in Scotland of a 13th-century castle. The four round towers, hall and chapel remains belong in substance to the original. The great gatehouse and other work is later, to the 16th century. It was the seat of the Earls of Mar, and played an important part in Scottish history until 1715 when it was dismantled.

586 KILDRUMMY CASTLE GARDENS 3E10

&
A
P

A97, 10m W of Alford. Apr-Oct, daily 0900-1700. Adult: 50p, child: 10p, under 4 years free. Children must be accompanied. Coach parties by arrangement. Dogs must be on leash. (Kildrummy Castle Garden Trust). Tel: Kildrummy (03365) 264/277/203.

The shrub and alpine garden in the ancient quarry are known to botanists for their interest and variety. A burn runs through the Den to the water garden with a shrub bank above it. A small museum and interesting old stones are displayed. The Kildrummy Castle Hotel is within the Trust area.

Killiecrankie: see No 772.

Kilmartin Sculptured Stones

587 KILMARTIN SCULPTURED STONES 4E4

A816, 7½m N of Lochgilphead. All reasonable times. Free. (AM) Tel: 031-226 2570.

In this typical West Highland churchyard are preserved a number of grave slabs and fragments of at least two crosses, one showing Christ crucified on the front and Christ in Majesty on the back. The cross dates from the 16th century.

The area north of the Crinan Canal (No 236) to Kilmartin has many reminders of both prehistoric and medieval times. These include: 1. Bronze Age cup-and-ring engravings at Ballygowan; 2. Bronze Age and earlier burial cairns at Dunchraigaig, Nether Largie, Ri Cruin and Kilmartin Glebe; 3. Two stone circles at Temple Wood.

Kilmeny Parish Church: see No 108.

KILMORY KNAP CHAPEL

588 KILMORY KNAP CHAPEL   4D5

Off road along E side of Loch Sween, 18m SW of Lochgilphead. All reasonable times. Free. (AM) Tel: 031-226 2570.

A typical small West Highland church with notable sculptured stones.

589 KILMORY CAIRNS   4F7

At S end of Arran, off A841. All times. Free.

Cairn Baan, 3½m NE of Kilmory village, is a notable Neolithic long cairn. ½m SW of A841 at the Lagg Hotel is Torrylin Cairn, a Neolithic chambered cairn. There are many other cairns in this area.

590 KILMUIR CROFT MUSEUM   2D8

Off A855, 20m NNW of Portree, Skye. Easter-Oct, Mon-Sat 0900-1800. Adult: 40p, child: 15p.

Four thatched cottages. Exhibits include a wall bed, farming and domestic implements, hand loom and a collection of old photographs and historical papers.

591 KILMUN ARBORETUM   4F4

By Forest Office on A880, 1m E of junction with A815. 5m N of Dunoon. All year. Daily, all day. Free. (FC)

A fascinating collection of tree species on a hillside to the northeast of Holy Loch within the Argyll Forest Park. (See No 52).

592 KILORAN GARDENS   4C4

Kiloran, Isle of Colonsay. Daily, all reasonable times. Free. Tel: Colonsay (095 12) 312 (Mrs E McNeill).

An island garden noted for its rhododendrons and shrubs, including embothriums and magnolias. Self-catering accommodation.

593 KILPHEDER WHEELHOUSE   2A10

2m W of A865 by Kilpheder at S end of Isle of South Uist. All times. Free.

Slight remains of an ancient circular dwelling, c 200 AD, divided into 'stalls' like the spokes of a wheel.

594 KILT ROCK   2D8

Off A855, 17m N of Portree, Skye. Seen from the road. Care should be taken not to go too near the edge of the cliff.

The top rock is composed of columnar basalt, the lower portion of horizontal beds, giving the impression of the pleats in a kilt. There is also a waterfall nearby.

595 KILWINNING ABBEY   4G6

Kilwinning, Ayrshire. All times. Free. (Historic Buildings and Monuments) Tel: 031-226 2570.

The ruins of a Tironensian-Benedictine Abbey. Most of the surviving buildings date from the 13th century.

596 KINDROCHIT CASTLE   3D11

Balmellan Road, Braemar. Free.

Ruins of ancient important fortification. Legend indicates that Malcolm Canmore built the first castle of Kindrochit in the 11th century. The existing remains stand above the Clunie and consist of walls and grass-grown embankments.

597 KING'S CAVE   4E7

On shore, 2m N of Blackwaterfoot on the west coast of Arran. All times. Free.

A two-mile walk along the shore from the golf course at Blackwaterfoot leads to a series of caves, the largest being the King's Cave. Said to have been occupied by Finn MacCoul and later by Robert the Bruce, this is one of the possible settings for the 'Bruce and the spider' legend. Carvings of figures are on the walls.

598 KINKELL CHURCH   3G10

On the E bank of the Don, 2m S of Inverurie, off B993. All reasonable times. Free. (AM) Tel: 031-226 2570.

The ruins of an early 16th-century parish church with some ornate details including a rich sacrament house of unusual design, dated 1524.

Kinloch Castle

599 KINLOCH CASTLE   2D11

Isle of Rhum, access by boat from Mallaig. Mar-Oct, as a hotel and hostel. Tours by arrangement with The Warden, White House, Kinloch, Rhum. (NCC) Tel: Mallaig (0687) 2037.

Extraordinary and magnificent residence built at the turn of the century for Sir George Bullough, still containing many of its sumptuous fittings. The island itself is a mountainous nature reserve where the Nature Conservancy Council have for some years conducted experiments in deer and forestry management.

600 KINNEFF CHURCH   3G12

Off unclassified road, E of A92, 2m N of Inverbervie. All reasonable times. Free. (Kinneff Old Church Preservation Trust)

Part of this historic church belonged to the original building in which were hidden the Crown Jewels of Scotland for nine years after being smuggled from Dunnottar Castle (see No 311) through Cromwell's besieging army in 1651. In the present church, which dates from 1738, are memorials to the parish minister, Rev James Grainger, who concealed the regalia under the flagstones of the church; and to the governor of the castle, Sir George Ogilvy of Barras.

601 KINNEIL HOUSE   6C6

Off A904, 4m NW of Linlithgow to the W of Bo'ness. Opening standard, except closed Tue afternoon and Fri. Adult: 50p, OAP/child: 25p. Group rates: 10% discount for parties of 11 or more persons. (AM) Tel: 031-226 2570.

In the grounds of this 16th/17th-century seat of the Dukes of Hamilton (which contains some of the finest contemporary wall paintings and decorated ceilings in Scotland) is the outhouse where James Watt developed his invention of the steam engine, the first being erected at a nearby colliery in 1765. (See also No 602).

**602 KINNEIL MUSEUM AND
ROMAN FORTLET**   6C6

♿
P
*In Bo'ness, 16m WNW of Edinburgh on A904 (adjacent to Kinneil
House). May-Sep, Mon-Sat 1000-1700. Free. (Falkirk District Council).
Tel: Falkirk (0324) 24911, ext 2472.*

These converted 17th-century stables contain a
museum of local industrial history, with displays of
Bo'ness pottery, examples of local cast-iron work and
salt pan implements. The history of Kinneil Estate is
presented in an interpretive exhibition, spanning the
Roman period to the Industrial Revolution. Kinneil
Roman Fortlet lies to the west of Kinneil House, and
its visible remains have been conserved for public
viewing.

603 KINROSS MUSEUM   6D4

High Street. May-Sep, Tues-Sat 1300-1700. Free.

Items relating to local history, including archaeological
finds, a display of local linen manufacturing, some
examples of peat cutting, and local military exhibits.

Kintail

604 KINTAIL   2G10

♿
*N of A87 between Lochs Cluanie and Duich, 16m E of Kyle of
Lochalsh. (NTS) Tel: (059 981) 219.*

Magnificent Highland scenery including the Five
Sisters of Kintail, peaks rising to 3,500 feet. Red deer
and wild goats. Visitor Centre at Morvich open 1 Jun
to end Sep, Mon-Sat 0900-1800, Sun 1300-1800.

605 KIPPEN CHURCH   5A4

♿
A
P
*Fore Road, Kippen, 10m W of Stirling. 0900-dusk. Free.
Tel: Kippen (078 687) 229.*

Beautifully renovated in 1925 under the direction of
Sir D Y Cameron, RA, this modern church with rich
interior furnishings is one of the most attractive of its
kind in Scotland. Attractive grounds attached to
church.

606 KIRK YETHOLM   5F7

Off B6352, 8m SE of Kelso.

Attractive village, with Town Yetholm, once famous
as the home of the Scottish gypsies, now the northern
end of the Pennine Way.

**607 KIRKCALDY MUSEUM AND
ART GALLERY**   6E5

♿
A
P
*By railway station. All year, Mon-Sat 1100-1700, Sun 1400-1700. Free.
Tel: Kirkcaldy (0592) 260732.*

The heritage of Kirkcaldy District in a unique
collection of fine Scottish paintings, a fascinating new
historical display and a full programme of changing
art, craft and local history exhibitions. Gallery shop for
crafts, cards and local publications.

Kirkwynd Cottages: see No 34.

608 KISIMUL CASTLE   2A11

& *On a tiny island in the bay by Castlebay, Isle of Barra. May-Sep, Wed*
A *and Sat afternoons only. Charge for boatman and admission to the castle.*
P *(The Macneil of Barra). Tel: Castlebay (08714) 336.*

For many generations Kisimul was the home and
stronghold of the Macneils of Barra, widely noted for
their lawlessness and piracy, and led by chiefs like
Ruari the Turbulent, 35th chief, who did not fear to
seize ships of subjects of Queen Elizabeth I of
England. The main tower dates from about 1120.
Restoration was commenced in 1938 by the 45th clan
chief, an American architect, and completed in 1970.

609 KITCHENER MEMORIAL   1A10

At Marwick Head, SW of Birsay, Orkney. All times. Free.

The cruiser *HMS Hampshire*, taking Lord Kitchener to
Russia was sunk in 1916 off the coast, close by this
point. (See also No 688).

610 KNAP OF HOWAR   1B9

W side of island of Papa Westray, 800 metres W of Holland House,
Orkney. All reasonable times. Free. (AM) Tel: 031-226 2570.

Only recently recognised as one of the oldest sites in
Europe, these two 5000-year-old dwellings have also
yielded many unusual artefacts—whalebone mallets
and a spatula and unique stone borers and grinders.

611 KNOCK CASTLE   2E10

& *Off A851, 12m S of Broadford, Isle of Skye. All reasonable times. Free.*

A ruined stronghold of the MacDonalds.

Knockan Cliff: see No 569.

612 KYLES OF BUTE   4F5

& *Narrow arm of the Firth of Clyde, between Isle of Bute and Argyll.*
Tel: 041-552 8391.

A 16-mile stretch of water which presents a constantly
changing view of great beauty. It can perhaps be best
appreciated from the A8003, Tighnabruaich to
Glendaruel road, where there are two view indicators.
The western one (Scottish Civic Trust) looks over the
West Kyle and identifies many features. The east
indicator (NTS) looks over Loch Ridden and the East
Kyle.

613 G & G KYNOCH   3E8

Isla Bank Mills, Keith. Mill Shop open Mon-Fri incl 0815-1215 and
1330-1630, Fri 1600. Mill Tours: Tues, Thu, starting 1430; other times
by arrangement. Free. Tel: Keith (05422) 2648/2603.

Woollen, spinning and weaving mill, established in
1788 on the banks of the River Isla, manufacturing
high quality wool fabrics for export to menswear and
ladieswear garment manufacturers as well as contract
furniture fabric manufacturers. Mill shop on premises
for sale of sundry items.

614 LADY GIFFORD'S WELL   5C6

& *At West Linton, 17m SSW of Edinburgh.*
Tel: West Linton (0968) 60346

The village of West Linton was well-known in former
days for its stonemasons. The figure on 'Lady Gifford's
Well' was carved in 1666. There are other carvings,
probably by the same hand, on a house across the
road, dated 1660 and 1678. There is a village
information and exhibition centre in the Raemartin
Square, open Apr-Oct 0900-1700 daily.

615 LADY KIRK   5F6

On B6470 4m E of Swinton. All reasonable times. Free.

The church was built by James IV c 1500 as a thanks-offering for his escape from drowning in the River Tweed. It was built entirely of stone to avoid the risk of fire.

---

616 LAGGANGAIRN STANDING STONES   4G10

9m N of Glenluce on Barrhill road, then 3m walk. All reasonable times. Free. (AM) Tel: 031-226 2570.

At Laggangairn (*Hollow of the Cairns*) the crosses on the two grey standing stones date from the Dark Ages. A slab with a simple Latin cross leans against a wall by the ruined farmhouse.

---

617 LAING MEMORIAL MUSEUM   6E2

High Street, Newburgh. May-Sep, daily 1100-1800. Free. (North East Fife District Council). Tel: Cupar (0334) 53722.

Museum with displays on the theme of Victorian Scotland — self-help, emigration, the antiquarian movement and the controversy of creation versus evolution.

---

618 WILLIAM LAMB MEMORIAL STUDIO   5E1

♿
P

Market Street, Montrose. Jul, Aug, Sun 1400-1700; or by arrangement. Free. Tel: Montrose (0674) 73232.

Studio of William Lamb, ARSA, noted Montrose sculptor and etcher, containing a selection of his works including heads of HRH Queen Elizabeth and HRH Princess Margaret as girls, and HRH The Queen Mother.

Land o' Burns Centre

619 LAND O' BURNS CENTRE   4G7

♿
T

Opposite Alloway Kirk, 2m S of Ayr. All year, daily, spring and autumn 1000-1800, summer 1000-2100, winter 1000-1700. Admission free; small charge for audio-visual display (Kyle and Carrick District Council). Tel: Ayr (0292) 43700.

This visitor centre has an exhibition area and an audio-visual display on the life and times of Robert Burns. Landscaped gardens.

---

620 LANDMARK VISITOR CENTRE   3C10

♿
T

Carrbridge, 9m W of Grantown-on-Spey. All year. (Woodland trails and pine forest nature centre) Adult: £1.35, child: 85p. (Multi-vision show) Adult: 90p, child: 45p. (Combined admission) Adult: £1.95, child: £1.10. Group rates: Adult: £1.75, child: 90p. Tel: Carrbridge (047984) 613 (0930-1700 winter), (0930-2130 summer).

This 'Landmark' Visitor Centre was the first of its kind in Europe. Ten thousand years of Highland history are shown in the triple-screen audio-visual theatre and a dramatic exhibition interprets the history of Strathspey. Now has sculpture park, tree-top trail and woodland maze. Adventure playground with giant slides and aerial net walkways. Also new pine forest nature centre. Craft and bookshop, restaurant, bar, snack bar, picnic area and plant centre. Free parking.

621 LAPIDARY WORKSHOPS   3G10

Garlogie School, Skene. All year, Mon-Sat (except Fri) 0900-1230, 1400-1730. Free.

Demonstrations of stone cutting and polishing.

622 LARGS MUSEUM   4G6

   Manse Court, Largs. Jun-Sep, Mon-Sat 1400-1700. Open at other times by arrangement. Donation box. (Largs and District Historical Society). Tel: Largs (0475) 687081 (Kirkgate House) or Largs (0475) 673731 (Secretary).

The museum holds a small collection of local bygones, with a library of local history books and numerous photographs.

Leadhills Library: see No 803.

623 LAUDER MEMORIALS   4F4

   Off A815, 3m SE of Strachur. All reasonable times. Free.

Sir Harry Lauder at one time resided at nearby Glenbranter House (now demolished) and during his stay his only son, John, was killed in World War I. Sir Harry erected an obelisk in his memory on a knoll a short distance N of Loch Eck. In the same enclosure is a Celtic Cross, a memorial to Lady Lauder who died in 1927.

624 LECHT SKI TOW   3D10

Off A939, 7m SE of Tomintoul. During ski-ing season only. Discount on application. (Lecht Ski Co Ltd). Tel: (09754) 240.

Ski tows operating to slopes on both sides of the Lecht Road, famous for its snowfalls. Licensed cafeteria, ski hire, ski school. Free car park.

625 LEGLEN WOOD   4H7

2m S of A758, 4m E of Ayr. All times. Free.

An attractive wood above the River Ayr which has associations with Burns' hero, William Wallace. Burns often visited the spot now marked by a cairn with inscription.

626 LEITH HALL   3F9

   A
   P
   T
B9002, 7m S of Huntly. (House) 1 May-30 Sep, daily 1400-1800. (last tour 1715). (Garden) All year, daily 0930-sunset. Adult: £1.40, child: 70p; group rates. Gardens and grounds by donation. (NTS)

The mansion house of Leith Hall is at the centre of a 263-acre estate which was the home of the head of the Leith and Leith-Hay family from 1650. The house contains personal possessions of successive Lairds, most of whom followed a tradition of military service. The grounds contain varied farm and woodlands. There are two ponds, a bird observation hide and three countryside walks, one leading to a hilltop viewpoint. Unique 18th-century stables; Soay sheep; ice house. Extensive and interesting informal garden of borders, shrubs and rock garden. Picnic area and tearoom.

627 LENNOXLOVE HOUSE 6G6

    A
    P
    T

On B6369, 1m S of Haddington. Apr-Sep, Wed, Sat, Sun 1400-1700; groups at other times by arrangement. Adult: £1.50, child: £1.00. Group rates: Adult: £1.00, child: 75p. Tel: Haddington (062 082) 3720.

Home of the Duke and Duchess of Hamilton. Originally named Lethington after its proprietor, Maitland of Lethington, Secretary to Mary, Queen of Scots. Later named after 'La Belle Stewart', Duchess of Lennox, who modelled for the original Britannia on the coinage of the 17th century. House has a threefold interest: its historic architecture; the association of the proprietors with the Royal House of Stewart; and the Hamilton Palace collection of portraits, furniture and porcelain. Tearoom, shop, gardens.

Leuchars Norman Church

628 LEUCHARS NORMAN CHURCH 6G2

    A

A919, 5½m NW of St Andrews. All reasonable times, Mar-Oct. Free. Tel: St Andrews (0334 83) 226.

Beautifully decorated 12th-century Norman chancel and apse, with unique 17th-century belltower.

629 LEWIS BLACK HOUSE 2C4

At Arnol, 15m NW of Stornoway, Isle of Lewis. Opening standard, except closed Sun. Adult: 50p, OAP/child: 25p. Group rates: 10% discount for parties of 11 or more persons. (AM) Tel: 031-226 2570.

A good example of a traditional type of Hebridean dwelling, built without mortar and roofed with thatch on a timber framework and without eaves. Characteristic features are the central peat fire in the kitchen, the absence of any chimney and the byre under the same roof. The house retains many of its original furnishings.

630 LEWIS CASTLE GROUNDS 2D5

    A

W of Harbour, Stornoway, Isle of Lewis. All reasonable times. Free. (Grounds only)

The modern castle, now a technical college (not open to the public), stands in the wooded grounds given to the town by Lord Leverhulme. Noted for their rhododendrons. Castle ground gardens and public park.

631 LEYDEN OBELISK AND TABLET 5E7

Denholm on A698 NE of Hawick. All times. Free. Tel: Denholm (045 087) 506.

The village was the birthplace of John Leyden (1776-1811), poet and orientalist, friend of Sir Walter Scott and also Sir James Murray, who edited the Oxford English Dictionary. An obelisk was set up in Leyden's memory in 1861 and a tablet on a cottage records his birth in 1776.

632 LHAIDHAY CAITHNESS CROFT MUSEUM 3D4

On A9, 1m N of Dunbeath. Easter-30 Sep, daily 0900-1700. Adult: 30p, child: 15p; group rates. Tel: Dunbeath (05933) 357.

An early 18th-century croft complex with stable, dwelling house and byre under one thatched roof with adjoining barn. Completely furnished in the fashion of its time. The barn has a notable crux roof. Picnic area.

633 LINCLUDEN COLLEGIATE CHURCH 5B9

Off A76, 1m N of Dumfries. Opening standard, except closed Thu afternoon and Fri. Adult: 50p, OAP/child: 25p. (AM) Tel: 031-226 2570.

A 15th-century Collegiate Church and Provost's House remarkable for heraldic adornment and for the tomb of Princess Margaret, daughter of Robert III. There is a motte in the grounds.

634 LINLITHGOW PALACE 6C6

S shore of loch, Linlithgow. Opening standard. Adult: £1.00, OAP/child: 50p. Group rates: 10% discount for parties of 11 or more persons. (AM) Tel: 031-226 2570.

The splendid ruined Palace overlooking the loch is the successor to an older building which was burned down in 1424. The Chapel and Great Hall are late 15th-century and the fine quadrangle has a richly-carved 16th-century fountain. In 1542 Mary Queen of Scots was born here while her father, James V, lay dying at Falkland Palace. In 1746 the palace was burned, probably by accident, when occupied by General Hawley's troops. George V held a court in the Lyon Chamber here in 1914.

635 LILLIE ART GALLERY 4H5

Milngavie, off A81, 8m N of Glasgow. All year, Tue-Fri 1100-1700, 1900-2100, Sat and Sun 1400-1700. Free. Tel: 041-956 2351.

A modern purpose-built art gallery with a permanent collection of 20th-century Scottish paintings, sculpture and ceramics, and temporary exhibitions of contemporary art. Alternative entrance with ramp.

636 LITTLEHAUGH AGRICULTURAL MUSEUM 3D8
(Ladycroft Agricultural Museum)

At Archiestown on the B9102 Grantown road. All year, dawn-dusk. Admission: 50p. (Mr and Mrs C W Spence)

A museum of the time when all the farm implements were worked by horses. There are life-size models of men and horses.

637 LIVINGSTON MILL FARM 6C7

Off A705 Kirkton, 1m W of Livingston. Apr-Sep, Sat & Sun 1000-1700, Mon-Fri by appointment; Oct-Mar, first Sat & Sun each month 1300-1600. Admission charge. Tel: (0506) 414957.

Restored 18th-century farm steading and watermill. Small agricultural museum, children's farm, play area, animal paddock, picnic/barbecue site and nature walks along the banks of the River Almond. Farm Kitchen, 95% access for disabled.

Livingstone National Memorial

638 LIVINGSTONE NATIONAL MEMORIAL 5A6

& *At Blantyre, A724, 3m NW of Hamilton. All year, daily 1000-1800,*
P *Sun 1400-1800. Adult: £1.00, OAP/child: 50p. Group rates: 1 adult free*
for every 10 persons and 10% discount. Tel: Blantyre (0698) 823140.

Shuttle Row is an 18th-century block of mill
tenements where David Livingstone, the famous
explorer/missionary was born in 1813, went to school
and worked while studying to become a doctor. The
National Memorial, containing very many interesting
relics of the Industrial Revolution and of Africa, is in
this building, now surrounded by parkland. The
Africa Pavilion illustrates modern Africa and a Social
History museum deals with agriculture, cotton
spinning and mining in Blantyre and district.
Tearoom, gardens, picnic area, play equipment and
paddling pool.

639 LOANHEAD STONE CIRCLE 3G9

¼m NW of Daviot, 5m NNW of Inverurie, off B9001. All reasonable
times. Free. (AM) Tel: 031-226 2570.

The best known example of a widespread group of
recumbent stone circles in east Scotland.

640 LOCH DOON CASTLE 4H8

From A713, 10m S of Dalmellington, take road to Loch Doon. All
reasonable times. Free. (AM) Tel: 031-226 2570.

This early 14th-century castle was devised to fit the
island on which it was originally built. When the
waters of the loch were raised in connection with a
hydro-electric scheme the castle was dismantled and re-
erected on the shores of the loch. The walls of this
massive building, once known as Castle Balliol, vary
from 7-9 feet thick and stand about 26 feet high.

**641 LOCH DRUIDIBEG NATIONAL NATURE
RESERVE** 2A9

In the N part of South Uist, Outer Hebrides. All year, daily. Free.
(NCC)

The most important surviving breeding ground of the
native greylag goose in Britain, in a typical example of
the Outer Hebrides environment, machair, fresh and
brackish lochs.

642 LOCH GARTEN NATURE RESERVE 3C10

Off B970, 8m NE of Aviemore. If Ospreys present, daily mid Apr-Aug
1000-2000 along signposted track to Observation Post. Other access into
bird sanctuary strictly forbidden Apr-Aug but elsewhere on the reserve
access unrestricted throughout the year. Free. (RSPB)
Tel: Aviemore (0479) 83694.

Ospreys, extinct in Scotland for many years, returned
here to breed in 1959. Their treetop eyrie may be
viewed through fixed binoculars from the Observation
Hut. The surrounding area owned by the RSPB,
includes extensive stretches of old Caledonian Pine
forest with rich and varied wildlife.

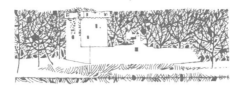

643 LOCH LEVEN CASTLE   **6D4**

On an island on Loch Leven, Kinross. Access by boat from Kinross.
Opening standard, closed winter. Adult: £1.00, OAP/child: 50p. (AM)
Tel: 031-226 2570.

The tower is late 14th or early 15th-century. Mary
Queen of Scots was imprisoned here in 1567 and from
it escaped eleven months later.

Loch Leven Nature Reserve: see No 970.

---

644 LOCH OF THE LOWES   **5B1**

 Off A923, 2m NE of Dunkeld. (SWT) Tel: Dunkeld (035 02) 337.

Loch with wooded fringe, varied habitats, water birds
and ospreys, hides and visitor centre, staff ranger and
observation hill. Wide range of provision for visitors
with special needs.

**645 LOCH OF KINNORDY NATURE
RESERVE**   **5D1**

On B951, 1m W of Kirriemuir, Angus. Apr-Aug, daily except Tues,
0900-2100; other times by arrangement. Admission: 60p. (RSPB)
Tel: 031-556 5624.

Fresh water marsh with large numbers of nesting
water birds. Small car park and two observation hides.

---

646 LOCH MORAR   **2E11**

SE of Mallaig.

Said to be the deepest loch in Scotland and the home
of Morag, a monster with a strong resemblance to the
Loch Ness Monster.

---

647 LOCH NAN UAMH CAIRN   **2E12**

Off A830, S of Arisaig.

The loch is famous for its association with Bonnie
Prince Charlie. The memorial cairn on the shore
marks the spot from which Prince Charles Edward
Stuart sailed for France on 20 September 1746 after
having wandered round the Highlands as a fugitive
with a price of £30,000 on his head.

---

648 LOCH NESS   **3A9**

SW of Inverness

This striking 24-mile-long loch in the Great Glen
forms part of the Caledonian Canal which links
Inverness with Fort William. For much of its length it
is over 700 feet deep. The loch contains the largest
volume of fresh water of any lake in the British Isles.
Famous world wide for its mysterious inhabitant, the
Loch Ness Monster. It is also ideal for cruising and
sailing. (See also Nos 649 and 862).

649 LOCH NESS MONSTER EXHIBITION CENTRE   3A9

♿
A
At Drumnadrochit on A82, 14m SW of Inverness. Peak season daily 0900-2130, off season times vary, please check. Adult: £1.35, OAP: 80p, child: 60p or 40p, student: 95p; group rates, family rate. Tel: Drumnadrochit (04562) 573.

A revised and greatly extended exhibition covers the fascinating story of the loch and its monster.

---

650 LOCHALSH WOODLAND GARDEN   2F9

♿
Off A87, 3m E of Kyle of Lochalsh. All year, daily. Adult: 45p, child: 20p. (NTS) Tel: Balmacara (059 986) 207.

A wide variety of native trees and shrubs and more exotic plants from Tasmania, New Zealand, the Himalayas, Chile, Japan and China in the grounds of Lochalsh House (not open to the public). There are pleasant walks and an ecology display in the coach house.

---

651 LOCH-AN-EILEAN VISITOR CENTRE   3C10

B970, 2½m S of Aviemore. May-Sep. Free.

This exhibition in a cottage by the loch traces the history of the native Scots Pine forest from the Ice Age until today, its management and conservation.

---

652 LOCHINDORB   3C9

Unclassified road off A939, 10m NW of Grantown-on-Spey.

On an island in this lonely loch stand the ruins of a 13th-century castle, once a seat of the Comyns. It was occupied in person by Edward I in 1303 and greatly strengthened. In 1336 Edward III raised the siege in which the Countess of Atholl was beleaguered by the Regent Moray's troops. In 1371 the castle became the stronghold of the 'Wolf of Badenoch', the vicious Earl of Buchan who terrorised the area. It was dismantled in 1456.

---

653 LOCHMABEN CASTLE   5C9

♿
A
Off B7020 on S shore of Castle Loch, by Lochmaben, 9m ENE of Dumfries. All reasonable times. Free. Tel: Dumfries (0387) 53862.

This castle was captured and recaptured twelve times and also withstood six attacks and sieges. James IV was a frequent visitor, and Mary Queen of Scots was here in 1565. Now a ruin, this early 14th-century castle is on the site of a castle of the de Brus family, ancestors of Robert the Bruce who is said to have been born here.

---

654 LOCHORE MEADOWS COUNTRY PARK   6D4

♿
T
Between Lochgelly and Ballingry on B920. (Country Park) At all times. (Park Centre) Summer 0800-2000, winter 0900-1700. (Fishery) 15 Mar-6 Oct. (Country Park facilities: rates on application); unemployed fishing and golf free, Mon-Fri 0900-1700. Tel: Ballingry (0592) 860086.

Green, pleasant countryside around large loch reclaimed from coal mining waste in the 1960s. Reclamation makes fascinating story told in slide show, displays and ranger guided walks. Plenty of scope for birdwatching, wildlife study, walks, picnics. Many ancient historical remains. Cafe and information in park centre. Activities include boat and bank fishing, sailing, windsurfing, canoeing, golf, horse riding, trim trail, wayfaring, self-guided trails, picnic areas and cafeteria. Wide range of provisions for visitors with special needs. Groups welcome.

655 LOCHRANZA CASTLE 4E6

On N coast of Isle of Arran. Opening standard. Free. Apply custodian. (AM) Tel: 031-226 2570.

A picturesque ruin of a castle erected in the 13th/14th centuries and enlarged in the 16th. Robert the Bruce is said to have landed here on his return in 1307 from Rathlin in Ireland at the start of his campaign for Scottish Independence.

656 LOCHTY PRIVATE RAILWAY 6G3

On B940 (Cupar-Crail road) 7m W of Crail. 18 June-4 Sep, Sun 1400-1700. Train fare: adult: 80p, child: 40p, group rates. (Lochty Private Railway Co)

This private railway operates a steam-hauled passenger train service between Lochty and Knightsward. Steam and diesel locomotives, passenger coaches and goods wagons.

657 LOCHWINNOCH COMMUNITY MUSEUM 4G6

&

Main Street, Lochwinnoch. Mon, Wed & Fri 1000-1300, 1400-1700 and 1800-2000; Tue & Sat 1000-1300 and 1400-1700. Closed Thu & Sun. Free. (Renfrew District Council Museums and Art Galleries Service). Tel: 041-889 3151 or Lochwinnoch (0505) 842615.

Lochwinnoch Community Museum features a series of changing exhibitions reflecting the historic background of local agriculture, industry and village life. There are occasional special exhibitions.

658 LOCHWINNOCH NATURE RESERVE 4G6

Largs Road, Lochwinnoch, 9m SW of Paisley. All year, Thu-Sun 1000-1715. Adult: 60p, child: 30p. School parties by arrangement. (RSPB) Tel: Lochwinnoch (0505) 842663.

Purpose built Nature Centre with observation tower, displays and shop. Two observation hides overlooking marsh reached by walk through woods. Third hide overlooking Barr Loch. Shop.

659 LOCHWOOD TOWER 5C8

A701 through Beattock then B7020 (Lochmaben road); site is 200 yds W of Lochwood crossroads. All times. Tel: Moffat (0683) 20620.

From the original 12th-century mote hill stronghold, sited 80 yds north of present tower, to the 15th/16th-century Border Peel Tower and adjacent buildings, Lochwood has seen many strongholds through centuries of Border wars and inter-clan feuds. It was finally abandoned both as a residence and as chief seat of the Johnstone clan in 1710. The ruins of the Tower and buildings are now being partly rebuilt to give an indication of their layout in the past.

660 LOGAN BOTANIC GARDEN 4F11

    Off B7065, 14m S of Stranraer. Daily Apr-Sep 1000-1700. 50p per car; group rates. Tel: Stranraer (0776) 86231.

Here a profusion of plants from the warm and temperate regions of the world flourish in some of the mildest conditions in Scotland. There are cabbage palms, tree ferns and many other Southern Hemisphere species. Salad bar, meals served all day.

661 LOGAN FISH POND 4F11

    Off B7065, 14m S of Stranraer. Easter-Sep, Mon, Wed-Fri and Sun 1000-1200, 1400-1730. Adult: 25p, child: 15p. (Sir Ninian Buchan-Hepburn, Bt). Tel: Ayr (0292) 268181

This tidal pool in the rocks, 30 feet deep and 53 feet round, was completed in 1800 as a fresh-fish larder for Logan House. Damaged by a mine in 1942, it was reopened in 1955. It holds some 30 fish, mainly cod, so tame that they come to be fed by hand.

662 LOUDOUN HALL 4G7

    Boat Vennal, off Cross in Ayr town centre. Mid Jul-end Aug, Mon-Sat 1100-1600 or by arrangement. Free, but donation box available. Group visits if booked can have guided walk of Ayr (approx 1 hour) with light refreshments. (Loudoun Hall Trustees). Tel: Ayr (0292) 282109.

A late 15th-century/early 16th-century town house built for a rich merchant, one of the oldest surviving examples of Burgh Architecture to remain in Scotland. For a period it was the town house of the Campbells, Earls of Loudoun, and the Moore family; both families played prominent parts in the life of Ayr. Local history publications for sale.

663 LUFFNESS CASTLE 6G5

    1m E of Aberlady on A198. By arrangement. Free. (Col and Mrs Hope). Tel: Aberlady (2277) 218.

A 16th-century castle with a 13th-century keep built on the site of a Norse camp. There are extensive old fortifications, an old moat and gardens.

664 LYTH ARTS CENTRE 3D3

    Signposted 4 miles off A9 between Wick and John o' Groats. 26 Jun-6 Sep, daily 1000-1800. Adult: 25p. (Mr W Wilson). Tel: Lyth (0955 84) 270.

Travelling exhibitions including Scottish fine art, crafts and tapestry. Snack bar, gardens.

665 McCAIG'S TOWER   **4E2**

On a hill overlooking Oban. All times. Free. Tel: Oban (0631) 63122.

McCaig was a local banker who tried to curb
unemployment by using local craftsmen to build this
tower from 1897-1900 as a memorial to his family. Its
walls are two feet thick and from 30-47 feet high. The
courtyard within is landscaped and the tower is
floodlit at night in summer. An observation platform
on the seaward side was added in 1983.

**666 HUGH MACDIARMID MEMORIAL
SCULPTURE**   **5D9**

*At Whita Hill Yett, approx 2m SWS of Langholm on the Langholm to
Newcastleton road. At any time. Tel: (0835) 22650.*

Steel and bronze sculpture by Jake Harvey to
commemorate the literary achievements of the
Langholm-born poet and Scots Revivalist. Nearby is
Malcolm Monument.

667 McDONALD'S MILL   **4E2**

*Off A816, ½m S of Oban. All year. Mon-Fri 0900-1930, Sat, Sun
0900-1700. Demonstrations weekdays 0900-1730. Free.
Tel: Oban (0631) 63081.*

Exhibition of the story of spinning and weaving, with
demonstrations of hand weaving. Tearoom.

668 FLORA MACDONALD'S BIRTHPLACE   **2A10**

*W of A865, 200 yds up farm track ½m N of Milton, Isle of South Uist.
All times. Free.*

A cairn on the top of a small hill marks the spot
where Flora Macdonald was born in 1722.

669 FLORA MACDONALD'S MONUMENT   **3B8**

Inverness Castle. All times. Free.

Monument to Flora Macdonald (1722-1790) on the
esplanade of the Victorian castle. Flora Macdonald is
famed for the help she gave to the Young Pretender in
June 1746, enabling him to escape from Benbecula to
Portree.

**670 SIR HECTOR MacDONALD'S
MEMORIAL**   **3A8**

*Mitchell Hill, Dingwall. All times. Free.
Tel: Dingwall (0349) 62391 (for keys to tower).*

An impressive monument erected to the memory of
General Sir Hector MacDonald, who was born near
Dingwall in the parish of Ferintosh in 1853. (See also
No 265).

671 McEWAN GALLERY   **3E11**

*On A939, 1m W of Ballater. Open all year, 1000-1800; other times by
arrangement. Free. Tel: Ballater (0338) 55429.*

An unusual house built by the Swiss artist Rudolphe
Christen in 1902, containing works of art, mainly of
the Scottish school. Occasional special exhibitions are
held. Also scarce Scottish, sporting and natural history
books.

672 RODERICK MACKENZIE MEMORIAL   **2H10**

1m E of Ceannacroc on A887, 13m W of Invermoriston. All times. Free.

A cairn on the south of the road commemorates
Roderick Mackenzie, who in 1746 feigned to be
Prince Charles Edward Stuart and was killed by
soldiers searching for the Prince after Culloden.

673 MACLAURIN GALLERY AND ROZELLE HOUSE 4G7

   P T *1½m S of Ayr, off road to Burns Cottage at Alloway. All year, Mon-Sat 1100-1700; Apr-Oct, Sun 1400-1700. Free. (Trustees of the late Mrs Mary Ellen Maclaurin with Kyle and Carrick District Libraries and Museums) Tel: Ayr (0292) 45447 or 43708.*

The gallery was formerly stables and servants' quarters attached to the mansion house. There are exhibitions of fine art, sculpture, craft and photography. Local history, especially military and civic relics, displayed in the house with a wide variety of art exhibitions. The gallery is set in extensive parkland with a nature trail. Coffee shop, Apr-Sep. Henry Moore bronze sculpture on display.

674 McLEAN MUSEUM AND ART GALLERY 4G5

   P *Greenock. All year, Mon-Sat 1000-1200, 1300-1700. Free. (Inverclyde District Council). Tel: Greenock (0475) 23741.*

A local museum with art collection, natural history, shipping exhibits, ethnographic material and items relating to James Watt, who was born in Greenock. Small shop. Parts of the building closed for renovation work. Wheelchair access at rear of building.

MacLellan's Castle

675 MacLELLAN'S CASTLE 5A11

Off High Street, Kirkcudbright. Opening standard. Adult: 50p, OAP/child: 25p. Group rates: 10% discount for parties of 11 or more persons. (AM) Tel: 031-226 2570.

A handsome castellated mansion overlooking the harbour, dating from 1582. Elaborately planned with fine architectural details, it has been a ruin since 1752. In Kircudbright also see the 16th/17th-century Tolbooth, the Mercat Cross of 1610, the Stewartry Museum (No 902) and Broughton House (No 119).

676 MACPHERSON MONUMENT 3B10

   A *Off old A9 (A86), 3m NE of Kingussie. All times. Free.*

Obelisk to James 'Ossian' Macpherson (1736-1796), Scottish poet and 'translator' of the Ossianic poems.

677 MacROBERT ARTS CENTRE 6A5

   T *University of Stirling. Group rates: 1 seat in 20 free. Cheap tickets for OAPs, students and UB40s. Tel: Stirling (0786) 61081 or 73171, ext 2543.*

A five-hundred seat theatre, art gallery and studio, providing all year theatre, opera, dance, films, concerts, conferences and exhibitions. Theatre bar. For details of events, contact the box office. Induction loop system.

678 MACHRIE MOOR STANDING STONES   4E7

1½m E of A841, along Moss Farm Road, S of Machrie on W coast of Arran. All reasonable times. Free. (AM) Tel: 031-226 2570.

These 15-feet high standing stones are the impressive remains of six Bronze Age stone circles. Some have now fallen. (See also No 714).

679 MAES HOWE   1B11

Off A965, 10m W of Kirkwall, Orkney. Opening standard. Adult: £1.00, child: 50p. Group rates: 10% discount for parties of 11 or more persons. (AM) Tel: 031-226 2570.

An enormous burial mound, 115 feet in diameter, dating back to c 2500 BC, and containing a burial chamber which is unsurpassed in Western Europe. In the 12th century Viking marauders broke into it in search of treasures and Norse crusaders sheltered from a storm in the Howe. They engraved a rich collection of Runic inscriptions upon the walls.

680 MAGNUM LEISURE CENTRE   4G6

&   *Harbourside, Irvine. All year, daily 0900-2300. Adult: 25p, child: 15p*
T   *(facilities extra). Tel: Irvine (0294) 78381.*

The centre, by the beach and in 150 acres of park, has two licensed bars, cafeteria, two swimming pools, an ice rink, squash courts, theatre, cinema and many other facilities.

681 MAISON DIEU   3F12

Off Market Street, Brechin. Opening standard. Free. (AM) Tel: 031-226 2570.

An interesting fragment of mid-13th-century ecclesiastical architecture.

682 MALLENY GARDENS   6D7

&   *In Balerno, off A70, 7½m SW of Edinburgh. 1 May-30 Sep, daily 1000-sunset. Adult: 60p, child: 30p. (NTS) Tel: 031-226 5922.*

Adjoining a 17th-century house (not open) is a garden with many interesting plants including a good collection of shrub roses. No dogs.

Manderston

683 MANDERSTON   5F5

Off A6105, 2m E of Duns. Mid May-Sep, Thu & Sun 1400-1730. House and grounds: £2.00; grounds only: £1. (1985 prices); groups by arrangement (Mr A Palmer) Tel: Duns (0361) 88450.

One of the finest Edwardian country houses in Scotland, with extensive estate buildings and gardens particularly noted for their rhododendrons. The house contains a silver staircase, thought to be unique. Tearoom, shop, gardens, stables and marble dairy.

684 MARJORIBANKS MONUMENT   5F6

At E entrance to Coldstream. All times. Free.

Obelisk with a stone figure of Charles Marjoribanks, elected the First Member of Parliament for Berwickshire after the passing of the Reform Act of 1832.

Mar's Wark

685   MAR'S WARK   **6A5**

At the top of Castle Wynd, Stirling. All times. Free. (AM)
Tel: 031-226 2570.

Mar's Wark is one of a number of fine old buildings
on the approach to Stirling Castle. Built c 1570 by the
first Earl of Mar, Regent of Scotland, it was a
residence of the Earls of Mar until the 6th Earl had to
flee the country after leading the 1715 Jacobite
Rebellion.

David Marshall Lodge: see No 794.

686   MARTELLO TOWER   **1B12**

Hackness, Island of Hoy, Orkney. All times. Can be viewed from the
outside only. (AM) Tel: 031-226 2570.

An impressive tower built during the Napoleonic and
American wars at the beginning of the 19th century.
The tower was renovated in 1866 and used again in
the First World War.

687   MARTYR'S MONUMENT   **4H10**

&   *Near Wigtown, A714, 7m S of Newton Stewart. All reasonable times.*
A   *Free. Tel: Newton Stewart (0671) 2431.*

A monument on the hill and a pillar on the shore of
Wigtown Bay where in 1685 two women, aged 18
and 63, were tied to stakes and drowned for their
religious beliefs during the persecution of the
Covenanters in 'the Killing Times'.

688   MARWICK HEAD NATURE RESERVE   **1A11**

Access along path N from Marwick Bay, Orkney. Any time. Free.
(RSPB) Tel: Kirkwall (0856) 850176.

Seabird cliffs with huge and spectacular colonies of
seabirds. Best time April-July. (See also No. 750).

689   MARY, QUEEN OF SCOTS HOUSE   **5E7**

&   *Queen Street, Jedburgh. Easter-Oct, Mon-Sat 1000-1200, 1300-1700,*
P   *Sun 1300-1700. Adult: 50p, OAP/child/student/UB40s: 35p. Group*
rates: 5% discount for parties of 20 or more persons. (Roxburgh District
Council). Tel: Jedburgh (0835) 63331.

A 16th-century bastel house in which Mary, Queen of
Scots is reputed to have stayed in 1566 when attending
the Court of Justice. Now a museum containing
several relics associated with the Queen. Delightful
gardens surround the house which also forms part of
the Jedburgh Town Trail.

690 MAXWELTON HOUSE 5B9

13m NW of Dumfries on B729, near Moniaive. (Garden): Apr-Sep, Mon-Thu 1400-1700. (Chapel): Apr-Sep, daily 1000-1800. (Annie Laurie's Boudoir): Jul-Aug, Mon-Thu 1400-1700. (House): by arrangement. Admission charge. (Mr Paul Stenhouse). Tel: Moniaive (084 82) 385.

The house dates back to the 14th/15th centuries. Originally it was a stronghold of the Earls of Glencairn and later the birthplace of Annie Laurie, to whom William Douglas of Fingland wrote the famous poem. Museum of early kitchen, dairy and small farming implements.

691 MAYBOLE COLLEGIATE CHURCH 3C12

In Maybole, S of A77. Not open to the public—can be viewed from outside. Free. (AM) Tel: 031-226 2570.

The roofless ruin of a 15th-century church, built for a small college established in 1373 by the Kennedies of Dunure.

692 MEAL AND FLOUR MILL 4G8

Off A9 at Blair Atholl Village. Apr Oct, Mon-Sat 1000-1800, Sun 1200-1800. Adult: 45p, child: 40p.

Built in 1613, the water mill produces a small amount of oatmeal—80 tonnes a year—and flour which is sold to shops and some used in the small wholemeal bakery at the mill. Tearoom. All home baking with mill products. Free car parking.

693 MEFFAN INSTITUTE 5D1

West High Street, Forfar. All year, Mon-Sat 0930-1900 (Thu and Sat 1700). Free. (Angus District Museums). Tel: Montrose (0674) 73232.

Display of material relating to Forfar and district, including local archaeology and local history, and watercolours by J W Herald.

694 MEGGINCH CASTLE GARDENS 6E2

A85, 10m E of Perth. Apr-Jun and Sep, Wed only 1400-1700, Jul and Aug, Mon-Fri 1400-1700. Adult: £1.00, child: 50p. (Capt and the Hon Mrs Drummond of Megginch). Tel: (082 12) 222.

The gardens around the 15th-century castle have daffodils, rhododendrons and 1,000-year-old yews. There is a double-walled kitchen garden, 16th-century rose garden and 19th-century flower parterre as well as the Gothic courtyard with pagoda-roofed dovecote. There is also an interesting example of topiary, including a golden yew crown. An 18th-century physic garden is currently being restored.

695 MEIGLE MUSEUM 5C1

In Meigle, on A94, 12m WSW of Forfar. Opening standard. Closed Sun. Adult: 50p, OAP/child: 25p. Group rates: 10% discount for parties of 11 or more persons. (AM) Tel: 031-226 2570.

This magnificent collection of 25 sculptured monuments of the Celtic Christian period, all found at or near the old churchyard, forms one of the most notable assemblages of Dark Age sculpture in Western Europe.

Meikleour Beech Hedge: see No 86.

696 MELLERSTAIN HOUSE 5E6

♿ P T

Off A6089, 8m NW of Kelso. Easter; 1 May-30 Sep, Sun-Fri 1230-1630. Admission charge; group rates. Tel: Gordon (057 381) 225.

This is one of the most attractive mansions open to the public in Scotland, with exceptionally beautiful interior decoration and plaster work. Began about 1725 by William Adam, it was completed between 1770 and 1778 by William's son Robert. There are attractive terraced gardens and pleasant grounds with fine views. Self-service tearoom, gift shop, lake, thatched cottage and garden.

697 MELROSE ABBEY 5E6

Main Square, Melrose. Opening standard. Adult: £1.00, OAP/child: 50p. Group rates: 10% discount for parties of 11 or more persons. (AM) Tel: 031-226 2570.

This Cistercian Abbey, founded in 1136, is notable for its fine traceried stonework. It suffered the usual attacks of all the Border abbeys during English invasions, but parts of the nave and choir dating from a rebuilding of 1385 include some of the best and most elaborate work of the period in Scotland. In addition to the flamboyant stonework, note on the roof the figure of a pig playing the bagpipes. There is an interesting museum in the Commendator's House, at the entrance.

698 MELROSE MOTOR MUSEUM 5E6

&
A
200 yards from Melrose Abbey, towards Newstead. Apr-Oct, daily 1000-1800; Nov-Mar, Sat and Sun 1000-1700, or by arrangement. Adult: 75p, child: 25p (under 5: free): group rates. Tel: Melrose (089 682) 2624.

Private collection with vehicles on loan, mainly vintage from 1909 to the late 1960s. Excellent motorcycles and bicycles with a quantity of old signs and items of memorabilia. Display cases of toy cars, cigarette cards, etc. Shop.

699 MELVILLE MONUMENT 6A2

1m N of Comrie, 6m W of Crieff. Access by footpath from parking place on Glen Lednock road. All times. Free.

The obelisk in memory of Lord Melville (1742-1811) stands on Dunmore, a hill of 859 feet, with delightful views of the surrounding country. The access path is linked to the scenic 4 mile Glen Lednock Circular Walk, running from Comrie and back through varied woodland (signposted).

700 MEMSIE BURIAL CAIRN 3H7

Near village of Memsie, 3m SSW of Fraserburgh. All reasonable times. Free. (AM) Tel: 031-226 2570.

A fine example of a large stone-built cairn probably dating to c 1500 BC.

Menstrie Castle

701 MENSTRIE CASTLE 6B4

&
A
Menstrie, A91, 5m E of Stirling. Exhibition Rooms: 1 May-30 Sep, Mon 1430-1630, Wed 0930-1200, Thur 1800-2000. Adult: 20p, child: 10p. Group rates: 10% discount for parties of 11 or more persons. (NTS) Tel: 031-226 5922.

The 16th-century restored castle was the birthplace of Sir William Alexander, James VI's Lieutenant for the Plantation of Nova Scotia. A Nova Scotia Exhibition Room (NTS) displays the coats of arms of 109 Nova Scotia Baronetcies.

702 MERTOUN GARDENS 5E7

St Boswells. Apr-Sep, Sat, Sun & Mon Public Holidays 1400-1800 (last entry 1730). Adult: 60p, OAP/child: 30p. Group rates: special terms available. Tel: St Boswells (0835) 23236.

20 acres of beautiful grounds with delightful walks and river views. Fine trees, herbaceous borders and flowering shrubs. Walled garden and well preserved circular dovecote thought to be the oldest in the county.

703 MIDHOWE BROCH AND CAIRN   1B10

On the W coast of the island of Rousay, Orkney. All reasonable times.
Free.

An Iron Age broch and walled enclosure situated on a
promontory cut off by a deep rock-cut ditch. Adjacent
is Midhowe Stalled Cairn 'an elongated ship of death'.
The island of Rousay has many other chambered tombs

---

704 THE MILL SHOP   3D8

  ♿
  T

Elgin. All year, Mon-Sat 0900-1730. (Johnstons of Elgin).
Tel: Elgin (0343) 7821.

Close to the ruins of Elgin Cathedral, the Mill Shop
offers a wide selection of products in cashmere and
wool by Johnstons of Elgin. Mill tours by
arrangement.

---

705 MILL OF TOWIE   3E8

  ♿
  P
  T

Drummuir, Keith, Banffshire. Mill: May-Oct 1030-1630.
Restaurant: May-Oct, Wed-Mon 1100-1500 and 1700-2100. Adult: £1,
OAP/child: 50p. Family ticket: £2.50. (Mr Rod Stewart).
Tel: Drummuir (054 281) 225.

Nestling in the hills beside the River Isla, the Mill of
Towie is being restored to full working order. Tours of
the 19th-century oatmeal mill by the miller. The grain
store has been renovated in traditional style and is now
a restaurant serving lunches, teas and suppers. Picnic
area beside the river.

Hugh Miller's Cottage

706 HUGH MILLER'S COTTAGE   3B7

  ♿
  P

Church Street, Cromarty, 22m NE of Inverness via Kessock Bridge.
28 Mar-30 Sep, Mon-Sat 1000-1200, 1300-1700 (June-Sep only, also
Sun 1400-1700). Adult: 65p, child: 30p. (NTS)
Tel: Cromarty (03817) 245.

The birthplace of Hugh Miller (1802-56)—
stonemason—became eminent geologist, editor and
writer. The furnished thatched cottage, built c 1711 by
his great grandfather, contains an exhibition and video
programme on his life and work.

---

707 MINARD CASTLE   4F4

Off A83, 14m S of Inveraray. May-Oct, Mon-Fri 1100-1600. Viewing
by appointment only, tel: Minard (055 66) 272. Free.

The castle is originally 16th century with subsequent
extensions and contains paintings of the Franco-
Scottish Royal House. There is an annual piping
contest.

---

708 MOFFAT MUSEUM   5C8

Moffat. Apr-Sep, weekdays (except Wed), 1030-1300, 1430-1700,
Sun 1430-1700. Adult: 30p, child: 15p. Family ticket: 75p.
(Moffat Museum Trust). Tel: Moffat (0683) 20868.

Situated in an old bakehouse in the oldest part of the
town. The Scotch oven is a feature of the ground
floor. No guide dogs.

709   MONIKIE COUNTRY PARK   **5D1**

&   *Off B961, 1m N of Newbiggin, 5m N of Dundee. All year, 1000-dusk.*
A   *Free. Charge for car park. (Tayside Regional Council).*
P   *Tel: Newbigging (082 623) 202.*

Country park situated on a reservoir complex of three
areas of water, constructed by the Dundee Water
Company over a span of 20 years from 1845. Ground
consists of parkland and mixed woodlands, and covers
185 acres. Woodland walks, watersports including
sailing and windsurfing courses. Children's play area,
rowing, sailing and windsurf hire, picnic areas with
barbecue site.

710   MONTROSE MUSEUM   **5E1**

&   *Montrose. Apr-Oct, Mon-Sat 1030-1300, 1400-1700; Jul, Aug also Sun*
A   *1400-1700; Nov-Mar, Mon-Fri 1400-1700, Sat 1030-1300 and*
P   *1400-1700. Free. Tel: Montrose (0674) 73232.*

Collection started 1836 by Montrose Natural History
and Antiquarian Society and housed in the present
building since 1842. Acquired by District Council in
1977 and reopened 1980 after complete renovations.
Four galleries display local and maritime history —
natural history and fine art.

711   MONUMENT HILL   **4F2**

&   *2m SW of Dalmally, off the old road to Inveraray. All times. Free.*
   Tel: Oban (0631) 63122.

Monument to Duncan Ban Macintyre (1724-1812),
the 'Burns of the Highlands', who was born near
Inveroran.

712   MORTLACH CHURCH   **3E9**

   Dufftown. Summer: daily 1000-1800 approx; Winter: daily 1000-1500
   approx (except during services). Donations. Tel: Dufftown (0390) 20380.

Founded c 566 AD by St Moluag. Part of present
building dates from 11th/12th century. In 1016 it was
lengthened by 3 spears length on the command of
King Malcolm after his victory over the Danes.
Believed to be of the oldest churches in continual use
for public worship. Sculptured stones in vestibule and
very fine stained glass. Battle stone in churchyard; old
watch tower.

713   MORTON CASTLE   **5B8**

   A702, 17m NNW of Dumfries. Closed to the public but may be viewed
   from the outside. (AM) Tel: 031-226 2570.

Beside a small loch, this castle was occupied by
Randolph, first Earl of Moray, as Regent for David II.
It afterwards passed to the Douglases and is now a
well-preserved ruin.

714   MOSS FARM ROAD STONE CIRCLE   **4E7**

   South side of Moss Farm Road, 3 miles N of Blackwaterfoot, E of A841,
   Isle of Arran. All reasonable times. Free. (AM) Tel: 031-226 2570..

Remains of a Bronze Age cairn and stone circle.
(See No 678).

715   MOTE OF MARK   **5B11**

   Off A710, 5m S of Dalbeattie. All reasonable times. Free.
   Tel: Dalbeattie (0556) 610117.

An ancient hill fort on the estuary of the River Urr at
Rockliffe, overlooking Rough Island, an NTS bird
sanctuary. This mote is one of the best preserved
examples in Scotland.

716 MOTE OF URR   5B10

Off B794, 5m NE of Castle Douglas. All reasonable times. Free.
Tel: Castle Douglas (0556) 2611.

An almost circular mound surrounded by a deep
trench. A good example of Norman 'motte-and-
bailey' fortification.

717 MOUSA BROCH   1G5

On the island of Mousa, accessible by boat from Sandwick, Shetland.
Daily bus service between Lerwick and Sandwick. Boat for hire; May-Sep
afternoons; also Sat and Sun mornings, and some evenings.
Opening standard. Free. (AM) Tel: 031-226 2570.

The best preserved example of the remarkable Iron
Age broch towers peculiar to Scotland. The tower
stands over 40 feet high. Its outer and inner walls
contain a rough staircase which can be climbed to the
parapet.

Muchalls Castle

718 MUCHALLS CASTLE   3G11

Off A92, 11m S of Aberdeen. May-Sep, Tue and Sun 1500-1700.
Adult: 30p, child: 10p. (Mr and Mrs A M Simpson).
Tel: Newtonhill (0569) 30217.

Overlooking the sea this tiny 17th-century castle was
built by the Burnetts of Leys in 1619. Ornate
plasterwork ceilings and fine fireplaces are features.
There is a secret staircase.

719 MUIRSHIEL COUNTRY PARK   4G6

Off B786, N of Lochwinnoch, 9m SW of Paisley. Free.
(Strathclyde Regional Council). Tel: Lochwinnoch (0505) 842803.

Attractive countryside featuring trails and walks in a
high valley above moorland, with picnic sites and an
information centre.

720 MULL AND IONA MUSEUM   4C1

Tobermory, Isle of Mull. Jun-Sep, Mon-Fri 1100-1700.
Adult: 30p, child: 10p. Tel: Tobermory (0638) 2182.

Local history museum, with Island exhibits in an old
Baptist Church.

721 MULL & WEST HIGHLAND NARROW GAUGE RAILWAY   **4D2**

♿
A
*29 Mar-5 Apr, then 3 May-27 Sep. Mon-Sat. Sun operates only when
Caledonian-MacBrayne are running a Sun service.
Fares—Adult: £1.00 return, 75p single; child: 70p return, 60p single.
Family return: 2 adults and 2 children (over 4 years old) £2.70.
Pre-booked groups of over 20: 10% discount on adult and child fares.
Family returns do not apply to group rates. Children under 4 years old
accompanied by their parents and not in a group and dogs: free.
See timetable. Railway available for charter by groups of not less than 30
at other times: dates and times by negotiation and by prior arrangement.
(Mull & West Highland Narrow Gauge Railway Co Ltd). Tel:
Craignure (06802) 494. (Out of season: (06803) 389/472).*

10¼″ gauge railway operating a scheduled service to
Torosay Castle and Gardens from Craignure (Old Pier)
Station. Steam and diesel-hauled trains, superb sea and
mountain panorama and woodland journey. Distance
1¼ miles, journey time 20 minutes. Souvenir shop at
booking office at Craignure. Tearoom at Torosay
Castle (opening shortly). Disabled must be able to get
in and out of wheelchairs.

722 MULL LITTLE THEATRE   **4C1**

Dervaig, Isle of Mull. Summer months only. Tel: Dervaig (06884) 267.

Officially the smallest professional theatre in the
country, according to the Guinness Books of Records,
providing a variety of performances in summer.

723 MUNESS CASTLE   **1H2**

*SE point of Isle of Unst, Shetland. Opening standard. Free.
Apply key-keeper. (AM) Tel: 031-226 2570.*

A late 16th-century building, rubble-built with fine
architectural detail.

Murray's Monument: see No 443.

724 MUSEUM NAN EILEAN STEORNABHAGH

Town Hall, Point Street, Stornoway. All year, Tues-Sat 1400-1730,   **2D4**
Thu 1400-1900. Free. Tel: Stornoway (0851) 3773.

The museum contains displays illustrating aspects of
the history of Lewis and the daily life and work of its
people with sections on archaeology, agriculture and
working life, domestic life, and fishing and the sea. A
further gallery is devoted to a changing programme of
temporary and travelling exhibitions.

725 MUSEUM OF THE CUMBRAES   **4G6**

♿
T
*Garrison House, Millport, Isle of Cumbrae. Jun-Sep, Tue-Sat 1000-1630.
Free. (Cunninghame District Council).
Tel: Millport (0475) 530741 (Mon-Fri only).*

A new museum with a collection of photographs and
objects illustrating the way of life of the island from
the earliest times. There is a special feature on
Victorian and Edwardian life, and cruising 'Doon the
Watter'.

726 MUSEUM OF DOLLS, TOYS AND VICTORIANA 3A8

Spa Cottage, The Square, Strathpeffer. Easter-Oct, weekdays 1000-1200 and 1300-1500 (in summer months). Also open 2000-2200 on Mon, Tues & Thu evenings. Other days/times, all year round: please telephone or call at cottage. Adult/OAP: 50p, child: 25p. (Mrs A Kellie). Tel: Strathpeffer (0997) 21549.

Private collection occupies one room in the owner's home, an 1840 cottage in the square in the spa village of Strathpeffer. Near the gate are the original Chalybeate and sulphur wells. Collection of dolls over 150 years old, games, toys, cradles, costume, baby robes, lace, bygones. More items are added each year. Owner gives spinning demonstrations during opening hours each day.

727 MUSEUM OF FLIGHT 6H5

By East Fortune Airfield, off B1347, 4½m S of North Berwick. Jul-Aug, daily 1000 -1600, and several open days. Free. (National Museums of Scotland). Tel: Athelstaneford (062 088) 308.

Aircraft on display at this World War II former RAF airfield range from a supersonic Lightning fighter to the last Comet 4 which was in airline service. The varied collection also includes a Spitfire and a 1930 Puss Moth. Special exhibitions relate to the development of fighter aircraft from 1914 to 1940 and to the airship R34 which flew from East Fortune to New York in 1919. Toilets, picnic area. Free car and coach park.

728 MUSEUM OF ISLAY LIFE 4B6

Situated in Port Charlotte. All year, Apr-Sep, Mon-Fri 1000-1700, Sat & Sun 1400-1700; Oct-Mar, Mon-Fri 1000-1630. Sat & Sun closed. Adult: 50p, OAP: 25p, child (up to 14 years old) and members: Free. (Islay Museum Trust). Tel: Port Charlotte (049 685) 538.

A varied collection of exhibits ranging from prehistoric to early 20th century. Also reference library and archives.

729 MUSEUM OF THE SCOTTISH LEAD MINING INDUSTRY 5B8

Goldscaur Road, Wanlockhead, on B797, 8m ENE of Sanquhar. Easter- Sep, daily 1100-1600. (Museum) Adult: 50p, child: 20p. (Mine) Adult: 50p, child: 20p. (Wanlockhead Museum Trust). Tel: (065 94) 387.

Indoor museum with mining and social relics. Visitor lead mine. Open air museum with beam engines, mines, smelt mill, but-and-ben cottages. Miners' Reading Society Library, founded 1756. Local gold, silver and minerals collection. (See also No 978).

730 MUSEUM OF SCOTTISH TARTANS 6A2

Drummond Street, Comrie, 6m W of Crieff. Apr-Oct, Mon-Sat 1000-1700, Sun 1400-1700; Nov-Mar, Mon-Fri 1100-1500, Sat 1000-1300, Sun by arrangement. Adult: 90p, child: 50p, family ticket: £2.00. Group rates: parties of over 20 persons: 50p per head. Curator tour of museum: £12.00. (Scottish Tartans Society). Tel: Comrie (0764) 70779.

The Scottish Tartans Society is the custodian of the largest collection in existence of material relating to tartans and Highland dress, historic costumes and artefacts; weavers cottage; dye plant garden. There is a research service on surnames, clans and tartans, and an archive of every known tartan.

731 MUTHILL CHURCH AND TOWER   **6B3**

At Muthill, A822, 3½m S of Crieff. All reasonable times. Free. (AM)
Tel: 031-226 2570.

Ruins of an important church of the 15th century, incorporating a 12th-century tower.

732 MYRETON MOTOR MUSEUM   **6G5**

   Off A198, 17m from Edinburgh and 6m SW of North Berwick. May-
P *Oct, daily 1000-1800; Nov- Apr, daily 1000-1700. Adult: 75p, child: 25p.*
T *(M J Mutch). Tel: Aberlady (087 57) 288.*

A varied collection of road transport, including motor cars from 1897, cycles from 1866, motorcycles from 1902, commercials from 1919, World War II military vehicles and automobilia. Catalogue and children's quiz book.

733 NAIRN FISHERTOWN MUSEUM   **3C8**

   Laing Hall, King Street. May-Sep, Tue, Thu and Sat 1430-1630;
A *Mon, Wed & Fri 1830-2030. Adult: 10p, child: 5p; group rates.*
T *Tel: Nairn (0667) 53331.*

A collection of photographs and articles connected with the Moray Firth and herring fishing industries during the steam drifter era. Exhibits on domestic life of the fishertown.

Neidpath Castle

734 NEIDPATH CASTLE   **5C6**

   A72, 1m W of Peebles. Thu before Easter-second Sun in Oct, Mon-Sat
1000-1300, 1400-1800, Sun 1300-1800. Adult: 75p, OAP: 50p,
child: 20p. Group rates: parties of 20 adults and over 60p per head
(by arrangement) (Lord Wemyss' Trust). Tel: Aberlady (087 57) 201.

In a beautiful valley among wooded hills, Neidpath Castle is dramatically situated high above the River Tweed. This medieval castle, with walls nearly 12 feet thick, contains a rock-hewn well and pit prison, and two of the three original vaults. It is also an interesting example of how such a fortress could be adapted to the more civilised living conditions of the 17th century. There are fine views from several levels, right up to the parapet.

735 NEPTUNE'S STAIRCASE 2G12
3m NW of Fort William off A830 at Banavie.

A series of 8 locks, built between 1805 and 1822, which raises Telford's Caledonian Canal 64 feet. (See No 151).

736 NESS HISTORICAL SOCIETY 2D3
(Comunn Eachdraidh Nis)
Old School, Lionel, Ness, Isle of Lewis. Open all Summer.
Adult: £1.00, child: 50p. (Ness Historical Society).

A permanent display of photographs and documents relating to local history with artefacts from domestic life, croft work and fishing. Videos and slides can be viewed on request.

737 NESS OF BURGI 1G6
On the coast at the tip of Scatness, about 1m SW of Jarlshof, S end of mainland Shetland. All reasonable times. Free. (AM) Tel: 031-226 2570.

A defensive stone-built structure of Iron Age date, which is related in certain features to the brochs.

738 NETHER LARGIE CAIRNS 4E4
½m SW of Kilmartin, Argyll. All reasonable times. Free. (AM)
Tel: 031-226 2570.

Three cairns, North (c 1800-1600 BC), Mid (c 1800-1500 BC) and South (c third Millennium BC).

739 NEW ABBEY CORN MILL 5B10
New Abbey, 6m S of Dumfries on A710. Opening standard, except closed Wed and Thu afternoon. Adult: 50p, OAP/child: 25p. Group rates: 10% discount for parties of 11 or more persons. (AM) Tel: 031-226 2570.

A late 18th-century water powered corn mill, still in working order and demonstrated regularly to visitors.

New Lanark

740 NEW LANARK 5B6
   1m S of Lanark. Group rates: 20p per head, minimum charge £2.50 per party. Tel: Lanark (0555) 61345.

The best example in Scotland of an industrial village, the product of the Industrial Revolution in the late 18th and early 19th centuries, now the subject of a major conservation programme. Founded in 1784 by David Dale and Richard Arkwright, it was the scene of early experiments in the paternalistic management and care for the workers, particularly by Robert Owen (1771-1858), Dale's son-in-law. Heritage trail. (See also No 412).

Newark Castle, Port Glasgow

741   NEWARK CASTLE, PORT GLASGOW   4G5

Off A8, through shipyard at E side of Port Glasgow. Opening standard (key-keeper Oct-Mar). Adult: 50p, OAP/child 25p. Group rates: 10% discount for parties of 11 or more persons. (AM) Tel: 031-226 2570.

A large, fine-turreted mansion house of the Maxwells, overlooking the River Clyde, still almost entire and in a remarkably good state of preservation, with a 15th-century tower, a courtyard and hall, the latter dated 1597.

742   NEWARK CASTLE, near SELKIRK   5D7

Off A708, 4m W of Selkirk. Entry on application to Buccleuch Estates, Bowhill, Selkirk. Free. (Buccleuch Estates). Tel: Selkirk (0750) 20753.

First mentioned in 1423, Newark or New Wark was so called to distinguish it from the older Auldwark Castle which stood nearby. This 5-storeyed oblong tower house, standing within a barmkin, was a royal hunting seat for the Forest of Ettrick; and Royal Arms of James I are on the west gable. In the courtyard 100 prisoners from the Battle of Philiphaugh (1645) were shot by Leslie. Care should be taken in the building.

Noltland Castle

743   NOLTLAND CASTLE   1B9

Isle of Westray, Orkney. Opening standard. Free. (AM) Tel: 031-226 2570.

Extensive ruins of a castle originally built in 1420 by Thomas de Tulloch, then the Governor. Later besieged by Sir William Sinclair of Warsetter, it fell into the hands of Gilbert Balfour of Westray, from whose time, around the mid 16th century, much of the building appears to date. It was partly destroyed in 1746. The stately hall, vaulted kitchen and fine winding staircase are impressive.

744 NORTH AYRSHIRE MUSEUM 4G6

In Saltcoats, past railway station. May-Aug, Mon-Sat, 1000-1600;
Sep-Apr, Thu, Fri, Sat, 1000-1600. Free. Tel: Saltcoats (0294) 64174.

A fine museum with both local and national exhibits
in a mid 18th-century Scottish church. Also exhibits
from the former maritime museum.

745 NORTH BERWICK LAW 6H5

S of North Berwick, off B1347. All times. Free.

The 613-ft volcanic rock is a fine viewpoint and is
crowned by a watch tower dating from Napoleonic
times, and an archway made from the jawbone of a
whale.

746 NORTH BERWICK MUSEUM 6H5

School Road. Easter-end May, Sat and Mon 1000-1300, 1400-1700, Fri
and Sun 1400-1700. Jun-Sep, Mon-Sat 1000-1300, 1400-1700, Sun
1400-1700. Free. (East Lothian District Council)

A compact museum with galleries devoted to natural
history, archaeology and the life of the North Berwick
area, housed on the upper floor of a former school.
Special exhibitions are arranged in June to August.

747 NORTH CARR LIGHTSHIP 6H3

East Pier, Anstruther. Apr-Sep, daily 1000-1730. Adult: 40p, child: 25p
(subject to change from Apr). (North East Fife District Council).
Tel: Cupar (0334) 53722, ext 435.

The lightship, stationed off Fife Ness from 1938-1975,
is now a floating museum and the only one of its
kind. All the interior fitments have been refurbished to
give a realistic impression of life on board.

748 NORTH EAST OF SCOTLAND AGRICULTURAL HERITAGE CENTRE (ADEN COUNTRY PARK) 3H8

On A950 between New Deer and Mintlaw, 9m W of Peterhead.
Tel: Mintlaw (07712) 2857.

A 230-acre estate, with original farm buildings totally
restored, creating a comprehensive and interpretive
leisure area. Audio-visual display, farm machinery
exhibition, woodland walks. Craft workers, knitwear
shop and Ranger Service. Restaurant.

749 NORTH GLEN GALLERY 5B10

Palnackie, 5m SE of Castle Douglas. Daily 1000-1800 by
arrangement. Adult: 40p, OAP/child: 10p. Advance notice for groups
recommended. Tel: Palnackie (055 660) 200.

Studio demonstrating the blowing of glass, assembly
of sculpture, welding and cutting of steel. Beautiful
view.

750 NORTH HOY NATURE RESERVE 1A11

Reached by boat from Stromness, Orkney. Access at all times. Free.
(RSPB). Tel: Kirkwall (0856) 850 176.

Extensive area of mountain and moorland with huge
seacliffs including Old Man of Hoy. Moorland birds
and large numbers of seabirds.

751 NORWOOD MUSEUM 1C11

Graemeshall House, Holm, Orkney. Sun, Tues, Wed & Thu 1400-1700
and 1800-2000 (groups by appointment). Adult: £1.00, child: 50p.
Tel: Holm (085 678) 217.

A large private collection of antiques featuring a
variety of rare and unusual pieces.

752 NOSS NATURE RESERVE 1G5

Isle of Noss, 5m E of Lerwick, Shetland. Access by inflatable boat each day (1000-1700) except Mon & Thu. Island open from mid-May until end of Aug; see local NCC staff of Shetland Tourist Board. Adult: 75p. (NCC) Tel: Lerwick (0591) 3434 or 3345.

Spectacular island with 600-feet cliffs and vast colonies of breeding auks, gulls and gannets. Modest display on natural history and restored Pony Pond (Shetland Pony Stud Farm) open to visitors.

Nova Scotia Room: see No 701.

753 OBAN GLASS 4E2

Lochavullin Estate, Oban. All year. Free. Factory Shop: Mon-Fri 0900-1700 (all year); Sat 0900-1200 (Summer only). Factory viewing: Mon-Fri 0900-1700 (all year). (Caithness Glass plc). Tel: Oban (0631) 63386.

See paperweight making from the raw materials stage through all the processes to the finished article. Visit the factory shop with an extensive range of glassware. Ample car/coach parking.

Old Blacksmith's Shop Visitor Centre

754 OLD BLACKSMITH'S SHOP VISITORS CENTRE 5D10

Gretna Green, just off A74 at English border. Daily, all year. (Museum) Admission: 30p; group rates. Tel: Gretna (0461) 38363/38224.

The old Blacksmith's Shop, famous for runaway marriages, has a museum with anvil marriage room and coach house. Gretna was once a haven for runaway couples seeking to take advantage of Scotland's then laxer marriage laws, when couples could be married by a declaration before witnesses; this was made illegal in 1940. Elopers can still, however, take advantage of Scots law permitting marriage without parental consent at 16. Among places where marriages took place were the Old Toll Bar (now bypassed) when the road opened in 1830, and the Smithy. Restaurant, bar and souvenir shop.

755 OLD BRIDGE HOUSE 5B9

Mill Road, Dumfries, at Devorgilla's Bridge. Apr-Sep, Mon-Sat 1000-1300, 1400-1700; Sun 1400-1700. Free. Tel: Dumfries (0387) 53374.

The house, built in 1662, now has rooms furnished in period style to illustrate life in Dumfries over the centuries. Devorgilla's Bridge was originally built in the 13th century by Devorgilla Balliol, who endowed Balliol College, Oxford.

756 OLD INVERLOCHY CASTLE 2G12

On NE outskirts of Fort William. Not yet open to the public—may be viewed from outside (AM) Tel: 031-226 2570.

A ruined 13th-century square building, with round corner towers. Nearby 19th-century Inverlochy Castle is now a hotel.

757 OLD MAN OF HOY 1A12

NW coast of Isle of Hoy, Orkney.

A 450-feet-high isolated stack (pillar) standing off the magnificent cliffs of NW Hoy. It can also be well seen from the Scrabster-Stromness ferry.

---

758 OLD PARISH CHURCH OF HAMILTON 5A6

  ♿ *Sat 1100, guided tour and coffee. Sunday worship 1115, (tour 1230); weekdays 1000-1200 (tour and coffee). Tel: Hamilton (0698) 420002.*

Present (1734) is the only church designed by William Adam. It is the oldest building in Hamilton still used for its original purpose and contains the Pre-Norman Netherton Cross and the Covenanters 'Heads' Memorial. Coffee with home baking, Sat 1100, Mon-Fri 1000-1200.

---

759 OLD PLACE OF MOCHRUM 4G10

Off B7005, 11m W of Wigtown. Not open to the public; can be seen from the road. Tel: Newton Stewart (0671) 2431.

Known also as Drumwalt Castle, this is mainly 15th and 16th century with two picturesque towers.

---

760 OLD SKYE CROFTER'S HOUSE 2E10

Luib, 7m NW of Broadford, Isle of Skye. Daily 1000-1800. Adult: 50p; child: 25p; group rates.

Thatched traditional dwelling house furnished in keeping with the early 19th century, including agricultural implements.

---

761 OLDMILLS 3D8

  ♿ *W end of Elgin off the A96. Wed-Sun 1030-1730, Adult: 30p,*
  P   *OAP/child: 15p. Group rates: 10 or more persons: 20p per head. (Moray District Council). Tel: Elgin (0343) 45121.*

The oldest and only remaining meal mill on the River Lossie. Its history can be traced back to a Royal Charter of 1230 granting its rights to the monks of Pluscarden Priory.

Orchardton Tower

762 ORCHARDTON TOWER 5B10

Off A711, 5½m SE of Castle Douglas. Opening standard. Free. Apply custodian at nearby cottage. (AM) Tel: 031-226 2570.

An example, unique in Scotland, of a circular tower house, built by John Cairns about the middle of the 15th century.

763 ORKNEY WIRELESS MUSEUM 1B12

              P

St Margaret's Hope, South Ronaldsay Island, 11m S of Kirkwall. 1 Apr-30 Sep, daily 1000-2000. Adult: 50p, child: 25p (under 12: free). (Mr James MacDonald). Tel: St Margaret's Hope (0856 83) 462.

Museum of wartime communications at Scapa Flow, with many of the instruments used by the thousands of service men and women posted here to protect the Home Fleet, shown in their proper context. Also many handsome wireless sets of the 1930s.
(See also No 860).

764 ORMISTON MARKET CROSS 6F6

At Ormiston, B6371, 7½m WSW of Haddington. (AM) Tel: 031-226 2570.

A 15th-century cross in the main street.

765 ORPHIR CHURCH 1B11

By A964, 8m WSW of Kirkwall. All times. Free. (AM) Tel: 031-226 2570.

The remains of Scotland's only circular medieval church, built in the first half of the 12th century and dedicated to St Nicholas. Nearby is the site of the Earl's Bu, a great hall of the Earls of Orkney.

Ospreys: see Nos 642 and 644.

766 OUR LADY OF THE ISLES 2A9

N of South Uist, Outer Hebrides. All reasonable times. Free.

On Reuval Hill—the Hill of Miracles—is the statue of the Madonna and Child, erected in 1957 by the Catholic community with contributions from all over the world. The work of Hew Lorimer, it is 30 feet high.

767 OUR LADY OF SORROWS 2A10

    A

Garrynamonie, South Uist, Western Isles. Daily till 1900. Free.
This modern church opened in 1964. There is a mosaic on the front of the building depicting Our Lady of Sorrows.

Paisley Abbey

768 PAISLEY ABBEY   **4H5**

♿ *In Paisley, 7m W of Glasgow. Outwith the hours of divine worship, open all year, Mon-Sat 1000-1500. Free. Group visits by arrangement. Tel: 041-889 7654 (0930-1230).*

A fine Cluniac Abbey Church founded in 1163. Almost completely destroyed by order of Edward I of England in 1307. Rebuilt and restored after Bannockburn and in the century following. In 1553 the tower collapsed, wrecking N-transept, crossing the choir; they lay open to the sky for 350 years while the nave alone was the parish church; but they were rebuilt and rejoined to the nave this century (1898-1907 and 1922-28). The choir contains a fine stone-vaulted roof, stained glass and the tombs of Princess Marjory Bruce and King Robert III. See the St Mirin Chapel with St Mirin carvings (1499). Note outside the Norman doorway, cloisters and Place of Paisley. The Barochan Cross, a weathered Celtic cross, 11 feet high and attributed to the 10th century, is also in the Abbey.

769 PAISLEY MUSEUM AND ART GALLERY   **4H5**

♿ *High Street, Paisley. All year, Mon-Sat 1000-1700. Free.*
A
P *Tel: 041-889 3151.*

The late 19th-century museum and art galleries house the world famous collection of Paisley Shawls. Displays trace the history of the Paisley pattern; the development of weaving techniques is explained and the social aspects of what was a tight-knit weaving community are explored. There are also fine collections of local history, natural history, ceramics and Scottish painting.

770 PALACERIGG COUNTRY PARK   **6A6**

♿ *Unclassified road, 2½m SE of Cumbernauld. All year. (Park) dawn to*
T *dusk. (Visitor Centre) winter 1000-1630, summer 1000-1800 (closed Tues). No dogs. Free. Pony-trekking—Adult: £3.50 per hour, child: £2.50 per hour. (Cumbernauld and Kilsyth District Council) Tel: Cumbernauld (0236) 20047.*

Wildlife includes roe deer, badger, fox and stoat. Also wolves, wildcats, and polecats in paddocks. Deer park, 18-hole golf course and pony-trekking. Children's farm being developed. Coffee shop open from 1100 daily in season (except Tues). Open at weekends in winter.

771 PARALLEL ROADS   **2H11**

Glen Roy, unclassified road off A86, 18m NE of Fort William.

These 'parallel roads' are hillside terraces marking levels of lakes dammed by glaciers during the Ice Age.

772 PASS OF KILLIECRANKIE   3C12

Off A9, 3m N of Pitlochry. NTS Visitor Centre: 28 Mar-30 Jun and 1 Sep-24 Oct, daily 1000-1800. Jul-Aug, daily 0930-1800. Adult: 10p, child: free. (NTS) Tel: Pitlochry (0796) 3233.

A famous wooded gorge where in 1689 the Government troops were routed by Jacobite forces led by 'Bonnie Dundee'. Soldier's Leap. NTS centre features the battle, natural history and ranger services. The Pass is on the network of Garry-Tummel walks, which extend for 20 miles in the area. Snack bar.

773 PEEL RING OF LUMPHANAN   3F10

A980, 11m NW of Banchory. All times. Free. (AM) Tel: 031-226 2570.

A major early medieval earthwork 120 feet in diameter and 18 feet high. There are links with Shakespeare's *Macbeth*.

774 PENKILL CASTLE   4G8

Old Dailly, 2½m NE of Girvan. Apr-Sep, by appointment only. Admission: £4.50, includes tour and light lunch. (Mr Wilson). Tel: Old Dailly (046 587) 261.

15th-century castle with impressive later additions. Fine furniture, tapestries and paintings. Favourite haunt of the pre-Raphaelites, an inspiration to Dante Gabriel Rossetti and his sister Christina and other well known visitors.

775 PERTH ART GALLERY AND MUSEUM   6D2

    ♾   A   *George Street. All year, Mon-Sat 1000-1300, 1400-1700. Free. Tel: Perth (0738) 32488.*

Collections of local history, fine and applied art, natural history, archaeology and ethnography. Changing programme of temporary exhibitions.

Perth Information Centre: see No 820.

776 PERTH REPERTORY THEATRE   6D2

    ♾   P   T   *High Street, Perth. Group concessions available, but variable. Tel: Perth (0738) 21031.*

An intimate Victorian theatre, built in 1900 in the centre of Perth, offering a variety of plays, musicals, etc. Induction loop for hard of hearing. Coffee bar and restaurant open during day and for performances.

777 PETER ANDERSON WOOLLEN MILL   5E6

Nether Mill, Galashiels. All year, Mon-Sat 0900-1700; also Jun-Sep, Sun 1200-1700. (Conducted tours) Apr-Sep, Mon-Fri at 1030, 1400. Free. Tel: Galashiels (0896) 2091.

Museum and exhibition of the past of Galashiels, showing all aspects of the growth of the town, including health, education, labour and textiles. Also tours of the manufacturing of tartans, tweeds, etc. Museum, mill tours and mill shop.

778 PETERHEAD ARBUTHNOT MUSEUM AND ART GALLERY   3H8

    ♾   *St Peter Street, Peterhead. All year, daily except Sun, 1000-1200, 1400-1700, Sat 1400-1700. Free. (North East of Scotland Museums Service). Tel: Peterhead (0779) 77778.*

The development of fishing and whaling, with Arctic exhibits, is featured. Local history, photographic and coin exhibitions.

779 PIER ARTS CENTRE   1A11

& Victoria Street, Stromness, Orkney. All year, Tues-Sat 1030-1230 and
P   1330-1700; Jul & Aug, Sun-Mon 1400-1700. Free.
    Tel: Stromness (0856) 850 209.

Former merchant's house (c 1800) adjoining buildings
(Pier Gallery) former coal store and fishermen's sheds
which has been converted into a gallery, housing
permanent collection of 20th-century paintings and
sculpture.

780 PIEROWALL CHURCH   1B9

At Pierowall, Island of Westray, Orkney. All reasonable times. Free.
(AM). Tel: 031-226 2570.

A ruin consisting of nave and chancel, the latter canted
out of alignment. There are some finely lettered
tombstones.

781 PINKIE HOUSE   6F6

& Off A1 at E end of Musselburgh. Mid Apr-mid Jul, mid Sep-mid Dec,
P   Tues 1400-1700. Free. (Loretto School). Tel: 031-665 2059.

Early 17th-century building with many later additions.
It is best known for its painted gallery (c 1630) and
plaster ceilings.

Pitlochry Festival Theatre

782 PITLOCHRY FESTIVAL THEATRE   5B1

& Off A9 bypass at Port-na-craig junction. May-Oct, open all day for
T   refreshments and art exhibitions.
    (Box Office) Tel: Pitlochry (0796) 2680.

Scotland's 'Theatre in the Hills' is now rehoused in a
magnificent new building by the River Tummel.
Opened by Prince Charles in 1981, it is a must for all
holidaymakers. A repertoire of five or six different
plays are presented each season, with concerts on most
Sundays. Catering and bar facilities. Coffee shop open
from 1000; lunch 1200-1400; restaurant 1830-2000.
Magnificent view from foyer and restaurant.

**783 PITLOCHRY POWER STATION
AND DAM**   5B1

& Off A9 at Pitlochry. Easter-end Oct, daily 0940-1730. Free.
A   (Exhibition: Adult: 30p, OAP/child: 15p. (North of Scotland Hydro-
P   Electric Board). Tel: Pitlochry (0796) 3152.

One of nine hydro stations in the Tummel Valley. The
dam created Loch Faskally where boating and fishing
are available. Salmon can be seen through windows in
the fish ladder. Exhibition and film inside power
station.

784 PITMEDDEN GARDEN AND MUSEUM OF FARMING LIFE 3G9

Outskirts of Pitmedden village on A920, 14m N of Aberdeen, off B999. (Garden) All year, daily 0930-sunset. (Museum) 1 May-30 Sep, daily 1100-1800. Adult: £1.10, child: 55p; group rates. (Garden only) Oct-Mar, Adult: 60p, child: 30p. (NTS) Tel: Udny (065 13) 2352.

The highlight is the 17th-century Great Garden originally laid out by Sir Alexander Seton, with elaborate floral designs, pavilions, fountains and sundials. The 'thunder houses' at either end of the west belvedere are rare in Scotland. The Museum of Farming Life contains a collection of agricultural and domestic implements. On the 100-acre estate is a woodland and farmland walk. Visitor Centre, tearoom, exhibition on formal gardens, picnic area.

785 PITSLIGO CASTLE 3G7

By Rosehearty, 3m W of Fraserburgh. All times. Free.

Ruined castle dating from 1424 which passed through various families to the 4th and last Lord Pitsligo who is remembered for his generosity to the poor and for his successful attempts to evade arrest after the '45 Jacobite rebellion. The ruins of the castle are interesting and impressive.

786 PITTENCRIEFF HOUSE MUSEUM 6D5

Pittencrieff Park, Dunfermline. May-Aug, daily except Tues 1100-1700. Tel: Dunfermline (0383) 722935 (May-Aug only) or Dunfermline (0383) 721814). Contact Ms Lin Collis, Curator.

The house, standing in a fine park, was built in 1610 for the Lairds of Pittencrieff, and was bought by Andrew Carnegie in 1902. There are displays of local history, costumes, and an art gallery.

787 PLUSCARDEN ABBEY 3D8

From B9010 at Elgin take unclassified road to Pluscarden, 6m SW. All year daily 0500-2030. Free. Tel: (034 389) 257 (0900-1100 and 1430-1700).

Originally a Valliscaulian house, the monastery was founded in 1230. In 1390 the Church was burned, probably by the Wolf of Badenoch who burned Elgin about the same time. It became a dependent priory of the Benedictines' Abbey of Dunfermline in 1454 until the suppression of monastic life in Scotland in 1560. Thereafter the buildings fell into ruins until 1948 when a group of Benedictine monks from Prinknash Abbey, Gloucester, returned to restore it. Monastic church services open to the public.

Poosie Nansie's

788 POOSIE NANSIE'S 4H7

Mauchline. Normal public house hours.

Ale-house in Burns' time which inspired part of his cantata *The Jolly Beggars*, and is still in use today.

789 PORTENCROSS CASTLE 4G6

At end of B7048 (off A78) near Largs. Not open to the public.

14th-century stronghold (1306) conferred on Sir
Robert Boyd of Kilmarnock by Robert II.

---

790 PRESTON MARKET CROSS 6F6

½m S of Prestonpans, 8m E of Edinburgh. All times. Free. (AM)
Tel: 031-226 2570.

An outstanding Scottish market cross, the only one
that still stands where and as it was built. The tall
shaft, surmounted by a unicorn, stands on a circular
structure with niches and a parapet. It was probably
erected by the Hamiltons of Preston after they
obtained the right to hold a fair in 1617.

Preston Mill

---

791 PRESTON MILL 6H6

& P
Off A1 at East Linton, 6m W of Dunbar. 28 Mar-30 Sep, Mon-Sat
1000-1230, 1400-1730, Sun 1400-1730 (Oct, closes 1630). 1 Nov-31
Mar, Sat 1000-1230, 1400-1630, Sun 1400-1630. Adult: 85p, child: 40p;
Group rates: Schoolchildren: 40p, no charge for accompanying teachers and
drivers. (NTS) Tel: 031-226 5922.

A picturesque water-mill, possibly the only one of its
kind still in working condition in Scotland. Nearby is
Phantassie Doocot (dovecot), originally containing 500
birds, and the Rennie Memorial, which contains a part
of John Rennie's Waterloo Bridge. (See also No 810).
An added attraction are the bantams, Chinese geese
and Muscovy ducks.

---

792 PRESTONPANS BATTLE CAIRN 6F6

&
E of Prestonpans on A198. All times. Free.

The cairn commemorates the victory of Prince Charles
Edward over General Cope at the Battle of
Prestonpans in 1745.

---

793 PRIORWOOD GARDENS 5E6

& A
In Melrose, by Abbey, on A6091. Open 28 Mar-30 Apr and
1 Nov- 24 Dec, Mon-Sat 1000-1300 and 1400-1730; 1 May-30 June and
1-31 Oct, Mon-Sat 1000-1730, Sun 1330-1730; 1 Jul-30 Sep, Mon-Sat
1000-1800, Sun 1330-1730. Admission by donation. (NTS)
Tel: Melrose (089 682) 2965.

A garden which specialises in flowers suitable for
drying. There is an NTS Visitor Centre. Picnic tables,
orchard walk, dry flower garden, NTS shop.

794 QUEEN ELIZABETH FOREST PARK 4H4

Between the E shore of Loch Lomond and the Trossachs. (FC)

In this 45,000 acres of forest, moor and mountainside there are many walks. On A821 is the David Marshall Lodge, a picnic pavilion and information centre. 'Duke's Road' from Aberfoyle to the Trossachs has fine views.

795 QUEENSBERRY AISLE 5B8

Durisdeer, unclassified road off A702, 6m N of Thornhill. All reasonable times. Free. Tel: Dumfries (0387) 53862.

Durisdeer church dates from 1699, and is noted for the elaborate monument, by Van Nost, to the second Duke of Queensberry (died 1711) and his duchess (died 1709).

796 QUEEN'S OWN HIGHLANDERS REGIMENTAL MUSEUM 3B8

Fort George, near Ardersier. Apr-Sep, Mon-Fri 1000-1800, Sun 1400-1800. Oct-Mar, Mon-Fri 1000-1600. Free. Tel: Inverness (0463) 224380.

Regimental museum with collections of medals, uniforms and other items showing the history of the Queen's Own Highlanders, Seaforth Highlanders and The Queen's Own Cameron Highlanders.

797 QUEEN'S VIEW, LOCH LOMOND 4H5

Off A809, 12m NNW of Glasgow.

From the west side of the road a path leads to a viewpoint where in 1879, Queen Victoria had her first view of Loch Lomond.

798 QUEEN'S VIEW, LOCH TUMMEL 5A1

On B8019, off A9, 8m NW of Pitlochry. Open at all times. Free.

A magnificent viewpoint along Loch Tummel to the peak of Schiehallion, 3,547 feet. Queen Victoria visited it in 1866. (See No 959). Toilets, car park and seasonal cafe.

799 QUIRAING 2D7

Off A855 at Digg, 19m N of Portree, Isle of Skye.

An extraordinary mass of towers and pinnacles into which cattle were driven during forays. A rough track zigzags up to the 'Needle', an imposing obelisk 120 feet high, beyond which, in a large amphitheatre, stands the 'Table', a huge grass-covered rock-mass. Impressive views.

800 QUOYNESS CHAMBERED TOMB IC10

E side of Els Ness, S coast of island of Sanday, Orkney. All reasonable times. Free. (AM) Tel: 031-226 2570.

A spectacular tomb with a main chamber standing to a height of about 13 feet. Analysis suggests that the tomb was in use about 2900 BC.

801 RAIDER'S ROAD 5A10

From A712 near Clatteringshaws Dam, or A762 at Bennan near Mossdale. June-Sep daily 0900-2100. £1 per car. (FC)

A 10-mile forest drive through the fine scenery of the Galloway Forest Park. (See also No 443)

802 RAMMERSCALES 5C9

On B7020, 2½m S of Lochmaben. 4-29 May, Sun, Tue, Thu 1400-1700; 3 Aug-14 Sep, alternate Sun and every Tue, Wed, Thu, or by arrangement in season. Adult: £1.00, child: 50p. (Mr A M Bell Macdonald). Tel: Lochmaben (038 781) 361.

A Georgian manor house begun in 1760 for Dr James Mounsey, personal physician to the Tsarina Elizabeth of Russia. Pillared hall and circular staircase. Some Jacobite relics, fine library and collection of modern works of art. Lovely policies, woodland walks and wonderful views of Annandale.

803 ALLAN RAMSAY LIBRARY 5B7

On B797 at Leadhills—enquire at Post Office. Tel: Leadhills (06594) 324 or 326.

Lead miners' subscription library, founded in 1741, with rare books, detailed 18th-century mining documents and local records. Tearoom nearby.

804 RANDOLPH'S LEAP 3C8

Off B9007, 7m SW of Forres.

The River Findhorn winds through a deep gorge in the sandstone, and from a path above are impressive views of the clear brown water swirling over rocks or in still dark pools. Randolph's Leap is the most striking part of this valley.

805 RAVENSCRAIG CASTLE 6E4

On a rocky promontory between Dysart and Kirkcaldy. Opening standard. Adult: 50p, OAP/child: 25p. Group rates: 10% discount for parties of 11 or more persons. (AM) Tel: 031-226 2570.

Imposing ruin of a castle founded by James II in 1460. Later it passed into the hands of the Sinclair Earls of Orkney. It is perhaps the first British castle to be symmetrically designed for defence by firearms.

806 RED CASTLE 5E1

Off A92, 7m S of Montrose. All times. Free.

This red stone tower on a steep mound beside the sandhills of Lunan Bay probably dates from the 15th century when it replaced an earlier fort built for William the Lion by Walter de Berkely to counter raids by Danish pirates. Robert the Bruce gave it to Hugh, 6th Earl of Ross, in 1328.

807 REEDIEHILL DEER FARM 6D3

Off A936, NW of Auchtermuchty, fork left onto Mournipea Road then 1½ miles. (Farm shop) Open all year. Guided tours by prior arrangement only. Adult: 60p. (Dr T J Fletcher). Tel: Auchtermuchty (0337) 28369.

Farm shop selling venison, deerskins and antlers, from the first commercial red deer farm in Britain in which the deer are fully domesticated and approachable. No dogs except guide dogs. Groups by prior arrangement.

808 REINDEER ON THE RANGE 3C10

Reindeer House, Loch Morlich. A951 from Aviemore; signposted from Loch Morlich Campsite. All year, daily (subject to weather), 1100 departure. Adult: £1.00, child: 50p. Tel: Cairngorm (047 986) 228.

Visitors may accompany the herdsman on his daily check of Britain's only herd of reindeer. For disabled visitors: reindeer can be brought to the car with prior notice.

809 RENNIBISTER EARTH HOUSE   1B11

About 4½m WNW of Kirkwall on the Finstown road (A965), Orkney. All reasonable times. Free. (AM) Tel: 031-226 2570.

An excellent example of the Orkney type of Iron Age souterrain or earth-house, consisting of a passage and underground chamber with supporting roof-pillars.

810 RENNIE'S BRIDGE   5F6

   Kelso. All times. Free. (Borders Regional Council).

A fine 5-arched bridge built over the River Tweed in 1803 by Rennie to replace one destroyed by the floods of 1797. On the bridge are two lamp posts from the demolished Old Waterloo Bridge in London, which Rennie built in 1811. There is also a fine view to Floors Castle (No 425).

811 RESTENNETH PRIORY   5D1

Off B9113, 1½m ENE of Forfar. All reasonable times. Free. (AM) Tel: 031-226 2570.

A house of Augustinian canons, probably founded by David I on the site of an earlier church, in an attractive setting. A feature of the ruins is the tall square tower, with its shapely broach spire, and an early doorway at its base.

Ring of Brodgar

812 RING OF BRODGAR   1B11

Between Loch of Harray and Loch of Stenness, 5m NE of Stromness, Mainland, Orkney. All times. Free. (AM) Tel: 031-226 2570.

Magnificent stone circle of 36 stones (originally 60) surrounded by a deep ditch cut into solid bedrock. Nearby are large mounds and other standing stones, notably the Comet Stone. (See also No 900).

813 ROB ROY'S GRAVE   4H3

Balquhidder Churchyard, off A84, 14m NNW of Callander. All reasonable times. Free.

Three flat gravestones enclosed by railings are the graves of Rob Roy, his wife and two of his sons. The church itself contains St Angus' Stone (8th century), a 17th-century bell from the old church and old Gaelic Bibles.

814 ROB ROY'S STATUE   3G10

Peterculter by A93. All times. Free.

Statue of Rob Roy standing above the Leuchar Burn can be seen from the bridge on the main road.

815 ROMAN BATH HOUSE 4H5

Roman Road, Bearsden, 5m NW of Glasgow. All times. Free. (AM)
Tel: 031-226 2570.

A Roman bath house built in the 140s AD for the use of the soldiers stationed in the adjacent Antonine Wall fort. The best surviving visible Roman building in Scotland. (See also No 35).

Prentice Pillar, Roslin

816 ROSSLYN CHAPEL 6E7

At Roslin, Off A703, 7½m S of Edinburgh. Apr-Oct, Mon-Sat 1000-1700. Adult: 75p, OAP: 50p, child: 30p. Group rates: 10% discount for parties of 20 or more persons. Tel: 031-440 2159.

This 15th-century chapel is one of Scotland's loveliest and most historic churches, renowned for its magnificent sculpture and Prentice Pillar. Coffee shop and craft shop.

817 ROTHIEMURCHUS ESTATE VISITOR CENTRE 3C10

1m from Aviemore. All year, 1000-dusk. Tel: Aviemore (0479) 810858.

Highland cattle, red deer, Caledonian pine forest, Cairngorm Nature Reserve, trout farm (feed the fish), fresh and smoked trout for sale. Design knitwear and crafts, estate tours, tractor and trailer rides.

818 ROTHESAY CASTLE 4F5

At Rothesay, Isle of Bute. Opening standard, except Oct-Mar closed Thu and Fri mornings. Adult: 50p, OAP/child: 25p. Group rates: 10% discount for parties of 11 or more persons. (AM) Tel: 031-226 2570.

One of the most important medieval castles in Scotland. Rothesay was stormed by Norsemen in 1240; their breach can still be detected. The walls, heightened and provided with four round towers in the late 13th century, enclose a circular courtyard unique in Scotland.

819 ROUGH CASTLE 6A6

Off B816, 6m W of Falkirk. All reasonable times. Free. (AM)
Tel: 031-226 2570.

The best preserved of the forts of the Antonine Wall, with ramparts and ditches easily seen. (See also No 35).

820   THE ROUND HOUSE   6D2

   Marshall Place, Perth. Apr & May, Mon-Fri 0900-1700, Sat 0900-1245;
 P *Jun-Sep, Mon-Fri 0900-1900, Sat 0900-1800, Sun 1200-1700; Oct-Mar,*
 T *Mon-Fri 0900-1245 and 1400-1700. Free.*
Tel: Perth (0738) 22900/27108.

The first Perth City waterworks, built in 1832 to a
design by Adam Anderson, Professor of Natural
Philosophy at St Andrews University and Rector of
Perth Academy. Restored in 1974 by Perth Town
Council. It is now used as the Tourist Information
Centre, and its special feature is a tape/slide
presentation of Perthshire. Free parking. Alternative
wheelchair entrance at side, please ring bell.

821   ROXBURGH CASTLE   5F7

Off A699, 1m SW of Kelso. All times. Free. Tel: Kelso (0573) 23333.

The earth works are all that remain of the once
mighty castle, destroyed by the Scots in the 15th
century, and the walled Royal Burgh which gave its
name to the county. The present village of Roxburgh
dates from a later period.

Royal Museum of Scotland: see Nos 360 and 361.

822   RUMBLING BRIDGE   6C1

A823 at Rumbling Bridge. Free. All reasonable times.

The River Devon is spanned here by two bridges, the
lower one dating from 1713, the upper one from 1816.
A footpath from the north side gives good access to
spectacular and picturesque gorges and falls, one of
which is known as the Devil's Mill. Another,
Cauldron Linn, is a mile downstream, whilst Vicar's
Bridge is a beauty spot a mile beyond this.

Ruthven Barracks

823   RUTHVEN BARRACKS   3B11

On B970, ½m S of Kingussie. All reasonable times. Free. (AM)
Tel: 031-226 2570.

Considerable ruins, on a site once occupied by a
fortress of the Wolf of Badenoch, of barracks built
1716-18 to keep the Highlanders in check, and added
to by General Wade in 1734. After the disaster of
Culloden, 1746, Prince Charles' Highlanders
assembled at Ruthven hoping he might take the field
again. When they realised the cause was hopeless, they
blew up the barracks.

Ruthven Castle: see No 555.

824   RUTHWELL CROSS   5C10
& *In Ruthwell Church, B724, 6½m W of Annan. All reasonable times.*
A *Free. (AM) Tel: Dumfries (0387) 53862.*

This preaching cross, which is 18 feet high, is carved
with Runic characters. It dates back to the 8th century
and is a major monument of Dark Age Europe.

825   ST ABB'S HEAD NATURE RESERVE   5F5
& *1m N of St Abbs. Best season Apr-Jul. Free (donations).*
P *Tel: Coldingham (039 03) 443.*

Spectacular cliffs with breeding seabirds, wild flowers,
magnificent views. Ranger Service (by prior
arrangement). Wheelchair access to Information
Centre.

826   ST ANDREWS CASTLE   6G2
Shore at St Andrews. Opening standard. Adult: 50p, OAP/child: 25p.
Group rates: 10% discount for parties of 11 or more persons. (AM) Tel:
031-226 2570.

The ruined castle, overlooking the sea, was founded in
1200 and rebuilt at several periods. Here Cardinal
Beaton was murdered in 1546, and the first round of
the Reformation struggle was fought out in the siege
that followed.

827   ST ANDREWS CATHEDRAL   6G2
Beside the castle at St Andrews. Charge for Museum and St Rule's
(Regulus') Tower. Opening standard. Adult: 50p, OAP: 25p, child: 25p.
Group rates: 10% discount for parties of 11 or more persons. (AM)
Tel: 031-226 2570.

The cathedral was once the largest church in the
country. The remains include parts of the east and
west gables, the south wall of the nave, and portions
of the choir and south transept, mostly built in the
12th and 13th centuries.

St Andrews University

828   ST ANDREWS UNIVERSITY   6G2
& *St Andrews town centre. Tel: St Andrews (0334) 76161.*
A
P The oldest university in Scotland, founded in 1412. See
the 15th-century Church of St Salvator, now the
chapel for the united colleges of St Salvator (1455) and
St Leonard (1512); St Mary's College (1537) with its
quadrangle; and the 16th-century St Leonard's Chapel.
Also in the town are St Mary's House built in 1523
and now St Leonard's School Library, and Holy
Trinity Church with a 16th- century tower and
interesting interior features. Guided tours operate
twice daily through the summer.

829 ST BEAN'S CHURCH 6B2

At Fowlis Wester, off A85, 5m NE of Crieff.

An attractive 13th-century church, restored in 1927, containing a finely carved Pictish stone cross. Opposite is Fowlis Wester Sculptured Stone, an 8th century Pictish stone with remarkably clear carvings, standing in the square of this attractive little village.

830 ST BLANE'S CHAPEL 4F6

8½m S of Rothesay, Isle of Bute. All reasonable times. Free. (AM) Tel: 031-226 2570.

Ruins of a chapel built c 1100. Nearby are the foundations of a monastery founded by St Blane in the 6th century.

831 ST BRIDE'S CHURCH 5B7

Douglas, 12m SSW of Lanark. Opening standard. Free. Apply key-keeper. (AM) Tel: 031-226 2570.

The restored chancel of this ancient church contains the tomb of the 'Bell the Cat' Earl of Angus (died 1514). The nearby tower (1618) has a clock of 1565 said to have been gifted by Mary, Queen of Scots.

832 ST BRIDGET'S CHURCH 6D5

Dalgety Bay, off A92, 3m E of N approach to Forth Road Bridge. All reasonable times. Free. Tel: 031-226 2570.

Ruins of an ancient church dedicated to St Bridget in 1244.

833 ST CLEMENT'S CHURCH 2B7

At Rodel, S end of Harris, Western Isles. All reasonable times. Free; apply key-keeper. (AM) Tel: 031-226 2570.

A cruciform church of c 1500 with rich decoration and sculptured slabs.

834 ST COLUMBA'S CAVE 4E5

1m N of Ellary on W shore of Loch Killisport (Caolisport), 10m SW of Ardrishaig. All times. Free.

Traditionally associated with St Columba's arrival in Scotland, the cave contains a rock-shelf with an altar, above which are carved crosses. A large basin, perhaps a Stone Age mortar, may have been used as a font. The cave was occupied from the Middle Stone Age. In front are traces of houses and the ruins of a chapel (possibly 13th century) and another cave is nearby.

835 ST CORMAC'S CHAPEL 4D5

Isle of Eilean Mor, E of Jura. All reasonable times. Free. (AM) Access: private launch to Eilean Mor (tel: Ormsary 239 evenings, Mr Rodgers). Tel: 031-226 2570.

This medieval chapel is 15 feet by 8 feet with an upper chamber only accessible by ladder. It contains a sculpture of a priest.

836 ST DUTHUS CHAPEL AND COLLEGIATE CHURCH 3B7

Tain. Chapel: All reasonable times. Free. Church: Open daily, enquire locally. Free.

The chapel was built between 1065 and 1256. St Duthus died in 1065 and was buried in Ireland, but 200 years later his remains were transferred to Tain. The chapel was destroyed by fire in 1427. St Duthus Church was built c 1360 by William, Earl and Bishop of Ross, in Decorated style, and became a notable place of pilgrimage. Folk museum and Clan Ross Centre in grounds.

837 ST FILLAN'S CAVE 6G4

Cove Wynd, Pittenweem, near harbour, 9m SSE of St Andrews. All year, 1000-1300, 1430-1730. Adult: 25p, child: free, group rates. (St John's Episcopal Church) Tel: (0333) 311495.

St Fillan's Cave gave Pittenweem (Pictish for *The Place of The Cave*) its name. In the 12th century, Augustinian monks from the Isle of May established the Priory, the Great House and the Prior's Lodging above the cave, cutting through the rock from the garden to the holy cave-shrine below. Restored and rededicated in 1935.

838 ST JOHN'S KIRK 6D2

♿ *St John Street, Perth. Tel: Perth (0738) 26159.*

A fine cruciform church largely dating from the 15th century, and restored 1923-28 as a war memorial. Here John Knox in 1559 preached his momentous sermon urging the 'purging of the churches from idolatry'. Wheelchair access via south door.

839 ST KILDA Map 2 Inset

♿ *110m W of Scottish mainland. Access difficult: NTS organises expeditions. (NTS leased to NCC) Tel: 031-226 5922.*

This remote and spectacular group of islands was evacuated in 1930. The cliffs at Conachair, 1397 feet, are the highest in Britain. The wildlife, some of which (eg Soay sheep, St Kilda mouse and wren) are unique, includes the world's biggest gannetry and myriads of fulmars and puffins. Remains of the primitive dwellings; working parties to maintain these visit in summer.

St Magnus Cathedral

840 ST MAGNUS CATHEDRAL 1B11

Kirkwall, Orkney. Mon-Sat 0900-1300, 1400-1700. Closed Sun (except for services). Free.

Founded by Jarl Rognvald in 1137 and dedicated to his uncle St Magnus. The remains of both men are in the massive central piers. The original building dates from 1137 to 1200 but additional work went on for a further 300 years. It is still in regular use as a Church, and contains some of the finest examples of Norman architecture in Scotland, with small additions in transitional styles and very early Gothic.

841 ST MAGNUS CHURCH 1B10

Isle of Egilsay, Orkney. All times. Free. (AM) Tel: 031-226 2570.

An impressive church, probably 12th-century, with a remarkable round tower of the Irish type, which still stands to a height of nearly 50 feet.

842 ST MARY'S CHAPEL, BUTE   4F5

A845, ½m S of Rothesay. Opening standard. Free. (AM)
Tel: 031-226 2570.

The remains of the late medieval Church of St Mary,
including two fine recessed and canopied tombs
containing effigies of a knight in full armour, and a
lady and child.

843 ST MARY'S CHAPEL, CROSSKIRK   3C2

Off A836, 6½m WNW of Thurso. All reasonable times. Free. (AM)
Tel: 031-226 2570.

A rudely-constructed chapel with very low doors
narrowing at the top in Irish style. Probably 12th
century.

St Mary's Chapel, Wyre: see No 208.

844 ST MARY'S CHURCH, AUCHINDOIR   3E9

Off A97, 11m SSW of Huntly. All reasonable times. Free. (AM)
Tel: 031-226 2570.

Ruins of one of the finest medieval parish churches
remaining in Scotland.

845 ST MARY'S CHURCH, GRANDTULLY   5B1

At Pitcairn Farm, 3m ENE of Aberfeldy, off A827. All times. Free.
(AM) Tel: 031-226 2570.

A 16th-century church, with a remarkable 17th-century
painted wooden ceiling of heraldic and symbolic subjects.

846 ST MARY'S COLLEGIATE CHURCH   6G6

  T *Sidegate, Haddington. 1 Apr-30 Sep, Mon-Sat 1000-1600, Sun*
1300-1600. Donations gratefully accepted. (Kirk Session of St Mary's).
Tel: Haddington (062 082) 5111.

14th-century medieval church. Choir and transepts
ruined for 400 years at seige of Haddington. Now
completely restorerd. John Knox heard Scots
Reformer, Wishart, preach his last sermon here before
going to the stake in St Andrews. Teas, bookshop,
guided tours. Toilets.

847 ST MARY'S LOCH   5D7

  Off A708, 14m ESE of Selkirk.

Beautifully set among smooth green hills, this three-
mile-long loch is now also used for sailing. On the
neck of land separating it from Loch of the Lowes at
the south end stands Tibbie Shiel's Inn, long kept by
Tibbie Shiel (Elizabeth Richardson, 1783-1878) from
1823, and a meeting-place for many 19th-century
literati. Beside the road towards the north end of the
loch is a seated statue of James Hogg, the 'Ettrick
Shepherd', author of the *Confessions of a Justified Sinner*
and a friend of Scott, who farmed in this district.
Tearoom and two hotels nearby.

848 ST MARY'S PLEASANCE   6G6

  Sidegate, Haddington. Open at all reasonable times. Free, but donations
welcome. (Haddington Garden Trust) Tel: Haddington (062 082) 3738
(Mon-Fri incl, 1000-1300 and 1400-1700).

These gardens of Haddington House have been
restored as a 17th-century garden, with rose and herb,
meadow, cottage and sunken gardens. The Pleached
Alley leads to St Mary's Gate and the restored
medieval church of St Mary's.

849 ST MICHAEL'S PARISH CHURCH 6C6

&♿ *Beside Linlithgow Palace, on S shore of the loch, Linlithgow. Oct-May, Mon-Fri 1000-1200, 1400-1600. Jun-Sep, daily 1000-1200, 1400-1600, and by arrangement. Free. Tel: Linlithgow (5) 842195.*

One of the finest examples of a medieval parish church in Scotland. Contemporary 'golden' crown by Geoffrey Clarke replaced the medieval crown which collapsed in 1820.

Church of St Monan

850 ST MONAN'S CHURCH 6G4

&♿
P
A
In St Monans, A917, 12m S of St Andrews. All reasonable times. Free. Tel: St Monans (033 37) 258.

Possibly a Ninianic foundation, c 400 AD. A place of healing from early times. David I was reputedly cured of an arrow wound here. It became a Royal Votive Chapel perhaps at that time. Alexander III initiated new building work c 1265. David II repaired and remodelled the Choir area in 1362 as a thanksgiving for deliverance from a storm at sea. James III gifted it to the Dominicans c 1460 and it became the Parish Church in 1646.

851 ST NINIAN'S CHAPEL, ISLE OF WHITHORN 4H11

At Isle of Whithorn, 3m SE of Whithorn. All times. Free. (AM) Tel: 031-226 2570.

Ruins of a 13th-century chapel on a site traditionally associated with St Ninian. On the shore by Kidsdale, 2m W, is St Ninian's Cave, with early Christian crosses carved on the rock.

852 ST NINIAN'S CHAPEL, TYNET 3E8

Tynet, 3m E of Fochabers on A98. All year, dawn-dusk. Free.

Built about 1755 by the Laird of Tynet, ostensibly for his own use as a sheepcote but in reality as a Mass centre for the Catholics of the neighbourhood. It has undergone many extensions and alterations since, the latest being in the 1950s under the direction of Ian G Lindsay, RSA. St Ninian's has the distinction of being the oldest post-Reformation Catholic church still in use, albeit from May to October only. Mass 1800 Sat, all year.

853 ST NINIAN'S ISLE 1G5

By B9102 off W coast of Mainland, Shetland. All times. Free.

Holy Well, foundations of chapel c 12th century and pre-Norse church where a hoard of Celtic silver was discovered (now in the Royal Museum of Scotland, Queen Street, Edinburgh). (See No 360).

854 ST PETER'S CHURCH   **3C3**

Near the Harbour at Thurso. All reasonable times. Free.

Ruins situated in the attractively restored old part of Thurso. Of medieval or earlier origin; much of the present church dates from the 17th century.

---

855 ST VIGEAN'S MUSEUM   **5E1**

Off A92, 1½m N of Arbroath. (AM) Tel: 031-226 2570.

A cottage museum containing Pictish gravestones which are among the most important groups of early Christian sculpture in Scotland. Attractive St Vigean's Church nearby.

---

856 SADDELL ABBEY   **4E7**

B842, 9m NNW of Campbeltown. All reasonable times. Free.

The abbey was built in the 12th century by Somerled, Lord of the Isles, or his son Reginald. Only the walls of the original building are left, with sculptured carved tombstones.

---

857 SANQUHAR MUSEUM   **5A8**

N end of High Street, Sanquhar. By arrangement, 42 High Street, tel: Sanquhar 303 (Mr T A Johnston). Free. (Nithsdale District Council) Tel: Dumfries (0387) 53374.

Items of local interest, displayed in one room of the old Tolbooth, a building designed by William Adam, dated 1735 and featuring a clock tower.

---

858 SANQUHAR POST OFFICE   **5A8**

Main Street, Sanquhar. Tel: Sanquhar (065 92) 201.

Britain's oldest post office, functioning in 1763, 20 years before the introduction of the mail coach service, and still in use today.

Scalloway Castle

859 SCALLOWAY CASTLE   **5G5**

6m W of Lerwick, Shetland. Opening standard. Free. (AM) Tel: 031-226 2570.

Built in 1600 by Earl Patrick Stewart, in medieval style. When the Earl, a notoriously cruel character, was executed in 1615, the castle fell into disuse.

---

860 SCAPA FLOW   **1B12**

Sea area, enclosed by the mainland of Orkney and the islands of Burray, South Ronaldsay, Flotta and Hoy.

It was a major naval anchorage in both wars and the scene of the surrender of the German Fleet in 1918. Today Scapa Flow is again a centre of marine activity as Flotta has been developed as a pipeline landfall and tanker terminal for North Sea Oil. Scapa Flow is considered one of the best dive sites in Europe. (See also Nos 763 and 916).

861 SCONE PALACE   6C1

& *Off A93 (Braemar Road), 2m NE of Perth. Easter-Oct, Mon-Sat*
A *1000-1730; Sun 1400-1730 (Jul & Aug 1100-1730), other times by*
P *arrangement. (House, grounds and pinetum) Adult: £2.20, child: £1.80.*
T *Group rates: £1.90. (Earl of Mansfield). Tel: Perth (0738) 52300.*

The present castellated palace, enlarged and
embellished in 1803, incorporates the 16th-century and
earlier palaces. It has notable grounds and a pinetum
and is still a family home. The Moot Hill at Scone,
known in the 8th century and earlier, was the site of
the famous coronation Stone of Scone, brought there
in the 9th century by Kenneth MacAlpine, King of
Scots. In 1296 the Stone was seized by the English and
taken to Westminster Abbey. The ancient Abbey of
Scone was destroyed by followers of John Knox.
Magnificent collection of porcelain, furniture, ivories,
18th-century clocks and 16th-century needlework. Full
catering facilities. Coffee shop, restaurant, produce and
gift shop, gardens, playground, banqueting, pinetum.
Parties of disabled visitors welcome.

862 SCOT II CRUISES   3B8

Departure point: top of Muirton Locks, Inverness. Signposted with thistle.
Afternoon Cruise: 1415 (21 Apr-26 Sep), Mon-Sat. Morning Cruise:
1015 (28 Apr-6 Sep), Mon-Sat. Evening Cruise: 1900 (2 June-8 Aug),
Mon-Fri. Adult: £5.00 and £3.00, OAP/child: £2.50 and £1.50.
Group rates available on request. (British Waterways Board).
Tel: Inverness (0463) 233140.

Scot II was built in 1932 originally as a Canal Tug. She
now cruises on the Caledonian Canal and Loch Ness,
offering an interest-packed voyage past Tomnahurich
Hill through swing bridges and locks, past a
lighthouse and out on to the beautiful Loch Ness to
historic Urquhart Castle. (See also No 969). Licensed
bar, snack bar, toilets.

863 SCOTLAND'S SAFARI PARK   6A4

& *At Blair Drummond on A84 between Stirling and Doune (exit 10 off*
T *M9). 20 Mar-6 Oct (approx), daily from 1000. Admission charge for car*
and occupants; alternatively, safari bus available for visitors without own
transport. Admission charge includes attractions inside. Last admission
1630 except Cinema (180). Group rates. For details of times and charges
Tel: Doune (0786) 841456 or 841396.

The collection includes lions, zebras, camels, a monkey
jungle, giraffes, tigers, antelopes, bison, Ankole cattle
and Pere David deer. There is a Pets Corner, aquatic
mammal shows, Boat Safari round chimp island and an
adventure playground. Self-service restaurant and bar,
ice cream kiosks. Drive through wild animal reserves.
Cinema (180). Giant astraglide, amusements, picnic
and barbecue areas, shops. Kennels for dogs and special
arrangements for groups of disabled visitors.

864 SCOTS DYKE   5D9

& *Off A7, 7m S of Langholm. All reasonable times. Free.*
Tel: Gretna (04613) 7834.

The remains of a wall made of clods of earth and
stones, which marked part of the border between
England and Scotland.

865 SCOTSTARVIT TOWER   6F3

Off A916, 3m S of Cupar. Opening standard. Free. (AM)
Tel: 031-226 2570.

A fine tower known to have been in existence in 1579.

**866 CAPTAIN SCOTT AND DR WILSON
CAIRN** 3E12

In Glen Prosen on unclassified road NW of Dykehead. All times. Free.

The cairn was erected in memory of the Antarctic
explorers, Captain Scott and Dr Wilson, who reached
the South Pole in 1912.

**867 SCOTTISH CRAFTS AND BEN NEVIS
EXHIBITION** 2G12

*Fort William. Easter-June 0900-1730; Jul & Aug 0900-2200;
Sep-Nov 0900-1730. Adult: 10p, child: free when accompanied by an
adult. Tel: Fort William (0397) 4406.*

A visual exhibition and large-scale model of Ben
Nevis, presented to explain all about Britain's highest
mountain. (See also No 91).

Scottish Fisheries Museum

868 SCOTTISH FISHERIES MUSEUM 6H3

*At Anstruther harbour, 10m SSE of St Andrews. All year, daily
Apr-Oct, 1000-1750, Sun 1400-1700; Nov-Mar, daily except Tue,
1400-1700. Adult: 85p, OAP/Child/UB40s: 35p. Group rates:
Adult: 35p, OAP/child: 20p. Tel: Anstruther (0333) 310625.*

16th to 19th-century buildings housing marine
aquarium, fishing and ships' gear, model and actual
fishing boats (including 'Fifie' and 'Zulu' in harbour),
fisher-home interiors, reference library, tearoom.

869 THE SCOTTISH HORSE MUSEUM 5B1

*The Cross, Dunkeld. Easter to mid Oct, daily 1030-1230, 1400-1700.
Adult: 30p. (Scottish Horse Trust). Tel: Dunkeld (035 02) 296.*

Exhibits, uniforms, photographs, maps and rolls of all
those who served in this Yeomanry Regiment.

**870 SCOTTISH MINING MUSEUM
PRESTONGRANGE SITE** 6F6

&
A
P
*At Morrisons' Haven, on B1348, 8m E of Edinburgh.
All year, Mon-Fri 1000-1630, Sat & Sun 1200-1700. Free.
(Scottish Mining Museum Trust). Tel: 031-665 9904.*

A former colliery site with 800 years of mining
history. Visitor Centre provides audio-visual
programme plus walk-through exhibition and displays
concerning mining and related industries at site.
Cornish Beam Pumping Engine House and
Exhibition Hall containing mining artefacts. Self-drive
Coal Heritage Trail to Lady Victoria Colliery. Also on
view are three steam locomotives, a steam navvy, a
colliery winding engine and remains of a Hoffman
Kiln. Special 'Steam Days' on first Sunday each month
Apr-Oct. Organised parties must book. Refreshments,
free car parking, picnic area, free leaflets.

871   SCOTTISH MUSEUM OF WOOLLEN TEXTILES   5D6

&   *On main road (A72) at Walkerburn, 9m ESE of Peebles. All year, Mon- Fri 1000-1700. Easter-end Sep, Sat 1100-1600, Sun 1200-1600. Adult: 25p, child: 15p, family ticket: 50p. (Clan Royal of Scotland) Tel: Walkerburn (089 687) 281 or 283 (0900-1500).*

This display features the growth of the Scottish textile trade, with many interesting exhibits. Group bookings by arrangement. Coffee and tea shop.

872   SCOTTISH RAILWAY PRESERVATION SOCIETY (FALKIRK)   6B6

&   *Wallace Street off Grahams Road. Falkirk. All year, Sat and Sun 1100-1700. Free. Tel: Falkirk (0324) 20790.*

Workshop for the restoration of locomotives and railway vehicles. There is a comprehensive collection, some of which are used on excursions.

Scottish Tartans Museum: see No 730.

873   SCOTTISH WHITE HEATHER FARM AND GARDENS   4F5

At Toward, 5m SW of Dunoon. All year, Mon-Sat 0900-1800, Sun by appointment. Free. Tel: Toward (036 987) 237 any time.

White heather sprays and plants. Also available: Alpines and rock plants, azaleas, conifers and rhododendrons. Visitors are invited to view the gardens.

874   SCOTT'S VIEW   5E6

B6356, 7m ESE of Galashiels.

A view over the Tweed to the Eildon Hills, beloved by Scott; here the horses taking his remains to Dryburgh for burial stopped as they had so often before for Sir Walter to enjoy this panorama.

875   DUNS SCOTUS STATUE   5F5

At Duns, in public park. All times. Free.

Duns was the birthplace of John Duns Scotus (1266-1308), a Franciscan who became a leading divine and one of the greatest medieval philosophers. It is said the word 'dunce' came into the English language as a result of criticism of his work after his death. (See No 956).

876   SEA LIFE CENTRE   4E2

&
A
T   *Barcaldine, on A828, 11m N of Oban. 1 Apr-31 Oct, daily. Adult: £1.60, OAP: £1.20, child: 90p. Group rates: parties of 10 or over 20p off adult rate, 30p off OAP rate and 10p off child rate. Tel: (063 172) 386.*

Britain's largest display of native marine life. Over 100 species including conger eels, octopus and seals. Both the aquarium and restaurant have a beautiful lochside setting.

877   SELKIRK GLASS   5E7

&
T   *Linglie Mill, Selkirk. All year, Mon-Thu 0900-1200, 1330-1700, Fri 0900-1200. Free. Tel: Selkirk (0750) 20954.*

Visitors are welcome at factory and showroom to see a range of paperweights and watch craftsmen at work. Coffee shop now open.

878   SETON COLLEGIATE CHURCH   6F6

Off A198, 13m E of Edinburgh. Opening standard, closed Tue. Adult:
50p, OAP/child: 25p. (AM) Group rates: 10% discount for parties of
11 or more persons. Tel: 031-226 2570.

An important ecclesiastical monument of the late 15th
century, with a fine vaulted chancel and apse.

---

879   SHAMBELLIE HOUSE MUSEUM OF
COSTUME   5B10

New Abbey, 6m S of Dumfries on A710. May-Sep, Thu-Sat, Mon
1000-1730, Sun 1200-1730. Free. Tel: New Abbey (038 785) 375.

A mid-Victorian small country house designed by
David Bryce housing the collection of European
fashionable dress made by Charles Stewart. Each year
there is a new display of material from the collection.

---

880   SHAWBOST FOLK MUSEUM   2C4

A858, 19m NW of Stornoway, Isle of Lewis. Apr-Nov, Mon-Sat,
1000-1800. Donation box. Tel: Stornoway (0851) 71 213.

Created under the Highland Village Competition
1970, the museum illustrates the old way of life in
Lewis. A Norse watermill has been restored; directions
at the museum.

---

881   SHETLAND CROFT HOUSE MUSEUM   1G6

Voe, Dunrossness, on unclassified road E of A970, 25m S of Lerwick.
1 May-30 Sep, Tue-Sun 1000-1300, 1400-1700. Adult: 50p, child: 20p.
(Shetland Museum). Tel: Lerwick (0595) 5057.

Typical mid-19th century thatched Shetland croft
house, complete with all outbuildings and working
water mill. Furnished in period style, c 1860.
Attendant in charge at all times.

---

882   SHETLAND MUSEUM   1G4

P

Lower Hillhead, Lerwick. All year, Mon, Wed & Fri 1000-1300,
1430-1700, 1800-2000. Tue & Sat 1030-1300, 1430-1700. Thu
1000-1300. Free. (Shetland Islands Council). Tel: Lerwick (0595) 5057.

The collection in this museum is entirely local in
character but international in interest. The theme is
the history of man in Shetland from pre-history to the
present day. Four continuous galleries are devoted to
archaeology, natural history, art and textiles, folk life
and shipping.

---

883   SIGNAL TOWER   5E1

Ladyloan, Arbroath. All year, Nov-Mar, Mon-Fri 1400-1700,
Sat 1030-1300 and 1400-1700; Apr-Oct, Mon-Sat 1030-1300 and
1400-1700; Jul-Aug, Sun 1400-1700. Free. Pre-booking for groups
essential. (Angus District Council).
Tel: Arbroath (0241) 75598 or Montrose (0674) 73232.

The museum collection relates to the history of
Arbroath, including fishing, the sea, flax industry,
Shanks lawnmowers, the Bell Rock lighthouse (for
which Signal Tower was once the shore base) and folk
life.

---

884   SS 'SIR WALTER SCOTT'   4H3

A

From Trossachs Pier, E end of Loch Katrine, 9m W of Callander.
Early May-late Sep, Mon-Fri 1045, 1345 and 1515, Sat 1400, Sun 1400
and 1530. Mid May-end Sep. Adult: £1.75 (am), £1.50 (pm), OAP/child:
£1.00 (am), 80p (pm). Charter of boat: £275. (Strathclyde Regional
Council Water Dept). Tel: 041-336 5333.

Regular sailings in summer from the pier to
Stronachlachar in this fine old steamer. Views include
Ben Lomond. Cafeteria, shop, Visitor Centre.

885 SIR WALTER SCOTT'S COURTROOM 5E7

Market Place, Selkirk. By application to: Ettrick and Lauderdale District Council, Paton Street, Galashiels. Jul-Aug, Mon-Fri 1400-1600, other times by appointment. Free. Tel: Selkirk (0750) 20096.

The bench and chair from which Sir Walter Scott, as Sheriff of Selkirk, administered justice for 30 years, are on display, with portraits of Scott, James Hogg, Mungo Park and Robert Burns, with ancient charters. Also displayed are paintings by Tom Scott.

Skara Brae

886 SKARA BRAE 1A11

7½m N of Stromness, Mainland, Orkney. Opening standard. Adult: £1.00, OAP/child: 50p. Group rates: 10% discount for parties of 11 or more persons. (AM) Tel: 031-226 2570.

A Neolithic village occupied from about 3000 BC to perhaps 2700 BC. The main period of settlement included eight or so houses joined by covered passages. Stone beds, fire places, cupboards and dressers survive. The inhabitants were farmers and herds who burned their dead in tombs like Quoyness (see No 800). The amazing preservation of the village is due to its inundation by sand which buried it for 4500 years until it was revealed by a storm in 1850.

887 SKELMORLIE AISLE 4G6

Bellman's Close, off main street, Largs. Opening standard, key-keeper in winter. Adult: 50p, OAP/child: 25p. Group rates: 10% discount for parties of 11 or more persons. (AM) Tel: 031-226 2570.

A splendid mausoleum of 1636, with painted roof, interesting tombs and monuments.

888 SKIPNESS CASTLE AND CHAPEL 4E6

Skipness, B8001, 10m S of Tarbert, Loch Fyne. Closed to the public but may be viewed from outside. (AM) Tel: 031-226 2570.

The remains of the ancient chapel and the large 13th-century castle overlook the bay.

889 SLAINS CASTLE 3H9

Off A975, 7m SSW of Peterhead. All reasonable times. Free.

Extensive ruins of a castle of 1664 to replace an earlier Slains Castle, 4 miles south; extended and rebuilt by the 9th Earl of Errol. Dr Johnson and James Boswell visited here in 1773. (Children should be accompanied by an adult.)

890 SMAILHOLM TOWER 5E7

Off B6404, 6m NW of Kelso. Opening standard, key-keeper in winter. Adult: 50p, OAP/child: 25p; group rates. (AM) Tel: 031-226 2570.

An outstanding example of a 16th-century Border peel tower built to give surveillance over a wide expanse of country. It is 57 feet high, in a good state of preservation and houses an exhibition of dolls and tapestries on the theme of Sir Walter Scott's 'Minstrelsy of the Scottish Border'. At nearby Sandyknowe Farm, Scott spent some childhood years.

891 SMITH ART GALLERY AND MUSEUM   6A5

♿
A
T

40 Albert Place, Stirling, ¼ m W of centre. All year. Wed, Thu, Fri, Sun 1400-1700, Sat 1030-1700. Free. Tel: Stirling (0786) 71917.

Room within a Victorian building with permanent display of Stirling's past and programme of temporary exhibitions. Sited below the Castle and 5 minutes' walk from the main shopping area, the Smith houses a display on the story of Stirling and features exhibitions and arts events. Well stocked shop. Set in its own grounds.

892 ADAM SMITH THEATRE   6E5

♿
T

Bennochy Road, Kirkcaldy. Tel: Kirkcaldy (0592) 260498.

Theatre with performances all year, named after Adam Smith, the economist who was born in Kirkcaldy in 1723.

893 THE SMOKEHOUSE   2G6

Achiltibuie. All year. Mon-Fri 0900-1730; Easter-Oct, Mon-Sat 0900-1730. (Keith Dunbar). Tel: Achiltibuie (085 482) 353.

A purpose-built specialist Smokehouse, close to the sea. A viewing gallery allows the visitor to see some of the aspects of curing and smoking of salmon, fish, meat and game.

894 SMOLLETT MONUMENT   4H5

On A82 N of Dumbarton at Renton. All times. Free.

A monument to Tobias Smollett (1721-1771), novelist and surgeon. Dr Johnson wrote the Latin epitaph to him in 1773.

Smoo Cave

895 SMOO CAVE   2H3

A838, 1½ m E of Durness. All reasonable times. Free.

Three vast caves at the end of a deep cleft in the limestone cliffs. The entrance to the first resembles a Gothic arch. The second cavern, access difficult, has a waterfall. The third is inaccessible.

896 SOUTER JOHNNIE'S COTTAGE   4G8

♿

At Kirkoswald, on A77, 4m W of Maybole. 28 Mar-30 Sep, daily 1200-1700, or by arrangement. Adult: 60p, child: 30p. (NTS) Tel: Kirkoswald (065 56) 603.

This thatched cottage was the home of the village cobbler (Souter) John Davidson at the end of the 18th century. Davidson and his friend Douglas Graham of Shanter Farm, known to Robert Burns in his youth in Kirkoswald, were later immortalised in Tam o' Shanter. The cottage contains Burnsiana and contemporary tools of the cobbler's craft.

897 SOUTH QUEENSFERRY MUSEUM 6D6

Old Burgh Chambers, High Street. May-Sep inclusive, certain afternoons by application to Burgh Chambers. Free.
Tel: 031-225 2424, ext 6689 (Huntly House Museum).

Displays relating to the former Royal Burgh of Queensferry, local crafts and industries, the Burry Man, the Queensferry Passage and the two great bridges across the Forth.

Staffa: see No 422.

898 STANEYDALE TEMPLE 1F4

3½m ENE of Walls, Shetland. All reasonable times. Free. (AM)
Tel: 031-226 2570.

A Neolithic or early Bronze Age hall, heel shaped and originally timber roofed.

899 STEINACLEIT CAIRN AND STONE CIRCLE 2D4

S end of Loch an Duin, Shader, 12m N of Stornoway, Lewis. All times. Free. (AM) Tel: 031-226 2570.

The fragmentary remains of a substantial house found beneath the peat; of unknown prehistoric date.

900 STENNESS STANDING STONES 1B11

Between Loch of Harray and Loch of Stenness, 5m NE of Stromness. Mainland, Orkney. All times. Free. (AM) Tel: 031-226 2570.

Four large upright stones are the dramatic remains of a stone circle, c 3000 BC, encircled by a ditch and bank. The area around Stenness is particularly rich in such remains. (See also Ring of Brodgar, No 812).

901 STEVENSON HOUSE 6G6

Near Haddington, East Lothian. House and Garden: 3 Jul-31 Jul: Thu, Sat & Sun; other times by arrangement. Groups welcome. Adult: £1.50, OAP: 75p, child (under 12): 50p. (Mrs J C H Dunlop). Tel: Haddington (062 082) 3376.

Although the mansion house dates from the 13th century, the present house dates mainly from the 16th century. It was altered both structurally and in decoration during the 18th century. The guided tour includes details of the history, furniture, pictures and china. Well landscaped gardens (both House Garden and Walled Kitchen Garden).

902 STEWARTRY MUSEUM 5A11

St Mary Street, Kirkcudbright. Easter-Oct, Mon-Sat 1100-1300, 1400-1600: Jul-Aug, 1100-1700. Adult: 50p, child: 25p (Stewartry Museum Association). Tel: Kirkcudbright (0577) 30797.

A museum depicting the life of the area with prehistoric articles, relics of domestic life and crafts of earlier days. Works of local artists are featured, especially Jessie M King (1875-1949). John Paul Jones, a founder of the American Navy who was born in the Stewartry and had varied associations with Kirkcudbright, is also the subject of a special display.

903 STIRLING BRIDGE 6A5

By A9 off Stirling town centre. All times. Free.

The Old Bridge built c 1400, was for centuries of great strategic importance as the 'gateway to the north' and the lowest bridging point of the River Forth.

904   STIRLING CASTLE   6A5

In central Stirling. Apr-Sep, Mon-Fri 0930-1715, Sun 1030-1645;
Oct-Mar, Mon-Sat 0930-1620, Sun 1230-1535. Adult: £1.20,
OAP/child: 60p. Group rates: 10% discount for parties of 11 or more
persons. (AM) Tel: 031-226 2570.

Stirling Castle on its 250-feet great rock has
dominated much of Scotland's vivid history. Wallace
recaptured it from the English in 1297; Edward I
retook it in 1304, until Bruce won at nearby
Bannockburn in 1314. Later it was a favourite Royal
residence: James II was born here in 1430 and Mary,
Queen of Scots and James VI both spent some years
here. Long used as a barracks, and frequently rebuilt,
the old towers built by James IV remain, as do the fine
16th-century hall, the splendid Renaissance palace of
James V, the Chapel Royal of 1594 and other
buildings. On castle hill there is a visitor centre (same
hours as castle; adult: 50p, child: 25p; NTS) which has
an audio-visual display as an introduction to the castle.

905   STONEHAVEN TOLBOOTH MUSEUM   3G11

At quay at Stonehaven. Jun-Sep, daily (except Tue) 1400-1700,
Mon, Thu, Fri and Sat 1000-1200. Free. (North-East of Scotland
Museums Service). Tel: Peterhead (0779) 77738.

This 16th-century former storehouse of the Earls
Marischal was later used as a prison. In 1748-49
Episcopal ministers lodged inside and baptised children
through the windows. The museum displays local
history, archaeology and particularly fishing.

906   STORR   2D8

2m walk from A855, 8m N of Portree, Isle of Skye.

A series of pinnacles and crags whose 2,360-feet
summit (3-4 hours) gives fine views of the Outer
Hebrides and Ross-shire mountains. The Old Man of
Storr, at the east end of the mountain, is a black
obelisk, 160 feet high, first climbed in 1955. Disabled
visitors can see Storr from the main road.

907   STRATHALLAN AERO PARK   6B3

Take B8062 from Auchterarder (Crieff road) or A822 from Muthill, then
follow airfield signs. 1 Apr-31 Oct, daily 1000-1800 (last admission
1730). Adult: £2.00, OAP/child: £1.50. Group rates for parties over 10
on request. (Strathallan Aero Park Ltd). Tel: Auchterarder (076 46) 2545

A collection of historic aircraft, predominantly World
War II era, dating back to 1930. There are flying
displays in summer. Licensed restaurant, cafeteria,
picnic area and children's play area, video cinema.

908   STRATHAVEN CASTLE   5A6

Kirk Street/Stonehouse Road, Strathaven, 14m W of Lanark.
All reasonable times. Free.

Also known as Avondale Castle, this ruin dates from
the 15th century.

909 STRATHCLYDE COUNTRY PARK 5A6

On both sides of M74 between Hamilton and Bothwell interchanges (A723 and A725). All year. Free (charges for facilities). Group rates on request. Tel: Motherwell (0698) 66155.

A countryside park with man-made loch, nature reserve (permit only), sandy beach and a wide variety of sporting facilities. Within the park is Hamilton Mausoleum, created in the 1840's by the 10th Duke of Hamilton, which has a remarkable echo and huge bronze doors. Tours start: summer, daily at 1500, also Sat and Sun at 1900; winter Sat and Sun at 1400 (groups by arrangement, tel: Motherwell (0698) 66155). Adult: 40p, child: 20p (subject to review).

910 STRATHISLA DISTILLERY 3E8

Keith. Mid Jun-end Aug, Mon-Fri 0900-1630. Free. (Chivas Bros Ltd). Tel: Keith (054 22) 7471 (0900-1700).

A typical small old-fashioned distillery, claimed to be the oldest established in Scotland, dating from 1786.

911 STRATHNAVER MUSEUM 3B3

Off A836, at Farr, near Bettyhill. Summer, Mon-Sat, 1400-1700. Donations (J and R McKay)

The former Farr Church (18th-century) now houses this museum of local history. This is historic Clan MacKay country and is associated with the Sutherland Clearances.

912 STRATHPEFFER VISITOR CENTRE AUDIO-VISUAL PROGRAMME 3A8

Apr-Sep. Programme shown every evening except Sat, 2030 and 2115. Adult: 95p, child: 40p, group rate: 80p. Tel: Strathpeffer (099 7) 21618.

Craft shops and audio-visual programme showing Highland wildlife in renovated Victorian railway station (1885). Tourist information and crafts. Alternative wheelchair entrance.

Strathspey Railway

913 STRATHSPEY RAILWAY 3C10

Aviemore (Speyside) to Boat of Garten. Access at Aviemore: cars in Dalfaber Road, pedestrians take underpass from Main Road at Bank of Scotland. Train Services Easter weekend—mid May Sun only. Weekends mid-May to mid-Oct; Jul-Aug, Mon-Thu; Jun, Mon 1200-1700 approx. 1st and 3rd class single and return fares, children half fare, under 5 free. Group rates: approx 10% reduction on standard fares (3rd class only). (Strathspey Railway Co Ltd). Tel: Aviemore (0479 83) 692.

The line is part of the former Highland Railway (Aviemore-Forres section) closed in 1965 and reopened 1978 after restoration work begun in 1972. Passenger steam train service run entirely by volunteers. Station buildings at Aviemore (Speyside) were brought from Dalnaspidal and the footbridge from Longmorn. Timetables available. Museum of small relics and other static rolling stock on display at Boat of Garten.

914 STRATHYRE FOREST INFORMATION CENTRE   **4H3**

   A84 at S end of Strathyre Village. Daily, May-30 Sep, 0900-1900. Free. (FC) Tel: Aberfoyle (087 72) 383.

An attractive display illustrating a working forest and also many forms of recreation and leisure to be enjoyed in Scotland's forests.

---

915 STROME CASTLE   **2F9**

Unclassified road off A896, NW shore of Loch Carron. Free. (NTS)

Scant ruins of an ancient castle, destroyed in 1602 after a long siege.

---

916 STROMNESS MUSEUM   **1A11**

   P   *Stromness, Orkney. All year, Mon-Sat 1100-1230, 1330-1700 (Thur 1100-1300 only); Jul-Aug 1030-1230, 1330-1700. Adult: 20p, child: 5p; group rates. (Orkney Natural History Society). Tel: Stromness (0856) 850025.*

A fine collection of preserved birds, eggs and Orkney shells. The maritime collection includes a selection of ship models and a permanent feature on the First World War German Fleet scuttled on Scapa Flow.

---

917 STRONE GARDENS   **4G3**

A815, 12m E of Inveraray. Apr-Oct, daily 0900-2100. Adult: £1, child: free. Group rates by arrangement. Tel: Cairndow (049 96) 284.

Rhododendrons, azaleas, daffodils and exotic shrubs. The Pinetum contains the tallest tree in Britain.

---

918 JOHN McDOUALL STUART MUSEUM   **6E4**

   Rectory Lane, Dysart, 2m N of Kirkcaldy. 1 Jun-31 Aug, daily 1400-1700. Free. (Kirkcaldy District Council). Tel: Kirkcaldy (0572) 260732.

A 17th-century building restored by the NTS as part of their 'little houses' scheme. Birthplace of the explorer John McDouall Stuart (1815-1866) who crossed Australia's desert heart in 1861. Permanent display relating to the explorer. Nearby are other NTS 'little houses' and the picturesque harbour.

The Study

919 THE STUDY   **6C5**

   In Culross. All year by arrangement: Apr and Oct, Sat & Sun 1400-1600. Adult: 70p, child: 35p. (The Study, Town House and audio-visual). (NTS) Tel: Newmills (0383) 880359.

Built in 1633, the tower contains a turnpike stair and a large room on the first floor houses a museum. Fine views of the Forth. Tearoom. (See also Nos 246, 247 and 952).

920 SUENO'S STONE 3C8

Beside B9011, 1m NE of Forres. All times. Free. (AM)
Tel: 031-226 2570.

One of the most remarkable early sculptured monuments in Scotland, 20 feet high with elaborate carving.

921 SUMMER ISLES 2F6

& *Isle of Tanera Mhor, off Achiltibuie, Ullapool, Wester Ross.*
A *Tel: Achiltibuie (085 482) 261.*
P

An attractive group of islands, the largest of which is Tanera Mhor. Ferries from Achiltibuie. Yacht anchorage available.

922 SUNTRAP 6D6

& *At Gogarburn, between A8 and A71, 6m W of Edinburgh. Garden all*
T *year, daily 0930-dusk. Advice centre all year, Mon-Fri 0930-1630;*
1 Apr-30 Sep, Sat and Sun 1430-1700. Adult: 50p, accompanied children
free. NTS members free. Tel: 031-339 7283.

A gardening advice centre, of particular interest to owners of small gardens, offering courses of instruction. Outlying department of Oatridge Agricultural College. Special section for disabled gardeners.

Sweetheart Abbey

923 SWEETHEART ABBEY 5B10

At New Abbey, A710, 7½m S of Dumfries. Opening standard.
Adult: 50p, OAP/child: 25p. Group rates: 10% discount for parties of
11 or more persons. (AM) Tel: 031-226 2570.

Founded in 1273 by Devorgilla in memory of her husband, John Balliol (she also founded Balliol College, Oxford), this beautiful ruin has a precinct wall built of enormous boulders. (See also No 755).

924 SYMINGTON CHURCH 4H7

Off A77 at Symington. All reasonable times. Free.

The small restored church has a trio of round-headed Norman windows, dating from the 12th century, and an ancient roof of open timber.

925 TAMDHU DISTILLERY 3D9

Off B9102 8m W of Craigellachie at Knockando. Easter-Sep 1000-1600.
Free. (The Highland Distilleries Co.) Tel: Carron (03406) 221.

Guided tour with large graphic display and views of distilling plant from viewing gallery.

926 THE TAMNAVULIN-GLENLIVET DISTILLERY 3D9

Tomnavoulin, 3½m NNE of Tomintoul on B9008. Daily 1000-1600. Free. Tel: Glenlivet (080 73) 442 (Lt Col R. Maddison).

Opened in May 1984, a visitor centre has been created by converting the old carding mill from which the distillery took its name. It comes from the Gaelic for 'mill on the hill'. The picnic area is well furnished in a level secluded area by the River Livet, close to walks.

927 TAM O'SHANTER MUSEUM 4G7

&
P

High Street, Ayr. Apr-Sep, Mon-Sat 0930-1700 (Jun-Aug, Sun 1430-1600). Oct-Mar, Mon-Sat 1200-1600. Adult: 35p, child: 20p, group rates: 20p. Tel: Ayr (0292) 269794 (0930-1700).

A brewhouse in Burns' time to which Douglas Graham of Shanter supplied malted grain and who was immortalised by Burns as *Tam o'Shanter*. Now a Burns Museum.

928 TANKERNESS HOUSE 1B11

&
T

Broad Street, Kirkwall, Orkney. All year, Mon-Sat 1030-1300, 1400-1700; also May-Sep, Sun 1400-1700. Free. (Orkney Islands Council). Tel: Kirkwall (0856) 3191.

Dating from 1574, this is a fine example of an Orkney merchant-laird's mansion, with courtyard and gardens. Now a museum of life in Orkney through 5,000 years, with additional special exhibitions. A fine garden with lawns, flowerbeds and shrubbery, gravel paths.

Tantallon Castle

929 TANTALLON CASTLE 6H5

A198, 3m E of North Berwick. Opening standard, except Oct-Mar closed Tue and alternate Weds. Adult: £1., OAP/child: 50p. Group rates: 10% discount for parties of 11 or more persons. (AM) Tel: 031-226 2570.

Extensive red ruins of a 14th-century stronghold of the Douglases, in magnificent clifftop setting. Although the castle withstood a regular siege by James V in 1528, it was eventually destroyed by General Monk in 1651.

930 TARVES MEDIEVAL TOMB 3G9

4m NE of Oldmeldrum, in the kirkyard of Tarves. All reasonable times. Free. (AM) Tel: 031-226 2570.

A fine altar-tomb of William Forbes, the laird who enlarged Tolquhon Castle. It shows an interesting mixture of Gothic and Renaissance styles. (see also No 941).

931 TAY BRIDGES 6F1

The present railway bridge carries the main line from
Edinburgh to Aberdeen. Built between 1883 and
1887, it replaces the first Tay Railway Bridge which
was blown down by a storm in 1879 with the loss of a
train and 75 lives after being in use for less than two
years.

The road bridge was opened in 1966, spanning the
River Tay from Dundee to Newport-on-Tay, a distance
of 1½ miles. It is made of box girders resting on 42
concrete piers, and took over three years to build.

932 TEALING EARTH HOUSE AND DOVECOT 6F1

*Off A929, 5m N of Dundee, ½m on unclassified road to Tealing and
Auchterhouse. All reasonable times. Free. (AM) Tel: 031-226 2570.*

A well-preserved example of an Iron Age souterrain or
earth-house comprising a passage and long curved
gallery and small inner chambers. Nearby is a fine
dovecote built in 1595.

933 TELFORD MEMORIAL 5D9

*At Westerkirk, B709, 6m NW of Langholm. All times. Free.
Tel: Langholm (0541) 30976.*

Memorial to Thomas Telford (1757-1834), the
engineer who was born in the valley of the Meggat
Water near Westerkirk. There are several reminders of
him nearby at Langholm.

934 TENTSMUIR POINT NATIONAL RESERVE 6G2

*S and W of Tayport between estuaries of rivers Tay and Eden. A919,
B945 from St Andrews or Tayport. (NCC)*

An area of foreshore (Abertay Sands) and inland area
of dunes, trees and marsh.

935 THIRLESTANE CASTLE 5E6

*Lauder, 28m S of Edinburgh on A68. 11 May-30 Jun, 3-30 Sep, Wed
and Sun; Jul and Aug, daily (not Fri), (grounds) 1200-1800, (castle)
1400-1700. Adult: £2, OAP/child: £1.50, family ticket £5. Group rates:
£1.50 per person for Castle and Museum. Tel: Lauder (05782) 254.*

Fine castle steeped in Scottish history, still the home of
the Maitland family after four centuries. Magnificent
17th-century state rooms. The Border Country Life
Museum is in the grounds. Tearoom, gift shop,
gadens, museum and castle. (See No 103).

Threave Castle

936 THREAVE CASTLE 5A10

N of A75, 3m W of Castle Douglas. Opening standard. Admission free. Ferry charge: adult: 50p, OAP: 25p, child: 25p. (AM) Tel: 031-226 2570.

Early stronghold of the Black Douglases, on an island in the Dee. The four-storeyed tower was built between 1639 and 1690 by Archibald the Grim, Lord of Galloway. In 1455 it was the last Douglas stronghold to surrender to James II.

937 THREAVE GARDENS AND WILDFOWL REFUGE 5A10

&

P

T

S of A75, 1m W of Castle Douglas. Gardens: all year, daily 0900-sunset. Walled garden and glasshouses: all year 0900-1700. Visitor Centre: 28 Mar-31 Oct. Adult £1.20, child: 60p. Group rates: 95p. Wildfowl refuge: access Nov-Mar. Tel: Bridge of Dee (055 668) 242.

The gardens of this Victorian mansion display acres of naturalised daffodils in April and May. There are peat, rock and water gardens and a visitor centre. The garden is of 60 acres and is at its best in June to August with good autumn colour in November. Threave Wildfowl Refuge nearby is a roosting and feeding place for many species of wild geese and ducks on and near the River Dee, access during November to March, to selected points only to avoid disturbance. Tearoom.

938 THURSO FOLK MUSEUM 3C3

&

T

Town Hall, Jun-Sep, Mon-Sat 1000-1300, 1400-1700, 1900-2100. Adult: 20p, OAP: 10p, child: 5p. Tel: Thurso (0847) 62875.

Exhibition of agricultural and domestic life, local trades and crafts with a room of an old Caithness cottage.

939 TINGWALL AGRICULTURAL MUSEUM 1G4

At Veensgarth off A971, 5m NW of Lerwick, Shetland. May-Sep, Tue, Thu, Sat 1000-1300, 1400-1700. Adult: 50p, child: 20p. Bus parties or callers outwith these hours by arrangement, tel: Gott 344. (Mrs J Sandison)

A private collection of tools and equipment used by the Shetland crofter, housed in a mid 18th-century granary, stables, bothy and smithy. Blacksmith's, wheelwright's, cooper's tools and craft shop.

940 TINNIS CASTLE 5C6

Off B712, 9m SW of Peebles. All reasonable times. Free. (Tod Holdings Ltd). Tel: 031-556 4518.

A sheepwalk leads to the ruin of Tinnis, built at the beginning of the 16th century. It was the home of the head of the clan Tweedies.

941 TOLQUHON CASTLE 3G9

Off B999, 7m ENE of Oldmeldrum. Opening standard. Adult: 50p, OAP/child: 25p. Group rates: 10% discount for parties of 11 or more persons. (AM) Tel: 031-226 2570.

Once a seat of the Forbes family, an early 15th-century rectangular tower, with a large quadrangular mansion of 1584-89. Two round towers, a fine carved panel over the door, and the courtyard are features. (See also No 930).

942 TOMATIN DISTILLERY 3B9

On A9 16m S of Inverness at Tomatin. Apr-Oct, Mon-Fri 1500. By arrangement. Free. Groups restricted to 15 persons except by prior arrangement. Tel: Tomatin (080 82) 234.

Demonstration of the process of whisky distilling. Off-sales facility: full range of products at advantageous rates.

943 TOMINTOUL MUSEUM 3D10

The Square, Tomintoul. Apr, May, Oct, Mon-Sat 0900-1730; Jun, Sep, Mon-Sat 0900-1800, Sun 1400-1800; July, Aug, Mon-Sat 0900-1900, Sun 1100-1900. Free. Tel: Forres (0309) 73701.

Displays on local history, folklife, a reconstructed farm kitchen, wildlife, climate, landscape and geology. Tourist Information Centre.

944 TOMNAVERIE STONE CIRCLE 3E10

4m NW of Aboyne. All times. Free. (AM) Tel: 031-226 2570.

The remains of a recumbent stone circle probably 1800-1600 BC. Unexcavated.

945 TONGLAND POWER STATION 5A10

By A711, 2m N of Kirkcudbright. Early May-end August, Mon-Sat 1000-1530, or by appointment. Free. (South of Scotland Electricity Board) Tel: Kirkcudbright (0557) 30114.

Hydro-electric power station and dam. Audio-visual programme.

946 TORHOUSE STONE CIRCLE 4H10

Off B733, 3½m W of Wigtown. All reasonable times. Free. (AM) Tel: 031-226 2570.

A circle of 19 boulders standing on the edge of a low mound. Probably Bronze Age.

947 TOROSAY CASTLE 4D2

A849, 1½m SSE of Craignure, Isle of Mull. Mid Apr-mid Oct, daily 1030-1700. (Castle and Gardens) Adult: £1.50, OAP/students: £1.20, child: 90p. (Gardens) Adult: 80p, OAP/students: 60p, child: 40p (1985 prices). Tel: Craignure (06802) 421.

The gardens and much of the house are open to the public. The Victorian castle is of Scottish Baronial architecture in a magnificent setting; its features include reception rooms and a variety of exhibition rooms. The 11 acres of Italian terraced gardens by Lorimer contain a statue walk and water garden. Served by a 10¼-inch gauge steam railway from Craignure Old Pier. (No 721). Tearoom.

948 TORPHICHEN PRECEPTORY 6C6

B792, 5m SSW of Linlithgow. Opening standard, except closed Fri and alternate Weds. Adult: 50p, OAP/child: 25p. Group rates: 10% discount for parties of 11 or more persons. (AM) Tel: 031-226 2570.

Once the principal Scottish seat of the Knights Hospitallers of St John. An exhibition depicts the history of the Knights in Scotland and overseas.

949 TORRIDON 2F8

Off A896, 9m WSW of Kinlochewe. Deer Museum and audio-visual display, 1 Jun-30 Sep, Mon-Sat 1000-1800, Sun 1400-1800. Deer Museum: Adult: 35p, child: 15p. Audio-visual: Donation box. (NTS) Tel: Torridon (044 587) 221.

Over 14,000 acres of some of Scotland's finest mountain scenery whose peaks rise over 3,000 feet. Of major interest also to geologists: Liathach (3,456 feet) and Beinn Eighe (3,309 feet) are of red sandstone, some 750 million years old and are topped by white quartzite some 600 million years old. The NTS Visitor Centre at the junction of A896 and Diabaig road has audio-visual presentations of wild life. At the Mains nearby is a static display of the life of the red deer. (See also No 87).

950 TORWOODLEE HOUSE 5DG

2m NW of Galashiels off A72. 1 May-30 Sep, by appointment. Admission: £1.50. Group rates: Over 20 persons in party: £1 each. Tel: Galashiels (0896) 2151.

A small Georgian mansion with Victorian alterations, which was built in 1783 by the 9th Laird, James Pringle. The Pringle family has lived at Torwoodlee since 1501 and still does.

951 TOWIE BARCLAY CASTLE 3G8

Off A947, 3m N of Fyvie. By prior arrangement. Tel: Auchterless (088 84) 347.

An ancient stronghold of the Barclays dating from 1136, recently reconstructed and winner of many major European restoration awards. The grounds contain a formal walled garden.

952 TOWN HOUSE, CULROSS 6C5

Sandhaven, Culross, 29, 30 Mar, 1 May-30 Sep, Mon-Thu 0930-1230, 1400-1700 (closed Fri), Sat, Sun 1400-1700, or by arrangement. (Town House, The Study and audio-visual) Adult: 40p, child: 20p. Group rates: 20p. (NTS) Tel: Newmills (0383) 880 359.

Built in 1526, with a double stair on the outside, it has a prison (criminals on the ground floor, witches in the attic) and was a meeting place for the Town Council. (See also Nos 246, 247 and 919). Tearoom.

953 TOWN MILL AND GRANARY, STRATHAVEN 5A6

Strathaven. (Club) Mon-Sat 1930-2300, Sat & Sun 1200-1430.

300-year-old grain mill and granary, originally owned by the Dukes of Hamilton, who vacated nearby Strathaven Castle in the early 1700s. Now attractively converted into an intimate theatre, club and arts centre, with much of the original atmosphere retained. Frequent shows at the theatre and arts centre throughout the year.

954 TRAPRAIN LAW 6H6

Off A1, 5m W of Dunbar. All times. Free.

734 feet high whale-backed hill, with Iron Age fortified site, probably continuing in use as a defended Celtic township until 11th century. A treasure of 4th-century Christian and pagan silver excavated here in 1919 is now in the Royal Museum of Scotland, Queen Street, Edinburgh. (See No 361).

Traquair House

955 TRAQUAIR HOUSE 5D6

B709, off A72, 8m ESE of Peebles. Open daily from Mon before Easter to 3rd Sun in Oct, 1330-1730. Also in Jul, Aug and 1st two weeks in Sep, 1030-1730. Admission charge. Group rates: £1.40 for parties of 20 or over (subject to alteration). (P Maxwell Stuart).
Tel: Innerleithen (0896) 830323.

Dating back to the 10th century, this is said to be the oldest continuously inhabited house in Scotland. Twenty-seven Scottish and English monarchs have visited it, including Mary, Queen of Scots, of whom there are relics. It was once the home of William the Lion who held court here in 1209. The well-known Bear Gates were closed in 1745, not to be reopened until the Stuarts should ascend the throne. Ale is regularly produced at the 18th-century brewhouse, and there are woodland walks and four craft workshops. Exhibitions are held during the summer months and the annual Traquair Fair is held the first weekend in August. Material available on cassette by arrangement. Restaurant/tearoom, gift shop, gallery, brewery, woodland and River Tweed walks and newly planted maze.

956 TRINITY TEMPLE (TEAMPULL NA TRIONAID) 2A8

Off A865, 8m SW of Lochmaddy, Isle of North Uist. All times. Free.

Ruins of a medieval college and monastery said to have been founded by Beathag, daughter of Somerled in the early 13th century, where Duns Scotus studied. (See No 875). Beside it is Teampull Clann A'Phiocair, the chapel of the MacVicars, teachers at the college; several ancient cup and ring marks; and the Field of Blood, site of a clan battle.

957 TUGNET ICE HOUSE 3E7

Spey Bay, 5m W of Buckie. Jun-Sep, daily 1000-1600. Free. (Moray District Council). Tel: Forres (0309) 73701 (Mr Morrison).

Permanent exhibition telling the story of the River Spey, its salmon fishing and wildlife, established in a historic ice house building, possibly the largest in Scotland, dated 1830.

958 TULLIBARDINE CHAPEL 6B3

Off A823, 5m SE of Crieff. All reasonable times. Free. Apply adjacent farmhouse. (AM) Tel: 031-226 2570.

Founded in 1446, this is one of the few rural churches in Scotland which was entirely finished and still remains unaltered.

959 TUMMEL FOREST CENTRE   **5A1**

♿ A P

On B8019, 6m NW of Pitlochry. Easter-end Sep, weekdays 1000-1730, Sun 1000-1730. Free. (FC) Tel: Pitlochry (0796) 3437.

Audio-visual slide show and presentation of various aspects of local history and industries. Forest walks, reconstructed Highland clachan and partly excavated ring fort. (See also No 798).

---

960 TURNBERRY CASTLE   **4G8**

Off A719, 6m N of Girvan. All reasonable times. Free.

The scant remains of the castle where Robert the Bruce was probably born in 1274.

---

961 TWEED BRIDGE   **5F6**

A697 at Coldstream, 9m ENE of Kelso. Tel: St Boswells (0835) 23301.

The 300 feet long bridge was built in 1776 by Smeaton and in the past was a crossing into Scotland for eloping couples taking advantage of Scotland's then-easier marriage laws.

---

962 TWEEDDALE MUSEUM   **5C6**

♿

High Street, Peebles. Mon, Tue, Thu, Fri 0900-1900, Wed 0900-1730. Free. (Tweeddale District Council). Tel: Peebles (0721) 20123.

Housed in the Chambers Institution, which was given to Peebles in 1859 by William Chambers, the publisher. The museum presents regularly changing displays on various themes of Tweeddale's heritage and culture.

---

963 TYNINGHAME HOUSE GARDENS   **6H5**

1m N of A1 between Dunbar and East Linton. 1 Jun-30 Sep, Mon-Fri 1030-1630. (1985 admission prices) Adult: 70p, OAP: 40p, child: 25p. (The Earl of Haddington) Tel: East Linton (0620) 860330.

Colourful herbaceous border, walled garden, terraced gardens and lovely 'secret' garden. Ruins of St Baldred's Church (Norman).

---

964 UI CHURCH   **2D5**

At Aignish, off A866, 2m E of Stornoway, Isle of Lewis. All reasonable times. Free.

Ruined church (pron. 'eye') containing some finely carved ancient tombs of the Macleods of Lewis.

---

965 ULLAPOOL MUSEUM   **2G6**

Quay Street, Ullapool. Apr-Oct, Mon-Sat 0900-1800. Free (donations appreciated). Tel: Ullapool (0854) 2356.

A collection of items of both local and general interest.

---

966 UNION CANAL   **6C6**

Tel: Broxburn (0506) 856624.

The canal was opened in 1822. It originally ran from Lothian Road, Edinburgh to lock sixteen on the Forth and Clyde Canal and was 31½ miles long. The canal runs through some attractive country and excursions by canal boat are available at Ratho and Linlithgow. The canal towing path makes a very pleasant walk and the three aqueducts over the Rivers Avon and Almond and the Water of Leith at Slateford are well worth a visit. (See also Nos 157 and 971).

967 UNION SUSPENSION BRIDGE 5G6

Across River Tweed, 2m S of Paxton on unclassified road.
(Borders Regional Council). Tel: St Boswells (0835) 22301.

This suspension bridge, the first of its type in Britain,
was built by Samuel Brown in 1820 and links England
and Scotland.

968 UNSTAN CHAMBERED TOMB 1B11

3½m NE of Stromness, by A965, Orkney. Opening standard. Free.
(AM) Tel: 031-226 2570.

A cairn containing a chambered tomb (over 6 feet
high) divided by large stone slabs. The type of pottery
discovered in the tomb is now known as Unstan
Ware.

Urquhart Castle

969 URQUHART CASTLE 3A9

2m SE of Drumnadrochit, on W shore of Loch Ness. Opening standard.
Adult: £1.00, OAP/child: 50p. Group rates: 10% discount for parties of
11 or more persons. (AM) Tel: 031-226 2570.

Once one of the largest castles in Scotland, the castle is
situated on a promontory on the banks of Loch Ness,
from where sitings of the 'monster' are most
frequently reported. The extensive ruins are on the site
of a vitrified fort, rebuilt with stone in the 14th
century. The castle was gifted by James IV, in 1509, to
John Grant of Freuchie, whose family built much of
the existing fabric and held the site for four centuries.
The castle was blown up in 1692 to prevent its being
occupied by Jacobites. (See also No 648).

970 VANE FARM NATURE RESERVE 6D4

On the S shore of Loch Leven, on B9097, off M90 and B996, 4½m S
of Kinross. Apr-Oct, daily 1000-1700, Nov-Mar, Sat and Sun 1000-1630.
Adult: 60p, child: 30p; school parties by arrangement. (RSPB)
Tel: Kinross (0577) 2355.

The Nature Centre is a converted farm building
equipped with displays designed to interpret the
surrounding countryside and the loch. Between the
last week of September and April, the area is a
favourite feeding and resting place for vast numbers of
wild geese and duck, and binoculars are provided for
observation. Also observation hide and nature trail.
Shop selling wide range of RSPB gifts. Car park with
picnic space. Path up Vane Hill through birchwoods
with impressive views.

'Victoria'

971 'VICTORIA'   **6C6**

&
A
Manse Road Basin, Linlithgow. Easter-end Sep, Sat and Sun 1400-1700.
Also day and evening charters by arrangement. Adult: 60p, child: 30p.
(Mrs L Alps). Tel: Linlithgow (5) 844916.

Replica of a Victorian steam packet boat offering half-
hour pleasure cruises on the Union Canal. Special rates
for school parties during the week. Disabled visitors
must be able to get out of wheelchairs. (See also Nos
966 and 157).

---

972 VICTORIA FALLS   **2F7**

&
Off A832, 12m NW of Kinlochewe, near Slattadale. All times. Free.

Waterfall named after Queen Victoria who visited
Loch Maree and area in 1877.

---

973 WADE'S BRIDGE   **5A1**

On B846, north of Aberfeldy. All times. Free.

The bridge across the River Tay was begun in 1733 by
General Wade with William Adam as architect. It is
considered to be the finest of all Wade's bridges. The
Black Watch Memorial is a large cairn surmounted by
a kilted soldier, erected close to the bridge in Queen
Victoria's Jubilee Year (1887). Easy access across lawn
to river bank.

---

974 JOHN WALKER & SONS   **4H7**

Hill Street, Kilmarnock, Ayrshire. Tours: Mon-Fri incl at 1015 and 1400.
Each tour lasts approximately two hours. Parties of up to 40 by prior
arrangement. Minimum age of 14 years. Free.

Whisky Blending and Bottling Plant with guided tours.

---

975 WALLACE MEMORIAL   **4H5**

On A737, 2m W of Paisley at Elderslie. All times. Free.

The town is the traditional birthplace of William
Wallace. A modern memorial has been erected near an
old house, perhaps on the site of the patriot's former
home.

---

976 WALLACE MONUMENT   **6A5**

&
P
Off A997 (Hillfoots Road), 1½m NNE of Stirling. Daily. Feb, Mar,
Oct, 1000-1630, closed Wed & Thu; Apr-Sep, 1000-1730; May, Jun, Jul,
Aug, 1000-1830. Adult: 80p, child: 40p. Group rates: 30p until 31 Mar
1986; rates for summer 1986 not yet fixed. (Stirling District Council).
Tel: Stirling (0786) 72140.

Commemorates William Wallace, who defeated the
English at the Battle of Stirling Bridge in 1297. Built
in 1870, with a statue of Wallace on the side of the
tower. There are two audio-visual displays, a cafe,
woodland walks and the Wallace Sword.

---

977 WALLACE TOWER   **4G7**

High Street, Ayr. By arrangement. Free.

The 113 feet high Wallace Tower, built in 1828, has a
statue of Sir William Wallace by a local self-taught
sculptor.

---

978 WANLOCKHEAD BEAM ENGINE   **5B8**

Wanlockhead Village, Dumfries and Galloway. At all times. Free.
Tel: 031-226 2570.

An early 19th-century wooden water-balance pump
for lead mining with the track of a horse engine beside
it. Nearby is the Museum of Scottish Lead Mines (See
also No 729).

979 WATERLOO MONUMENT 5E7

Off B6400, 5m N of Jedburgh. All times. Free. No access to interior. Tel: Jedburgh (0835) 62201 (Lothian Estates Office).

This prominent landmark on the summit of Penielheugh Hill (741 feet) was built in 1815 by the Marquess of Lothian and his tenants. Can be seen from a walk from the Woodland Centre. (See No 995).

980 PS 'WAVERLEY' 4G5

Rates and full details of departure points and times from Waverley Excursions Ltd, Anderston Quay, Glasgow G3 8HA. Tel: 041-221 8152.

Historically one of the most interesting vessels still in operation in the British Isles, the *Waverley* is the last paddle steamer to be built for service on the Clyde, and now the last sea-going paddle steamer in the world. A variety of cruises from Glasgow and Ayr along the Clyde Coast, with meals, bar and light refreshments available.

Weaver's Cottage

981 WEAVER'S COTTAGE 4H5

A
P
At Kilbarchan, off A737, 5m W of Paisley. 28 Mar-31 May, 1 Sep-30 Oct, Tue, Thu, Sat and Sun 1400-1700; 1 Jun-31 Aug, daily 1400-1700. Adult: 60p, child: 30p. (NTS) Tel: Kilbarchan (050 57) 5588.

In the 18th century Kilbarchan was a thriving centre of handloom weaving. The cottage is preserved as a typical weaver's home of the period, with looms, weaving equipment and domestic utensils. Attractive cottage garden.

982 WELL OF THE SEVEN HEADS 2H11

Off A82 on the W shore of Loch Oich. All times. Free.

A curious monument inscribed in English, Gaelic, French and Latin and surmounted by seven men's heads, stands above a spring and recalls the grim story of the execution of seven brothers for the murder of the two sons of a 17th century chief of Keppoch.

West Highland Museum

983 WEST HIGHLAND MUSEUM   2G12

♿
A
P

Cameron Square, Fort William. All year, Mon-Sat 1000-1300,
1400-1700 (Jun and Sep 0930-1730, Jul and Aug 0930-2100).
Adult: 35p, child: 15p. Fort William (0397) 2169.

Historical, natural history and folk exhibits, local
interest and a tartan section. Jacobite relics including a
secret portrait of Prince Charles Edward Stuart.

984 THE WEST PORT   6G2

St Andrews, at W end of South Street. All times. Free. (AM)
Tel: 031-226 2570.

One of the few surviving city gates in Scotland. Its
building contract is dated 1589 although it was
completely renovated in 1843. It now consists of a
central archway protected from above by battlements
between two semi-octagonal turrets with gun loops.

985 WESTQUARTER DOVECOT   6B6

In Westquarter, 2m E of Falkirk, off A9. May be viewed from outside
only. (AM) Tel: 031-226 2570.

A rectangular dovecot of considerable architectural
merit. Over the entrance doorway there is a heraldic
panel dated 1647 containing the arms of Sir William
Livingstone of Westquarter.

986 WESTSIDE CHURCH   1B9

Bay of Tuquoy, south coast of island of Westray, Orkney. All reasonable
times. Free. (AM) Tel: 031-226 2570.

A 12th-century church, with nave and chancel, the
former lengthened in the latter Middle Ages.

987 WHITEN HEAD   3A3

5m N of A838 and 6m E of Durness. No road access; boat trips from
Durness in summer.

A splendid perpendicular cliff with a fine series of
caves.

Whithorn Priory and Museum

988 WHITHORN PRIORY AND MUSEUM   4H11

Main Street, Whithorn, 10m S of Wigtown. Opening standard.
Adult: 50p, OAP/child: 25p. Group rates: 10% discount for parties of
10 or more persons. (AM) Tel: 031-226 2570.

Here St Ninian founded the first Christian Church in
Scotland in 397. The present priory ruins date from
the 12th century. Early Christian crosses, some carved
in the rock, others now displayed in the museum
attached to the priory, are notable.

989 WICK HERITAGE CENTRE 3E3

     *Bank Row, Wick. Jun-Sep, Tue-Sat 1000-1230, 1400-1700; Sun
P
T 1400-1700 or by arrangement for groups. Adult: £1.00, OAP/child: 50p.
(Wick Society). Tel: Wick (0955) 3385.*

Prize-winning exhibition of the herring fishing
industry and domestic life. Gardens and tearoom.

990 WIDEFORD HILL CAIRN 1B11

*2½m W of Kirkwall on W slope of Wideford Hill, Orkney. All
reasonable times. Free. (AM) Tel: 031-226 2570.*

A cairn with three concentric walls surrounding a
passage and megalithic chamber.

991 WIGTOWN DISTRICT MUSEUM 4F10

*Old Town Hall, George Street, Stranraer. All year, Mon-Fri 1000-1700,
Sat 1000-1300, 1400-1700. Free. (Wigtown District Council).
Tel: Stranraer (0776) 5088.*

A local history museum with changing exhibitions.
Free town trail leaflets available. Shop. Information on
town trail which can be followed by wheelchair users.

992 WIGTOWN MUSEUM 4F10

*County Buildings, Wigtown. May-end Sep, Mon, Wed, Fri, 1400-1600.
Free. Tel: Stranraer (0776) 5088.*

Town Museum telling the story of Wigtown martyrs.
New signposts to points of interest in Wigtown.
Shop. Information on town trail which can be
followed by wheelchair users.

993 WINTON HOUSE 6F6

*B6355, 6m SW of Haddington. Open by prior arrangement, to parties
only or people very specially interested. Adult: £1.30, child: 65p.
(Sir David and Lady Ogilvy). Tel: Pencaitland 340222.*

A gem of Scottish Renaissance architecture dating
from 1620. Associations with Charles I and Sir Walter
Scott. Beautiful plaster ceilings, unique carved stone
chimneys, fine pictures and furniture. Personally
conducted tours.

994 WOOD OF CREE NATURE RESERVE 4H10

*On minor road from Minigaff, 4m NW of Newton Stewart. Can be
viewed at any time from road or paths through the wood. Free. (RSPB)
Tel: Newton Stewart (0671) 2861*

One of the finest areas of remaining native oak and
birch woodland in Scotland with woodland birds and
flowers.

995 THE WOODLAND CENTRE 5E7

     *At Monteviot, 3m N of Jedburgh at junction of A68 and B6400. Easter-
P
T end Oct, Sun, Wed & bank holiday Mons only; Jul, Aug, Sun-Thu
1300-1730; or by prior arrangement for parties. Adult: 80p, child: 40p.
Group rates: 10% discount for booked parties. (Marquis of Lothian)
Tel: Jedburgh (0835) 62201 (Lothian Estates Office)*

An interpretation centre, based on the old home farm
of a large country estate. The major theme is the use
of woodlands and timber. Exhibitions, woodland
walks, pinery, games and puzzles, shop, slide show,
adventure play area, tearoom, parking. (See also No 995).

996 WOODSIDE STUDIO GALLERY 5B10

     *William Street, Dalbeattie. All year, daily, 0930-1900. Free.
A
P (J C Sturgeon)*

Exhibition of large selection of original paintings of
subjects including Galloway landscapes, for sale. Also
craft gifts and framing. Car parking.

997 WOOL STONE   6H6

♿ A

In Stenton, B6370, 5m SW of Dunbar. All reasonable times. Free.

The medieval Wool Stone, used formerly for the weighing of wool at Stenton Fair, stands on the green. See also the 14th century Rood Well, topped by a cardinal's hat, and the old doocot.

---

998 YARROW KIRK   5E7

A708, W from Selkirk.

A lovely valley praised by many writers including Scott, Wordsworth and Hogg, who lived in this area. Little Yarrow Kirk dates back to 1640, Scott's great-great-grandfather was minister there. The nearby Deuchar Bridge (not now in use) was built in 1653. On the hills around Yarrow are the remains of ancient Border keeps.

---

999 YESTER PARISH CHURCH   6G7

♿ A

Gifford, B6369, 5m SSE of Haddington. All reasonable times. Free.

The Dutch-looking church dates from 1708, and in it is preserved a late mediaeval bell, and also a 17th-century pulpit. A tablet near the church commemorates the Rev John Witherspoon (1723-94), born at Gifford, principal of Princeton University, USA, and the only cleric to sign the American Declaration of Independence. No guide dogs.

1000 'PARAFFIN' YOUNG EXHIBITION   6B6

Situated at the BP Information Centre, Grangemouth. Apr-30 Sep, Mon-Fri 0900-1700. Free. (Forth Valley Tourist Board). Tel: Linlithgow (0506) 844600.

Exhibition tracing the life of James 'Paraffin' Young and the development of the shale oil industry. Shows the processes involved in making paraffin.

Younger Botanic Garden

1001 YOUNGER BOTANIC GARDEN   4F4

♿ *A815, 7m NNW of Dunoon. Apr-Oct daily 1000-1800. Adult: 20p, child: 10p. Group rates: 10% discount for parties of 11 or more persons if party voucher requested on arrival. Tel: Dunoon (0369) 6261.*

Extensive woodland gardens featuring conifers, rhododendrons, azaleas, many other shrubs and a magnificent avenue of Sierra redwoods.

Clan Tartan Centre

JAMES PRINGLE at
Woollen Mill

Find your

Scottish heritage

on Pringle's archive

computer.

Do you have a clan to your name?

You can find out, in seconds, on Pringle's Archive Computer at the CLAN TARTAN CENTRE.

And you don't need to be a MacDonald or a Campbell, to be a Scot.

Such names as Oliver, Pollock, Bisset, Bowie and Hannay are as Scottish as Bonnie Prince Charlie.

The Pringle's Archive Computer gives you fascinating facts like your clan origins, Chief, tartans and heraldic crest.

And we have a unique film presentation which tells you all about the history and mystery of tartan.

In fact, about the only thing we can't tell you is how to play the bagpipes.

70-74 Bangor Road, Leith, Edinburgh.
Telephone 031-553 5100/5161.

185

188

THE MILL
BLAIR ATHOLL

WORKING CORN MILL

Weekdays   10.00 am to 6.00 pm

Sundays   12 noon to 6.00 pm

GRANARY TEA ROOM

Visit one of Scotland's smallest attractions.

Nestled at the foot of the beautiful Campsie Hills lies the tiny Glengoyne distillery.

It produces one of Scotland's rarest whiskies. Glengoyne 10 year old single malt.

The history of the distillery goes back to 1833.

The history of the area back to the days when Rob Roy reputedly hid in an ancient oak stump less than 1/2 mile from the distillery.

Glengoyne Distillery.

Conducted tours Mon-Fri 10.30am. 11.15am. 12.00. 2.00pm and 3.30pm (April-October). Large parties of 10 or more please telephone 041-332 6361.

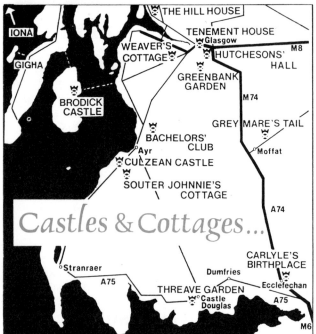

THIRLESTANE CASTLE, LAUDER, BERWICKSHIRE. Magnificent State Rooms with exquisite 17th-century ceilings and beautiful family treasures. Also the Border Country Life Museum within the Castle, showing the development of life in the Borders of bygone days. Visitors to Scotland should not miss the opportunity of visiting this wonderful family home. Signed off the A68 and A697, 28 miles south of Edinburgh.

Open: 11 May-30 June and all September, Wednesdays and Sundays July and August. Every day except Fridays. Castle and Museum: 2-5 pm. Grounds: 12-6 p.m.

DUMFRIES MUSEUM, Church Street, Dumfries
Natural and human history of Dumfries and Galloway.
Open all year.   Admission Free.

CAMERA OBSCURA
Dumfries Museum, Church Street, Dumfries
1836 astronomical instrument giving views of the town
and surrounding area.
Open April-September.   Adults 50p. Children 25p.

BURNS HOUSE, Burns Street, Dumfries
House in which Robert Burns lived for the three years
prior to his death in 1796.
Open all year.   Adults 30p. Children 15p.

OLD BRIDGE HOUSE, Mill Road, Dumfries
Victorian and Edwardian period rooms.
Open April-September.   Admission Free

OPENING HOURS
Mon-Sat 10 a.m.-1 p.m.   2 p.m.-5 p.m.
(Sun 2 p.m.-5 p.m. April-September only)
Closed Mondays October-March

LYTH ARTS CENTRE. Local and touring exhibitions of contemporary fine art in an old village school 4 miles off the A9, between Wick and John O' Groats. 26 June-6 Sept 10 am-6pm daily. Homemade food.

Dalmeny House

Home of the Earl and Countess of Rosebery

Set on the shores of the Firth of Forth 7 miles from Edinburgh containing

The Rothschild Collection Superb French 18 Century furniture, tapestries, Sevres porcelain and paintings from the Earl's English home, Mentmore.

The Rosebery Collection Prime Minister Rosebery's important collection of portraits, 17th Century furniture, Goya tapestries, Burns and Racing mementos

The Napoleon Room Furniture and paintings associated with the Emperor

Open May-Sept. Sun-Thurs. 2-5.30 Teas
Admission £1.50, children and students £1.00, OAP's £1.20, Party rates.
Full details The Administrator Tel: 031 331 1888

Enjoy the famous

SEA·LIFE

EXPERIENCE

in the beautiful surroundings of Argyll

See seals from the underwater observatory and hundreds of other fascinating sea creatures displayed in ideal viewing conditions.

ATTRACTIONS FOR 1986 INCLUDE THE SUPERB NEW SHORELINE RESTAURANT

Delicious home baked fare & salad table. Lovely surroundings & wonderful views.

OPEN EVERY DAY, 9am–6pm (till 8pm July/August)
ON THE A828 11 MILES NORTH OF OBAN
NEW GIFT SHOP · FREE PARKING

Sea life Centre

MORE THAN EVER THE WEST COAST'S LEADING ATTRACTION

EARLSHALL CASTLE & GARDENS
Leuchars by St Andrews, Fife

Earlshall is a romantic 16th-century castle that is also a family home. Open Easter Saturday, Sunday and Monday from 2 p.m. to 6 p.m., thereafter Thursdays to Sundays inclusive from 2 p.m. to 6 p.m. Last admission to the castle 5.15 p.m. Closes for the season the last Sunday in September at 6 p.m. Gift Shop, Tearoom, Nature Trail, Picnic Facilities, Free Coach and Car Park. Special evening visits catered for on Thursdays and Fridays in season, when visitors are shown parts of the castle not normally on view. Please phone 033483 205 for further details and special rates.

CAIRNGORM
A JOURNEY TO THE SUMMIT

A ride on the chairlift up to 3,600 feet at Cairngorm leads to Britain's most spectacular view–Ben Nevis can be clearly seen in the West and on Midsummer Day Ben Wyvis in the North may still be snow-capped.

As one of the highest mountains in Britain, Cairngorm stands over 4,000 feet high.

Restaurant and bar facilities of a high standard are located in the Day Lodge at the main Cairngorm car-park. In addition there is a well-stocked shop, where visitors can purchase mementoes. In the Winter, visitors will find ski equipment and at reasonable prices ski and clothing hire facilities in the Day Lodge.

Cairngorm Chairlift
Aviemore, Inverness-shire
Telephone (Cairngorm) 047-986 261

The Day Lodge

INDEX

198 Antiquities

198 Monuments

198 Churches, Cathedrals, Abbeys and Chapels

199 Castles

200 Stately Homes and Mansions

200 Other Historic and Notable Buildings

201 Museums

202 Art Galleries, Public Buildings, etc.

203 Theatres and Art Centres

203 Visitor Centres

203 Leisure Centres

203 Robert Burns and the Burns Heritage Trail

203 Bridges

204 Scotland at Work

204 Gardens

204 Scenic and Nature Interest

ANTIQUITIES

21 Aberlemno Sculptured Stones
22 Abernethy Round Tower
35 Antonine Wall
49 Ardestie and Carlungie Earth Houses
47 Ardoch Roman Camp
81 Barsalloch Fort
96 Blackhammer Cairn
113 Brechin Round Tower
118 Brough of Birsay
130 Burghead Well
140 Burnswark
147 Cairnpapple Hill
152 Callanish Standing Stones
183 Castlelaw Fort
186 The Caterthuns
189 The Chesters Fort
200 Clava Cairns
202 Clickhimin Broch
211 Columba's Footsteps
218 Corrimony Cairn
220 Coulter Motte
244 Cullerie Stone Circle
248 Culsh Earth House
250 Cuween Hill Cairn
267 Dogton Stone
277 Drumtrodden
286 Dun Carloway Broch
287 Dun Dornadilla Broch
288 Dunadd Fort
317 Dwarfie Stane
318 Dyce Symbol Stones
319 Eagle Stone
325 Eassie Sculptured Stone
393 Edinshall Broch
497 Glenelg Brochs
516 Grain Earth House
521 Grey Cairns of Camster
525 Gurness Broch
538 Haylie Chambered Tomb
574 Jarlshof
581 Kempock Stone
582 Kilberry Sculptured Stones
584 Kildalton Crosses
587 Kilmartin Sculptured Stones
589 Kilmory Cairns
593 Kilpheder Wheelhouse
610 Knap of Howar
616 Laggangairn Standing Stones
639 Loanhead Stone Circle
678 Machrie Moor Standing Stones
679 Maes Howe
700 Memsie Burial Cairn
703 Midhowe Broch and Cairns
714 Moss Farm Road Stone Circle
715 Mote of Mark
716 Mote of Urr
717 Mousa Broch
737 Ness of Burgi
738 Nether Largie Cairns
773 Peel Ring of Lumphanan
800 Quoyness Chambered Tomb
809 Rennibister Earth House
812 Ring of Brodgar
815 Roman Bath House
819 Rough Castle
824 Ruthwell Cross
837 St Fillans Cave
853 St Ninian's Isle
864 Scots Dyke
886 Skara Brae
898 Staneydale Temple
899 Steinacleit Cairn and Stone Circle
900 Stenness Standing Stones
920 Sueno's Stone
932 Tealing Earth House and Dovecote
944 Tomnaverie Stone Circle
946 Torhouse Stone Circle
954 Traprain Law
968 Unstan Chambered Tomb
988 Whithorn Priory and Museum
990 Wideford Hill Cairn

MONUMENTS

26 Alexander III Monument
88 Bell Obelisk
105 Boswell Museum and Mausoleum
121 Bruce's Stone
122 Bruce's Stone
133 Burns Family Tombstones and Cairn
207 Cobb Memorial
215 Commando Memorial
345 Edinburgh, Greyfriars Bobby
381 Edinburgh, Scott Monument
419 Fettercairn Arch
424 Flodden Monument
438 Fyrish Monument
501 Glenfinnan Monument
535 Keir Hardie Statue
545 Highland Mary's Monument
546 Highland Mary's Statue
552 James Hogg Monument
577 Keith Statue
609 Kitchener Memorial
623 Lauder Memorials
631 Leyden Obelisk and Tablet
638 Livingstone National Memorial
647 Loch Nan Uamh Cairn
659 Lochwood Tower
666 Hugh MacDiarmid Memorial Sculpture
668 Flora Macdonald's Birthplace
669 Flora Macdonald Monument
670 MacDonald Tower
672 Roderick Mackenzie Memorial
676 Macpherson Monument
684 Marjoribanks Monument
687 Martyrs' Monument
699 Melville Monument
711 Monument Hill
790 Preston Market Cross
792 Prestonpans Battle Cairn
813 Rob Roy's Grave
814 Rob Roy's Statue
866 Captain Scott and Dr Wilson Cairn
875 Duns Scotus Statue
894 Smollett Monument
930 Tarves Medieval Tomb
933 Telford Memorial
975 Wallace Memorial
976 Wallace Monument
977 Wallace Tower
979 Waterloo Monument
982 Well of Seven Heads

CHURCHES, CATHEDRALS, ABBEYS AND CHAPELS

3 Abercorn Church
18 Aberdeen (Old), St Machar's Cathedral
20 Aberlady Church
28 Alloway Kirk
38 Arbroath Abbey
42 Ardchattan Priory
43 Ardclach Bell Tower
55 Athelstaneford Church
60 Auld Kirk
70 Balmerino Abbey
84 Beauly Priory
85 Bedrule Church
94 Biggar Kirk
95 Birnie Church
108 Bowmore Round Church
113 Brechin Round Tower
118 Brough of Birsay
153 Cambuskenneth Abbey
160 Carfin Grotto
181 Castle Semple Collegiate Church
187 Chapel Finian

188 Church of St Mahew
190 Church of the Holy Rude
191 Church of St Moluag
192 Cille Barra
210 Collegiate Church of St Nicholas
232 Crathie Church
237 Croick Church
239 Cross Kirk
240 Crossraguel Abbey
242 Cruggleton Church and Castle
246 Culross Abbey
253 Dalmeny Kirk
258 The Dean's House
259 Deer Abbey
261 Deskford Church
268 Dornoch Cathedral
278 Dryburgh Abbey
290 Dunblane Cathedral
302 Dundrennan Abbey
303 Dunfermline Abbey
305 Dunglass Collegiate Church
307 Dunkeld Cathedral
316 Durness Old Church
333 Edinburgh, Canongate Kirk
347 Edinburgh, High Kirk of St Giles
351 Edinburgh, Kirk of the Greyfriars
355 Edinburgh, Magdalen Chapel
375 Edinburgh, St Cuthbert's Church
376 Edinburgh, St John's Church
377 Edinburgh, St Mary's Cathedral
378 Edinburgh, St Triduana's Chapel
394 Edrom Norman Arch
400 Elgin Cathedral
406 Eynhallow Church
427 Fogo Church
435 Fortrose Cathedral
440 Fyvie Church
456 Glasgow Cathedral
480 Glasgow, St Andrew's Parish
    Church
481 Glasgow, St David's 'Ramshorn'
    Church
482 Glasgow, St Vincent Street
    Church
507 Glenluce Abbey
558 Inchcolm Abbey
559 Inchmahome Priory
563 Inveraray Bell Tower
571 Iona
573 Italian Chapel
575 Jedburgh Abbey
580 Kelso Abbey
588 Kilmory Knap Chapel
595 Kilwinning Abbey
598 Kinkell Church
600 Kinneff Church
605 Kippen Church
615 Lady Kirk
628 Leuchars Norman Church
633 Lincluden College
691 Mayboke Collegiate Church
697 Melrose Abbey
712 Mortlach Church
731 Muthill Church and Tower
758 Old Parish Church of Hamilton
765 Orphir Church
767 Our Lady of Sorrows
768 Paisley Abbey
780 Pierowall Church
787 Pluscarden Abbey
795 Queensberry Aisle
811 Restenneth Priory
813 Rob Roy's Grave
816 Rosslyn Chapel
827 St Andrews Cathedral
829 St Bean's Church
830 St Blane's Chapel
831 St Bride's Church
832 St Bridget's Church
833 St Clement's Church
835 St Cormac's Chapel
836 St Duthus Chapel and Church
838 St John's Kirk
840 St Magnus Cathedral
841 St Magnus Church

842 St Mary's Chapel, Bute
843 St Mary's Chapel, Crosskirk
844 St Mary's Church, Auchindoir
845 St Mary's Church, Grandtully
846 St Mary's Collegiate Church
849 St Michael's Parish Church
850 St Monan's Church
851 St Ninian's Chapel, Isle of
    Whithorn
852 St Ninian's Chapel, Tynet
854 St Peter's Church
856 Saddell Abbey
878 Seton Collegiate Church
887 Skelmorlie Aisle
923 Sweetheart Abbey
924 Symington Church
948 Torphichen Preceptory
956 Trinity Temple
958 Tullibardine Chapel
964 Ui Church
986 Westside Church
998 Yarrow Kirk
999 Yester Parish Church

CASTLES

11th Century
335 Edinburgh Castle

12th Century
 48 Ardrossan Castle
161 Carleton Castle
181 Castle Sween
208 Cobbie Row's Castle
260 Delgatie Castle
283 Duffus Castle
284 Dumbarton Castle
460 Glasgow, Crookston Castle
596 Kindrochit Castle
608 Kisimul Castle
904 Stirling Castle
951 Towie Barclay Castle
960 Turnberry Castle

13th Century
 98 Blair Castle
104 Bothwell Castle
115 Brodick Castle and Gardens
163 Carnasserie Castle
176 Castle Moil
266 Dirleton Castle
273 Drum Castle
280 Duart Castle
314 Dunstaffnage Castle
315 Dunvegan Castle
397 Eilean Donan Castle
439 Fyvie Castle
530 Hailes Castle
543 Hermitage Castle
585 Kildrummy Castle
652 Lochindorb
655 Lochranza Castle
663 Luffness Castle
713 Morton Castle
734 Neidpath Castle
756 Old Inverlochy Castle
818 Rothesay Castle
821 Roxburgh Castle
826 St Andrews Castle
888 Skipness Castle

14th Century
 19 Aberdour Castle
 74 Balvenie Castle
166 Carrick Castle
174 Castle Lachlan
182 Castle Tioram
185 Cawdor Castle
194 Clackmannan Castle
235 Crichton Castle
243 Culcreuch Castle
257 Dean Castle
311 Dunnottar Castle
336 Edinburgh, Craigmillar Castle

417 Fast Castle
640 Loch Doon Castle
643 Loch Leven Castle
653 Lochmaben Castle
789 Portencross Castle
929 Tantallon Castle
969 Urquhart Castle

15th Century
50 Ardvreck Castle
58 Auchindoun Castle
97 Blackness Castle
104 Borthwick Castle
159 Cardoness Castle
170 Castle Campbell
214 Comlongon Castle
226 Craignethan Castle
270 Doune Castle
313 Dunsgaith Castle
455 Glasgow, Cathcart Castle
555 Huntingtower Castle
583 Kilchurn Castle
742 Newark Castle, Selkirk
743 Noltland Castle
759 Old Place of Mochrum
762 Orchardton Tower
774 Penkill Castle
785 Pitsligo Castle
805 Ravenscraig Castle
806 Red Castle
908 Strathaven Castle
915 Strome Castle
941 Tolquhon Castle

16th Century
41 Ardblair Castle
116 Brodie Castle
131 Burleigh Castle
163 Carnasserie Castle
168 Carsluith Castle
171 Castle Fraser
175 Castle Menzies
177 Castle of Park
180 Castle Stalker
184 Castles Girnigoe and Sinclair
216 Corgarff Castle
222 Craig Castle
231 Crathes Castle
274 Drumcoltran Tower
279 Dryhope Tower
298 Dundee, Claypotts Castle
322 Earlshall Castle
354 Edinburgh, Lauriston Castle
395 Edzell Castle and Garden
398 Elcho Castle
448 Gilnockie Tower
464 Glasgow, Haggs Castle
520 Greenknowe Tower
526 Gylen Castle
556 Huntly Castle
579 Kellie Castle
675 MacLellan's Castle
701 Menstrie Castle
707 Minard Castle
723 Muness Castle
741 Newark Castle, Port Glasgow
865 Scotstarvit Tower
890 Smailholm Tower
940 Tinnis Castle

17th Century
110 Braemar Castle
225 Craigievar Castle
227 Craigston Castle
275 Drumlanrig Castle
326 Eden Castle
450 Glamis Castle
611 Knock Castle
718 Muchalls Castle
859 Scalloway Castle
889 Slains Castle
935 Thirlestane Castle
936 Threave Castle

18th Century
249 Culzean Castle
396 Eglinton Castle
425 Floors Castle
564 Inveraray Castle

19th Century
63 Ayton Castle
71 Balmoral Castle
312 Dunrobin Castle
599 Kinloch Castle
947 Torosay Castle

STATELY HOMES AND MANSIONS

2 Abbotsford House
41 Ardblair Castle
65 Bachuil
68 Balbithan House and Gardens
71 Balmoral Castle
98 Blair Castle
107 Bowhill
115 Brodick Castle and Gardens
119 Broughton House
225 Craigievar Castle
227 Craigston Castle
231 Crathes Castle and Garden
249 Culzean Castle
252 Dalmeny House
260 Delgatie Castle
273 Drum Castle
275 Drumlanrig Castle
280 Duart Castle
281 Duff House
312 Dunrobin Castle
315 Dunvegan Castle
354 Edinburgh, Lauriston Castle
366 Edinburgh, Palace of
       Holyroodhouse
397 Eilean Donan Castle
416 Fasque
423 Finlaystone
425 Floors Castle
450 Glamis Castle
514 Gosford House
529 Haddo House
548 The Hill House
549 Hill of Tarvit
553 Hopetoun House
554 House of the Binns
564 Inveraray Castle
579 Kellie Castle
599 Kinloch Castle
626 Leith Hall
627 Lennoxlove House
663 Luffness Castle
683 Manderston
690 Maxwelton House
696 Mellerstain
701 Menstrie Castle
718 Muchalls Castle
781 Pinkie House
802 Rammerscales
861 Scone Palace
901 Stevenson House
947 Torosay Castle
950 Torwoodlee House
951 Towie Barclay Castle
955 Traquair House
993 Winton House

OTHER HISTORIC AND NOTABLE BUILDINGS

11 Aberdeen, Marischal College
13 Aberdeen, Mercat Cross

14 Aberdeen, Provost Skene's House
17 Aberdeen (Old), King's College
53 Argyll's Lodging
80 Barrie's Birthplace
92 Bernera Barracks
100 Boath Doocot
123 Michael Bruce's Cottage
162 Carlyle's Birthplace
164 Carnegie Birthplace Memorial
194 Clackmannan Tower
229 Crail Tolbooth
247 Culross Palace
295 Dundee, Camperdown
297 Dundee, Howff Burial Ground
308 Dunkeld Little Houses
309 Dunmore Pineapple
320 Earl Patrick's Palace and Bishop's Palace
321 Earl's Palace, Birsay
328 Edinburgh, Acheson House
334 Edinburgh, Canongate Tolbooth
337 Edinburgh, Cramond
339 Edinburgh, Dean Village
343 Edinburgh, Georgian House
344 Edinburgh, Gladstone's Land
346 Edinburgh, George Heriot's School
349 Edinburgh, Huntly House
352 Edinburgh, John Knox's House
353 Edinburgh, Lamb's House
365 Edinburgh, Parliament House
391 Edinburgh, White Horse Close
411 Falkland Palace
421 Finavon Doocot
428 Fordyce
430 Fort Charlotte
431 Fort George
436 Foulden Tithe Barn
458 Glasgow, City Chambers
462 Glasgow, George Square
467 Glasgow, Hutchesons' Hall
470 Glasgow, Merchants House
473 Glasgow, Necropolis
476 Glasgow, Provan Hall
477 Glasgow, Provand's Lordship
483 Glasgow School of Art
485 Glasgow, Stirling's Library
486 Glasgow, The Stock Exchange—Scottish
487 Glasgow, Templeton's Carpet Factory
488 Glasgow, Tenement House
524 Guildhall
527 Haddington
542 The Hermitage
561 Innerpeffray Library
601 Kinneil House
614 Lady Gifford's Well
634 Linlithgow Palace
662 Loudoun's Hall
665 McCaig's Tower
667 MacDonald's Mill
681 Maison Dieu
685 Mar's Wark
686 Martello Tower
689 Mary Queen of Scots House
706 Hugh Miller's Cottage
739 New Abbey Corn Mill
754 Old Blacksmith's Shop and Visitor Centre
761 Oldmills
764 Ormiston Market Cross
766 Our Lady of the Isles
820 The Round House
823 Ruthven Barracks
828 St Andrews University
858 Sanquhar Post Office
885 Sir Walter Scott's Courtroom
919 The Study
952 Town House, Culross
984 West Port
985 Westquarter Dovecote
997 Wool Stone

MUSEUMS

Clan and Tartan

195 Clan Donald Centre
196 Clan Donnachaidh Museum
197 Clan Macpherson Museum
379 Edinburgh, Scotland's Clan Tartan Centre
404 Exhibition of the Scottish Highlander
730 Museum of Scottish Tartans

Folk and Agriculture

30 Alyth Folk Museum
34 Angus Folk Museum
56 Atholl Country Collection
59 Auchindrain Museum
324 Easdale Island Folk Museum
382 Edinburgh, Scottish Agricultural Museum
404 Exhibition of the Scottish Highlander
420 Fife Folk Museum
426 Fochabers Folk Museum
494 Glencoe and North Lorn Folk Museum
498 Glenesk Folk Museum
519 Greenhill Covenanters' House
544 Highland Folk Museum
590 Kilmuir Croft Museum
629 Lewis Black House
632 Lhaidhay Caithness Croft Museum
636 Littlehaugh Agricultural Museum
657 Lochwinnoch Community Museum
720 Mull and Iona Folklore Museum
760 Old Skye Crofter's House
881 Shetland Croft House Museum
939 Tingwall Valley Agricultural Museum
981 Weaver's Cottage

General and Miscellaneous

6 Aberdeen, James Dun's House
36 Appin Wildlife Museum
124 John Buchan Centre
172 Castle Jail
198 Jim Clark Memorial Trophy Room
223 Craigcleuch Scottish Explorers Museum
234 Creetown Gem Rock Museum
271 Doune Motor Museum
291 Henry Duncan Cottage Museum
294 Dundee, Broughty Castle Museum
329 Edinburgh, Braidwood and Rushbrook Fire Museum
357 Edinburgh, Museum of Childhood
360 Edinburgh, National Museums of Scotland (Antiquities)
361 Edinburgh, National Museums of Scotland
367 Edinburgh, Philatelic Bureau
374 Edinburgh, St Cecilia's Hall
380 Edinburgh, Scotmid Transport Collection
385 Edinburgh, Lady Stair's House
388 Edinburgh University Collection of Musical Instruments
389 Edinburgh Wax Museum
442 Galloway Deer Museum
464 Glasgow, Haggs Castle
466 Glasgow, Hunterian Museum
469 Glasgow, C R Mackintosh Museum
472 Glasgow, Museum of Transport
531 Halliwell's House
537 Hawick Museum
539 Heatherbank Museum of Social Work
541 Heritage of Golf
617 Laing Memorial Museum

695 Meigle Museum
698 Melrose Motor Museum
726 Museum of Dolls, Toys and
    Victoriana
727 Museum of Flight
732 Myreton Motor Museum
751 Norwood Museum
763 Orkney Wireless Museum
855 St Vigean's Museum
879 Shambellie House
882 Shetland Museum
907 Strathallan Air Museum
918 John McDouall Stuart Museum
957 Tugnet Ice House

Local History

75 Banchory Museum
76 Banff Museum
83 Baxters Visitor Centre
103 Border Country Life Museum
112 Brechin Museum
125 Buckhaven Museum
128 Burghead Museum
141 Burntisland Museum
142 Bute Museum
209 Coldstream Museum
228 Crail Museum
265 Dingwall Town Hall
282 Dufftown Museum
285 Dumfries Museum
293 Dundee, Barrack Street Museum
304 Dunfermline District Museum
349 Edinburgh, Huntly House
401 Elgin Museum
405 Eyemouth Museum
409 Falconer Museum
410 Falkirk Museum
441 Gairloch Heritage Museum
449 Gladstone Court Street Museum
474 Glasgow, People's Palace
518 Great Glen Museum
523 Groam House Museum
528 Haddington Museum
532 Hamilton District Museum
536 John Hastie Museum
557 Huntly Museum
567 Inverkeithing Museum
570 Inverurie Museum
572 Isle of Arran Heritage Museum
603 Kinross Museum
622 Largs Museum
693 Meffan Institute
708 Moffat Museum
710 Montrose Museum
728 Museum of Islay Life
733 Nairn Fishertown Museum
736 Ness Historical Society
744 North Ayrshire Museum
746 North Berwick Museum
755 Old Bridge House
786 Pittencrieff House Museum
857 Sanquhar Museum
897 South Queensferry Museum
902 Stewartry Museum
905 Stonehaven Tolbooth Museum
911 Strathnaver Museum
916 Stromness Museum
928 Tankerness House
938 Thurso Folk Museum
943 Tomintoul Museum
962 Tweeddale Museum
965 Ullapool Museum
983 West Highland Museum
989 Wick Heritage Museum
991 Wigtown District Museum
992 Wigtown Museum

Maritime

8 Aberdeen Fish Market
12 Aberdeen Maritime Museum
126 Buckie Maritime Museum
151 Caledonian Canal
157 Canal Museum
236 Crinan Canal
293 Dundee, Barrack Street Museum
294 Dundee, Broughty Castle
    Museum
301 Dundee, Unicorn
433 Forth/Clyde Canal
461 Glasgow, Custom House Quay
472 Glasgow, Museum of Transport
733 Nairn Fishertown Museum
868 Scottish Fisheries Museum
882 Shetland Museum
883 Signal Tower
905 Stonehaven Tolbooth Museum
916 Stromness Museum
966 Union Canal
971 'Victoria'
989 Wick Heritage Centre

Industrial

30 Alford Valley Railway
93 Biggar Gasworks
101 Bonawe Iron Furnace
102 Bo'ness and Kinneil Railway
157 Canal Museum
201 Click Mill
515 Grangemouth Museum
517 Grampian Transport Museum
602 Kinneil Museum and Roman
    Fortlet
638 Livingstone National Memorial
656 Lochty Private Railway
729 Museum of the Scottish Lead
    Mining Industry
740 New Lanark
803 Allan Ramsey Library
870 Scottish Mining Museum
871 Scottish Museum of Woollen
    Textiles
872 Scottish Railway Preservation
    Society (Falkirk)
913 Strathspey Railway
978 Wanlockhead Beam Engine
981 Weavers Cottage
1000 Paraffin Young Exhibition

Regimental

9 Aberdeen, Gordon Highlanders
    Regimental Museum
54 Argyll and Sutherland
    Highlanders Museum
69 Balhousie Castle (Black Watch
    Museum)
154 Cameronians (Scottish Rifles)
    Regimental Museum
209 Coldstream Museum
213 Combined Operations Museum
373 Edinburgh, Royal Scots
    Dragoon Guards Display Rooms
478 Glasgow, Regimental
    Headquarters of the Royal
    Highland Fusiliers
796 Queen's Own Highlanders
    Regimental Museum
869 Scottish Horse Museum

MUSEUMS, ART GALLERIES, PUBLIC BUILDINGS, ETC.

4 Aberdeen Art Gallery and
    Museum
32 An Lanntair Gallery
38 Arbroath Art Gallery
212 Colzium House and Park
264 Dick Institute
297 Dundee, McManus Galleries
328 Edinburgh, Acheson House
340 Edinburgh, Richard Demarco
    Gallery
342 Edinburgh, Fruit Market
    Gallery
358 Edinburgh, National Gallery of
    Scotland

359 Edinburgh, National Library of Scotland
363 Edinburgh, New Town Conservation Centre
364 Edinburgh, Outlook Tower and Camera Obscura
368 Edinburgh, Register House
372 Edinburgh, Royal Scottish Academy
383 Edinburgh, Scottish National Gallery of Modern Art
384 Edinburgh, Scottish National Portrait Gallery
386 Edinburgh, Talbot Rice Arts Centre
390 Edinburgh, West Register House
408 Fair Maid's House Gallery
451 Glasgow Art Gallery and Museum
454 Glasgow, The Burrell Collection
458 Glasgow, City Chambers
465 Glasgow, Hunterian Art Gallery
466 Glasgow, Hunterian Museum
471 Glasgow, Mitchell Library
475 Glasgow, Pollok House
484 Glasgow, Scottish Design Centre
534 Harbour Cottage Gallery
568 Inverness Museum and Art Gallery
607 Kirkcaldy Museum and Art Gallery
618 William Lamb Studio
635 Lillie Art Gallery
664 Lyth Arts Centre
671 McEwan Gallery
673 Maclaurin Gallery and Rozelle House
674 McLean Museum and Art Gallery
769 Paisley Museum and Art Gallery
775 Perth Art Gallery and Museum
778 Peterhead Arbuthnot Museum and Art Gallery
779 Pier Arts Centre
891 Smith Art Gallery and Museum
996 Woodside Studio Gallery

THEATRES AND ARTS CENTRES

10 Aberdeen, His Majesty's Theatre
143 The Byre Theatre
233 Crawford Centre for the Arts
300 Dundee Repertory Theatre
327 Eden Court Theatre
350 Edinburgh, King's Theatre
362 Edinburgh, Netherbow Arts Centre
370 Edinburgh, Royal Lyceum
387 Edinburgh, Traverse Theatre Club
457 Glasgow, Citizens Theatre
459 Glasgow, Collins Gallery
468 Glasgow, King's Theatre
489 Glasgow, Theatre Royal
490 Glasgow, Third Eye Centre
677 MacRobert Arts Centre
722 Mull Little Theatre
776 Perth Repertory Theatre
782 Pitlochry Festival Theatre
892 Adam Smith Theatre
953 Town Mill and Granary

VISITOR CENTRES

77 Bannockburn
87 Beinn Eighe National Nature Reserve
90 Ben Lawers
91 Ben Nevis
109 Braeloine Interpretive Centre

155 Camperdown Wildlife Centre
195 Clan Donald Centre
245 Culloden Moor
249 Culzean Country Park
254 Darnaway Farm Visitor Centre
255 David Marshall Lodge
331 Edinburgh, Butterfly Farm
412 Falls of Clyde Centre
415 Farigaig Forest Centre
493 Glencoe and Dalness
566 Inverewe Gardens
578 Kelburn Country Centre
619 Land o' Burns Centre
620 Landmark Visitor Centre
649 Loch Ness Monster Exhibition
651 Loch-an-Eilean Visitor Centre
754 Old Blacksmith's Shop and Visitor Centre
772 Pass of Killiecrankie
817 Rothiemurchus Estate Visitor Centre
876 Sea Life Centre
912 Strathpeffer Visitor Centre
949 Torridon
959 Tummel Forest Centre
970 Vane Farm Nature Reserve
995 The Woodland Centre

LEISURE CENTRES

33 Anderson's Storybook Glen
62 Aviemore Centre
89 Bell's Sports Centre
205 Coasters Arena
356 Edinburgh, Meadowbank Stadium
680 Magnum Leisure Centre

BURNS AND THE BURNS HERITAGE TRAIL

28 Alloway Kirk
60 Auld Kirk
64 Bachelors' Club
120 Brow Well
132 Burns Cottage and Museum
133 Burns Family Tombstones and Cairn
134 Burns House, Dumfries
135 Burns House Museum, Mauchline
136 Burns Mausoleum
137 Burns Monument, Alloway
138 Burns Monument and Museum, Kilmarnock
139 Murison Burns Collection
257 Dean Castle
385 Edinburgh, Lady Stair's House
403 Ellisland Farm
471 Glasgow, Mitchell Library
512 Globe Inn
540 Heckling Shop and Glasgow Vennel
545 Highland Mary's Monument
546 Highland Mary's Statue
619 Land o' Burns Centre
625 Leglen Wood
788 Poosie Nansie's
896 Souter Johnnie's House
927 Tam o' Shanter Museum

BRIDGES

5 Aberdeen, Bridge of Dee
15 Aberdeen (Old), Bridge of Balgownie
114 Bridge of Carr
169 Cartland Bridge
193 Clachan Bridge

224 Craigellachie Bridge
306 Dunkeld Bridge
432 Forth Bridges
447 Garvamore Bridge
810 Rennie's Bridge
822 Rumbling Bridge
903 Stirling Bridge
931 Tay Bridges
961 Tweed Bridge
967 Union Suspension Bridge
973 Wade's Bridge

SEE SCOTLAND AT WORK

8 Aberdeen Fish Market
27 Alford Valley Railway
57 Auchentoshan Distillery
67 Balbirnie Craft Centre
72 Balnakeil Craft Village
99 Blowplain Open Farm
117 Brook Cottage Workshop
148 Caithness Glass, Perth
149 Caithness Glass, Wick
151 Caledonian Canal
156 Camphill Village Trust
203 Cloch Lighthouse
206 Coats Observatory
221 'Countess Fiona'
236 Crinan Canal
241 Cruachan Pumped Storage Power Station
263 John Dewar
269 Dornoch Craft Centre
272 Dounreay Nuclear Power Establishment
299 Dundee, Mills Observatory
330 Edinburgh, Brass Rubbing Centre
338 Edinburgh Crystal Visitor Centre
341 Edinburgh, Fountain Brewery
371 Edinburgh, Royal Observatory
402 Andrew Elliot
418 MV 'Ferry Queen'
452 Glasgow, The Barras
487 Glasgow, Templeton's Carpet Factory
496 Glendronach Distillery
499 Glenfarclas Distillery
500 Glenfiddich Distillery
502 Glengarioch Distillery
504 Glengoyne Distillery
505 Glen Grant Distillery
506 The Glenlivet Distillery
509 Glenruthven Weaving Mill
511 Glenturret Distillery
551 Hjaltasteyn
560 Ingasetter
613 G & G Kynoch
621 Lapidary Workshops
637 Livingston Mill Farm
656 Lochty Private Railway
692 Meal and Flour Mill
704 The Mill Shop
705 Mill of Towie
721 Mull and West Highland Narrow Gauge Railway
747 North Carr Lightship
749 North Glen Gallery
753 Oban Glassworks
777 Peter Anderson Woollen Mill
783 Pitlochry Power Station and Dam
791 Preston Mill
862 Scot II Cruises
873 Scottish White Heather Farm
877 Selkirk Glass
884 SS Sir Walter Scott
893 The Smokehouse
910 Strathisla Distillery
913 Strathspey Railway
925 Tamdhu Distillery
926 Tamnavulin-Glenlivet Distillery
942 Tomatin Distillery
945 Tongland Power Station
966 Union Canal
971 'Victoria'
974 John Walker & Sons
980 PS 'Waverley'
1000 Paraffin Young Exhibition

GARDENS

7 Aberdeen, Duthie Park Winter Gardens
16 Aberdeen (Old), Cruikshank Botanic Gardens
23 Achamore House Gardens
31 An Cala
37 Arbigland
40 Ardanaiseig Gardens
44 Ardencraig Gardens
49 Arduaine Gardens
51 Ardwell House Gardens
68 Balbithan House and Garden
78 Bargany Garden
79 Barguillean Garden
111 Branklyn Garden
115 Brodick Castle Garden
165 Carradale House Gardens
173 Castle Kennedy Gardens
195 Clan Donald Centre
204 Cluny House Gardens
212 Colzium House and Park
230 Crarae Glen Garden
231 Crathes Castle and Gardens
249 Culzean Country Park
256 Dawyck Botanic Gardens
276 Drummond Castle Gardens
322 Earlshall Castle and Gardens
369 Edinburgh, Royal Botanical Gardens
395 Edzell Castle and Garden
411 Falkland Castle and Gardens
423 Finlaystone
444 Galloway House Gardens
445 Gargunnock Garden
453 Glasgow, Botanic Gardens
463 Glasgow, Greenbank Garden
549 Hill of Tarvit
550 The Hirsel
553 Hopetoun House
562 Innes House Gardens
565 Inveresk Lodge Garden
566 Inverewe Gardens
576 Kailzie Gardens
579 Kellie Castle and Gardens
586 Kildrummy Castle and Gardens
591 Kilmun Arboretum
592 Kiloran Gardens
650 Lochalsh Woodland Gardens
660 Logan Botanic Garden
682 Malleny Gardens
694 Megginch Castle Grounds
702 Mertoun Gardens
784 Pitmedden Garden
793 Priorwood Gardens
848 St Mary's Pleasance
917 Strone Gardens
922 Suntrap
937 Threave Gardens and Wildfowl Refuge
963 Tyninghame House Gardens
1001 Younger Botanic Gardens

SCENIC AND NATURE INTEREST

1 Abbey St Bathans Trout Farm
24 Achray Forest Drive
25 Ailsa Craig
29 Almondell Country Park
45 Ardessie Fisheries
52 Argyll Forest Park
61 Aviemore Bird Garden
73 Balranald Nature Reserve
82 Bass Rock

86 Beech Hedge
87 Beinn Eighe National Nature Reserve
90 Ben Lawers
91 Ben Nevis
99 Blowplain Open Farm
127 Bullers of Buchan
128 The Burg
145 Caerlaverock National Nature Reserve
146 Cairngorm Chairlift
150 Calderglen Country Park
155 Camperdown Wildlife Centre
158 Cape Wrath
167 Carsaig Arches
179 Castle Semple Country Park
199 Clatto Country Park
217 Corrieshalloch Gorge
219 Corryvreckan Whirlpool
238 Crombie Country Park
251 Dalkeith Park
255 David Marshall Lodge
262 Devil's Beef Tub
289 Dunaverty Rock
292 Duncansby Head
295 Dundee, Camperdown
310 Dunnet Head
323 Eas Coul Aulin
331 Edinburgh, Butterfly Farm
332 Edinburgh, Calton Hill
337 Edinburgh, Cramond
339 Edinburgh, Dean Village
348 Edinburgh, Hillend
364 Edinburgh, Outlook Tower and Camera Obscura
392 Edinburgh Zoo
399 Electric Brae
407 Fair Isle
412 Falls of Clyde Centre
413 Falls of Glomach
414 Falls of Shin
415 Farigaig Forest Centre
418 MV 'Ferry Queen'
422 Fingal's Cave
434 Fortingall Yew
437 Fowlsheugh Nature Reserve
442 Galloway Deer Museum
443 Galloway Forest Park
446 Gartmorn Dam
479 Glasgow, Rouken Glen
491 Glasgow, Victoria Park and Fossil Grove
492 Glasgow Zoo
493 Glen Coe and Dalness
495 Glencoe Chairlift
503 Glengoulandie Deer Park
508 Glenmore Forest Park
510 Glenshee Chairlift
513 Goatfell
522 Grey Mare's Tail
533 Handa Island Nature Reserve
542 The Hermitage
547 Highland Wildlife Park
569 Inverpolly National Nature Reserve
578 Kelburn Country Centre
594 Kilt Rock
597 King's Cave
604 Kintail
606 Kirk Yetholm
612 Kyles of Bute
624 Lecht Ski Tow
630 Lewis Castle Grounds
637 Livingston Mill Farm
641 Loch Druidibeg National Nature Reserve
642 Loch Garten Nature Reserve
644 Loch of the Lowes
645 Loch of Kinnordy Nature Reserve
646 Loch Morar
648 Loch Ness
651 Loch-an-Eilean Visitor Centre
654 Lochore Meadows Country Park
657 Lochwinnoch Nature Reserve
661 Logan Fish Pond

688 Marwick Head Nature Reserve
709 Monikie Country Park
719 Muirshiel Country Park
745 North Berwick Law
748 North East of Scotland Agricultural Heritage Centre
750 North Hoy Nature Reserve
752 Noss Nature Reserve
757 Old Man of Hoy
770 Palacerigg Country Park
771 Parallel Roads
772 Pass of Killiecrankie
794 Queen Elizabeth Forest Park
797 Queen's View, Loch Lomond
798 Queen's View, Loch Tummel
799 Quiraing
801 Raiders Road
804 Randolph's Leap
807 Reediehill Farm
808 Reindeer on the Range
817 Rothiemurchus Estate Visitor Centre
822 Rumbling Bridge
825 St Abbs Head
834 St Columba's Cave
837 St Fillan's Cave
839 St Kilda
847 St Mary's Loch
860 Scapa Flow
862 Scot II Cruises
863 Scotland's Safari Park
864 Scots Dyke
874 Scott's View
876 Sea Life Centre
884 SS 'Sir Walter Scott'
895 Smoo Cave
906 Storr
909 Strathclyde Country Park
914 Strathyre Forest Information Centre
921 Summer Isles
934 Tentsmuir Point National Nature Reserve
937 Threave Wildfowl Refuge
949 Torridon
959 Tummel Forest Centre
970 Vane Farm Nature Reserve
971 'Victoria'
972 Victoria Falls
980 PS 'Waverley'
987 Whiten Head
994 Wood of Cree Nature Reserve

Burns Heritage Trail

The places and people associated with Scotland's national bard, Robert Burns, have been highlighted in the Burns Heritage Trail, which has been developed by the Scottish Tourist Board with local authorities and other organisations.

In the peaceful surroundings of the Land o' Burns Centre in Alloway by Ayr, there is a lively and colourful multi-screen presentation of Burns' life, which is an exciting beginning or end to a tour of the places mentioned. There are opportunities to learn about the problems and successes of life in Burns' time at Kilmarnock, Tarbolton, Mauchline, Ayr, Alloway, Kirkoswald, Ellisland, Irvine, Dumfries and other places.

The attractive countryside of the south west of Scotland, while steeped in Burns, also offers much active and inactive leisure, whether sporting, lazing on the beach, or visiting historic buildings.

Fishing Heritage Trail

The sea has always played a vital part in the life of Scotland, this country with its wandering coastline and hundreds of islands.

Today, for holidaymakers it means golden beaches, boat trips and birdwatching; but for those who live on the coast it means a tradition of earning a living from the sea. You can learn about this tradition in the charming fishing villages and ports on the coast and in the fascinating museums which preserve it, by following Scotland's Fishing Heritage Trail, which runs the length of the east coast from the Borders to Shetland.

A Taste of Scotland

Food in Scotland is treated with pride and there are many delicious traditional dishes.

Start the day with the substantial Scottish breakfast, an enjoyable occasion where you can sample porridge, kippers, oatcakes and butteries. At afternoon tea, home baking comes into its own with scones and jam, shortbread and cakes. Or there is high tea a Scottish speciality consisting of one large main course plus plates piled high with home baking. Keep an eye open for places which serve fresh local produce — salmon, trout, shellfish, venison and grouse.

More information is available from Tourist Information Centres.

Published by the Scottish Tourist Board, P.O. Box 705, Edinburgh EH4 3EU.
Printed by Scotprint Ltd., Musselburgh.